TALES OF THE FLYING TIGERS

Books by Daniel Ford

Looking Back From Ninety: The Depression, the War, and the Good Life that Followed

Cowboy: The Interpreter Who Became a Soldier, a Warlord, and One More Casualty of Our War in Vietnam

Flying Tigers: Claire Chennault and His American Volunteers, 1941-1942

Poland's Daughter: How I Met Basia, Hitchhiked to Italy, and Learned About Love, War, and Exile

A Vision So Noble: John Boyd, the OODA Loop, and America's War on Terror

The Lady and the Tigers (with Olga Greenlaw)

Glen Edwards: The Diary of a Bomber Pilot

The Only War We've Got: Early Days in South Vietnam

The Country Northward: A Hiker's Journal

Novels

Michael's War: A Story of the Irish Republican Army

Remains: A Story of the Flying Tigers

The High Country Illuminator: A Tale of Light and Darkness and the Ski Bums of Avalon

Incident at Muc Wa: A Story of the Vietnam War

Now Comes Theodora: A Story of the 1960s

Thank you for buying this book. For more about the author and his work, or to sign up for an occasional electronic newsletter, visit the website at danfordbooks.com

TALES OF
THE FLYING TIGERS

Five Books About the American Volunteer Group, Mercenary Heroes of Burma and China

Daniel Ford

虎

Warbird Books

Revised and Updated 2022

TALES OF THE FLYING TIGERS revised edition copyright © 2012, 2022 by Daniel Ford. The following images reproduced with permission of the copyright holders: P-40B three-view from Richard Ferriere, R.T. Smith photographs from Brad Smith, diagram of Christmas raid from Dai Nippon Kaiga, Burma map from Japan Defense Agency, Ki-27 suicide dive from Konnichi no Wadaisha. The cover shows the "blood chit" identification patch sewn to the jackets of AVG pilots. Other images from Noel Bacon, Jim Lansdale, Tom Cleaver, National Air and Space Museum Archives, and the author's collection. Calligraphy by Eileen Chow. In different form, portions of "100 Hawks for China" first appeared in *Air & Space Smithsonian*, and "First Blood for the Flying Tigers" in *America in WW2*, and are used by permission of those magazines.

All rights reserved. No part of this book may be reproduced or transmitted in any form or by any means, graphic, electronic, or mechanical, including photocopying, recording, taping or on any information storage or retrieval system, without the written permission of the copyright holders. For information, write Warbird Books, 433 Bay Road, Durham NH 03824 USA.

ISBN 978-1530249930

Contents

100 Fair Pilots
Recruiting the Flying Tigers / 1
100 Pilots (plus 10) / 4
About Those Combat Claims / 60

100 Hawks for China
How the Planes Reached China / 65
RAF Pilot's Manual / 76
Tye Lett's Allison Engine Notes / 113
What We Know About the Hawks / 119

First Blood for the Tigers
Why Doesn't He Blow Up? / 126

Rising Sun Over Burma
Flying Tigers and Wild Eagles / 137
Air Battle for Rangoon / 147
Numbers Are Not Important / 158
South Burma Falls / 166
Duel Over Loiwing / 177
Last Days in Burma / 186

AVG Confidential
Becoming a Flying Tiger / 191
The 'Confidential' Interview / 200
The Tigers Come Home / 219

Back Matter
Notes and Sources / 223
About the Author / 229

Noel Bacon before his first flight in the P-40, September 1941

100 Fair Pilots: The Men Who Became the Flying Tigers

Recruiting the Flying Tigers

CLAIRE CHENNAULT retired from the U.S. Army Air Corps as a captain and sailed for China in 1937 to become air advisor to the dictator Chiang Kai-shek. A few weeks after he arrived, the armed forces of Japan attacked China, first at the old capital of Beijing and then at the seaport of Shanghai where Chennault and most foreigners were based. He watched from the ground (and sometimes from the air) as Japanese fighter planes all but destroyed the Chinese Air Force. For more than two years, Russian planes and pilots kept China from defeat, but by 1940 the Soviet dictator Joseph Stalin began withdrawing his air units, fearing they'd soon be needed to fend off a German invasion from the west.

"Boy," Chennault wrote to a friend in the U.S. Army Air Corps, early in the Sino-Japanese War, "if the Chinese only had 100 good pursuit planes and 100 fair pilots, they'd exterminate the Jap air force!" This was the formula he took with him to Washington in the fall of 1940, to lobby for an American unit to replace the Russians.

One hundred planes and pilots were duly authorized by the White House, the project to be financed by an American loan. The men would be released from the U.S. Army, Navy, and Marines and go to work for a front organization, the Central Aircraft Manufacturing Company. About two hundred technicians and administrative staff would also be hired, mostly from the military but some from civilian life. Finally, CAMCO would sign up ten U.S. Army flight instructors to go to China and select fledgling aviators for future training in the United States. Since Chennault commanded both institutions — the American Volunteer Group and the Chinese Air Force Flight School — the barrier between them was very permeable, with one AVG pilot transferring to the flight school soon after he arrived, and eight flight instructors eventually joining the combat squadrons.

For many of the military men, going to work for CAMCO and the

CAF meant a tripling of their pay. As a further incentive, the fighter pilots were promised a combat bonus of $500 for every Japanese warplane they shot down — the equivalent, in purchasing power, of more than $10,000 in our much depreciated greenbacks. (In 1940, a factory-fresh Cadillac sedan could be had for $1,350.)

As matters turned out, one of Chennault's "fair pilots" had flown as a mercenary during the Spanish Civil War. That hadn't bothered the U.S. Army, and of course it didn't bother the AVG recruiters. But the State Department felt differently. Americans weren't supposed to fight in foreign armies, so with bureaucratic logic the department ruled that he couldn't get a passport to join the Chinese Air Force since he'd violated his earlier passport by joining the Spanish Air Force! So it was that in the summer and fall of 1941, a total of 109 American pilots actually set sail for Burma, the entry port for China, in what AVG veterans liked to regard as their country's first clandestine military operation.

Some quit because of the climate and living conditions in Burma, where the fighter pilots would train. Others may have gone home because they were frightened by the specifications of the new "Type Zero" Japanese Navy fighter, the Mitsubishi A6M, though as matters turned out they would never have met the Zero in combat. And one or two might have joined the AVG in order to get out of the U.S. military and go to work for an airline, a profession that seemed safer, less stressful, and more remunerative.

And three were killed in training accidents.

Of those who stayed and survived, not everyone had the right stuff to fly a Curtiss P-40 fighter — what the British, from whose Lend-Lease allocation the AVG fighters were taken, called a Tomahawk. The P-40 had a thousand-horsepower engine, narrow landing gear, and a "taildragger" configuration – two main wheels forward and a small tail wheel aft – that made it difficult to land and even to taxi on the ground. In the end, Chennault had about sixty Tomahawk-qualified pilots when combat operations began that December.

The AVG training base at Kyedaw airfield near Toungoo, north of the capital city and seaport of Burma, was only a few minutes' flying time from the Thai border. And the kingdom of Thailand was occupied by the Japanese on December 8, 1941, the same day (west of the International Date Line) that they attacked the Hawaiian Islands,

Malaya, and the Philippines. Honoring an earlier promise to the British, Chiang Kai-shek ordered one AVG squadron — about twenty planes and planes, plus a skeleton ground crew — to go to Rangoon to help the Royal Air Force defend the city. The other two squadrons flew off to Kunming in southwestern China, as did some critical staff, and most of the remaining personnel set off over-land on the "Burma Road," China's lifetime ever since the Japanese had cut off all other supply routes. A small force kept Kyedaw open as a backup and repair base for the squadron at Mingaladon airport outside Rangoon.

The fighting began on December 20 — at Kunming, to everyone's surprise. Then Rangoon too came under attack, and the fliers of the American Volunteer Group won immortality as the "Flying Tigers." Over the next six months, British and Chinese armies would be defeated in Burma, and the AVG would fall back to China, to be replaced in July 1942 by uniformed airmen of the U.S. Army's 23rd Fighter Group.

Chennault of course was wrong in his prediction of what it would take to "exterminate the Jap air force." Tens of thousands of planes and fair pilots — and almost four years of total war — would be needed for that. Like most westerners, he hugely underestimated the fighting and manufacturing ability of the Japanese, and he assumed that the fighters and bombers of the Imperial Japanese Navy were the only weapons his pilots would have to worry about. In fact, the American Volunteer Group never met a navy fighter in combat, regularly mistaking the Imperial Army's similar though less awesome Nakajima Hayabusa for the Zero.

But the job was done eventually, and it was the Flying Tigers — Chennault's irregulars — who showed the way.

With every year that goes by, it seems, we learn a bit more about those "100 fair pilots" and 10 flight instructors who went to Burma and China in the summer and fall of 1941. In consequence, this little encyclopedia will always be a work in progress. If you have anything to add about any of these men, please write or email me at the addresses given at the back of the book. — *Daniel Ford*

100 Pilots (Plus 10)

A FIGHTER ACE, as understood in most air forces, is a pilot credited with five or more air-to-air victories. Over the past hundred years, some 60,000 men (and in recent years a few women) have flown fighter planes in U.S. service, of whom only 1,447 have earned the distinction of ace, including 19 of the AVG Flying Tigers. For each of these men, I provide a list of his victories by date.

In the biographies that follow, the 100 men recruited as fighter pilots for the American Volunteer Group are shown in roman type, whether or not they ever qualified in the Curtiss P-40. The ten CAF flight school recruits are shown in italics, even if they eventually joined the AVG combat squadrons.

In the text, I sometimes have occasion to mention the Japanese Army Air Force units that met the AVG in combat. The basic force was the *sentai*, which is sometimes translated as "regiment" but is actually more like an American or British group, commanded by a major and containing three squadrons. The Japanese units, however, were smaller than their Allied equivalents — say 35 aircraft to a sentai, including a small headquarters flight. A *chutai* is a squadron (sometimes operating independently) of about 10 planes.

Frank Adkins of Miami Beach, Florida, joined from the U.S. Navy. As a wingman in the 3rd Squadron, he was credited with a Nakajima Ki-43 *Hayabusa* (Falcon) fighter shot down over Hsipaw, Burma, in April 1942. He may have flown the group's photo ship while at Kunming. He served to the AVG's disbandment and afterward flew for CNAC, the Chinese transport airline. He apparently returned to the U.S. toward the end of 1942 and along with Ken Jernstedt joined Republic Aviation in Farmingdale, New York, making four Flying Tigers working as test pilots for the P-47 Thunderbolt fighter-bomber.

John Dean Armstrong was recruited from USS *Ranger*, where he flew a Grumman Wildcat for VF-4. Known as "Dean" to his family, he was "Army" to his squadron mates. He was killed in a mock dogfight with Gil Bright on September 8, 1941, when their planes collided over Toungoo. He was buried there, to be exhumed postwar, reburied briefly in India, and transferred in 1947 to the Punchbowl Cemetery in Hawaii, by which time his identity had been forgotten. In 2005, after a family reunion, two nieces began to search for him in hopes of bringing him home to Kansas, finally identifying his remains through DNA testing along with those of Pete Atkinson and Maax Hammer. All three were repatriated and buried with honors in 2017.

Peter Atkinson was assigned to the 8th Pursuit Group at Mitchel Field, New York, when he signed up for the AVG. He too was killed in a training accident at Toungoo, on October 25, 1941, and like Armstrong was finally brought home for burial seventy-six years later.

Noel Bacon, born 1917 in Randalia, Iowa, graduated from Iowa State Teachers College and taught high school for a year before he joined the Navy in 1939. He was another of the USS *Ranger* Wildcat pilots when recruited for the AVG. As a wingman in the 2nd Squadron, he was credited with 3 Nakajima Ki-27 Nate fighters shot down over Rangoon in January 1942. He went on leave the following month, apparently because of illness in his family. His CAMCO bonus account shows him with 3.50 enemy aircraft destroyed, since he'd shared the credit for one plane destroyed on the ground in a strafing attack.

Instead of returning to Burma, Bacon decided to marry his sweetheart and rejoin the U.S. Navy. Following the protocol adopted after the Pearl Harbor attack, Chennault gave him a "dishonorable discharge" toward the end of May, so Bacon was never recognized as a Flying Tiger by the AVG veterans' group or the U.S. Air Force when it decorated the Tigers in 1991. (Curiously, the Chinese honored him with a Cloud Banner medal, though it's unlikely he actually collected it.) He served aboard the flagship of an aircraft carrier group and remained in the Navy postwar, retiring as a captain. He died in Florida in 1996.

See page 191 for more about Noel Bacon.

Percy Bartelt of Waseca, Minnesota, was an engineering graduate of Iowa State University. He was commissioned in the U.S. Army Corps of Engineers but in time resigned to become an aviation cadet in the Navy. He flew the Brewster F2A Buffalo and Grumman F4F Wildcat for Fighting Three on USS *Saratoga*. When he signed up for the AVG, like many of the Navy pilots, he was assigned to the 2nd

Squadron, serving at Rangoon in January 1942. He flew a Tomahawk with the fuselage number 45.

In his weeks at Rangoon, Bartelt was credited with 7 Japanese aircraft, though 2 of those were Nakajima Nates destroyed on the ground while strafing an airfield in Thailand. He resigned in March 1942 and thus received a "dishonorable discharge" from Chennault. He was the only ace to be so treated, and there is no photograph of him in the AVG records. He returned to the Navy as a lieutenant and served as a flight instructor until hospitalized with a lung infection. He received a medical discharge in 1951 and worked for the state of Minnesota until retirement in 1974. He died in North Dakota in 1986.

In May 2015, Bartelt's family received the Congressional Gold Medal granted to all American fighter aces, though he had earlier been denied the Silver Star given to Flying Tiger veterans in the 1990s. The record shows him in a five-way tie as the AVG's fifteenth-ranking ace with 5 air-to-air victories, all achieved in a two-day period at Rangoon:

- 23 January 1942: 3 Ki-30 Ann light bombers
- 24 January 1942: 2 Ki-27 Nate fighters

William Bartling of Middletown, Indiana, graduated from Purdue as a chemical engineer in 1938. He joined the Navy and flew a dive bomber off USS *Wasp*. In the AVG, he flew with the 1st Squadron at Rangoon, racking up 7.27 victories there and in China according to his CAMCO bonus account. He was awarded a Five Star Wing Medal by the Chinese and was one of the AVG pilots who volunteered two extra weeks' service in China to ease the transition to the 23rd Fighter Group. Afterward he flew for CNAC. Postwar, he was an executive at National Skyway Freight Corporation, which morphed into the Flying Tiger Line, the most successful of the "non-scheduled" airlines established by veterans flying war-surplus aircraft (in this case, Douglas C-47s with a rather bemused shark-face painted on). He died in 1979. He too was tied for 15th place among AVG aces, with 5 air-to-air victory claims:

- 23 January 1942: 1 Ki-27 Nate fighter
- 28 January 1942: 1 Ki-27 Nate fighter
- 9 May 1942: 1 Ki-46 Dinah observation plane
- 12 June 1942: 1 Ki-45 Toryu fighter + 1 Ki-27 Nate fighter

Bartling's May 9 encounter involved the first plane ever lost by the 18th Independent Chutai, which had been flying reconnaissance missions over China for four years. It was piloted by Captain Hideharu Takeuchi.

Marion Baugh *of Beverly Hills, California, was one of the Air Corps instructors recruited as a check pilot for the Chinese Air Force Flight School at Yunnan-yi, west of Kunming. On January 3, 1942, he was killed in the crash of his Ryan trainer on a routine flight between Yunnan-yi and Kunming.*

Albert (Ajax) Baumler was the recruit Chennault would have most liked to see, only to have him become the 100th Flying Tiger — the man who never sailed to Burma. Born 1914 in Bayonne, New Jersey, he enlisted in the Army in 1913, and two years later was accepted for flight training, only to be washed out when he crashed a trainer at Kelly Field. He became a civilian airline pilot instead. When Spanish army troops rebelled against the left-wing Republican government, Baumler sailed for Spain and offered his service as a mercenary pilot, flying Russian-built Polikarpov fighters for the government forces. He was credited with 4.5 Italian and German planes shot down. He then returned to the U.S. Army Air Corps and was assigned to Eglin Field where he was recruited for the AVG.

The redoubtable Ruth Shipley, who ran the State Department passport office, evidently didn't get the message that the group had the President's blessing. Since Baumler had violated the provisions of his earlier passport by serving in a foreign military, she refused to give him another. So the AVG transports sailed without him, and it wasn't until the spring of 1942 as a captain in the U.S. Army Air Forces that he finally caught up with Chennault in China. He was credited with 4.5 enemy aircraft as a member of the 23rd Fighter Group, for a lifetime total of 9 planes shot down from the three Axis air forces.

Donald Bernsdorf was a Navy or Marine Corps pilot when recruited for the AVG. There is almost no mention of him in the group's records. He didn't accompany his squadron when it went down to Rangoon because Chennault didn't think he was ready for combat. Perhaps for that reason, he resigned and went home in January 1942. He may have later worked as a test pilot for Eastern Aircraft Division of General Motors, which built Grumman FM-1 Wildcats and TBM-1 Avengers.

Lewis Bishop was born 1915 in Dekalb Junction, New York. After two years at Oklahoma Military Academy, he joined the Navy and earned his wings. He was a flight instructor at Pensacola when recruited for the AVG. He was married, and his daughter was born not long after he reached Burma and began training as a P-40 pilot with the 2nd Squadron. His CAMCO bonus account credits him with 5.2 enemy aircraft. His air-to-air victories included two Nakajima Ki-43 Hayabusa fighters, plus a one-fifth share of an observation plane, shot down in March 1942. In May, flying a bomb-equipped P-40E — called "Kittyhawk" by the Tigers, using the British terminology — he took part in a raid against the Japanese airfield at Hanoi, northern Vietnam, where he was credited with three Nakajima Nate fighters destroyed on the ground.

A few days later, on a return visit to what was then known as French Indochina, Bishop led a flight of Kittyhawks including one flown by Colonel Robert Scott, the designated commander of the 23rd Fighter Group that would replace the AVG. Bombing the railroad yards at Lao Kay at an altitude of 500 feet, Bishop was apparently hit by ground fire. His Kittyhawk on fire, he bailed out and landed safely, only to fall into Japanese hands. He suffered three miserable years as a prisoner of war in China before escaping from the train that was moving him to a camp in Manchuria. He made his way back to Chennault and eventually the United States. Postwar, he returned to active duty with the Navy but was medically retired in 1948. He died in 1987.

John Blackburn, *born 1918 in Amarillo, Texas, was one of the Army flight instructors who signed up to be a CAF check pilot at Yunnan-yi, and he was also the first of them to transfer to the AVG and qualify in a Tomahawk, which he did in January 1942. At Rangoon the following month with the 1st Squadron, he was credited with two Nakajima Ki-27 Nates shot down. But on April 28, 1942, testing the guns on a new P-40E, he dove into Lake Kunming, the victim of target fixation or perhaps the Kittyhawk's tendency to "mush" in a dive. His body was recovered a month later, and in 2003 the wreck of his aircraft was located in what is now known as*

Lake Danchi, buried in silt so deep it could not be lifted. A Sino-American team has tried to recover it, but without success at this writing.

Morris Bohman of Lewiston, Idaho, was a Navy pilot when he joined the AVG but evidently did not make the grade as a P-40 pilot. He resigned in November 1941 and may have served later with the U.S. Army Air Forces (USAAF).

Harry Bolster was an Army flight instructor recruited as a CAF check pilot. When the flight school closed in the spring of 1942, he qualified as a wingman in the AVG 2nd Squadron and flew his first mission on May 11, strafing a Japanese truck column on the China-Burma border. On July 3 — in theory the last full day of the American Volunteer Group — he escorted B-25 Mitchell bombers and was credited with a Nakajima Nate in the air and another on the ground. He was one of those who volunteered to stay on duty for two weeks after the AVG disbanded. He then rejoined the U.S. Army and was killed in the crash of a flight-test Fisher P-75A at Eglin Field, Florida, on October 10, 1944, four days after the USAAF terminated the plane's development program.

Charles Bond was born in Dallas in 1915. As a high-school student, he joined the ROTC and eventually the Texas National Guard. In 1935 he joined the Army in hopes of qualifying for West Point Preparatory School — a route for enlisted men to attend the U.S. Military Academy. Failing to win an appointment, he tried again as a flying cadet. He succeeded in becoming an officer, but was disappointed to be assigned to the 2nd Bomb Group at Langley Field, Virginia, instead of flying "pursuit" as every young pilot dreamed of doing. He was ferrying Lockheed Hudson light bombers to Canada when an AVG recruiter caught up with him. The British awarded him the Distinguished Flying Cross for his services in Burma, and the Chinese a Seven Star Wing Medal.

After his AVG tour — which included two weeks' extra service during the transition to the 23rd Fighter Group — he became a career officer, stationed in England during the war and retiring from the Air Force with the rank of major general. He published his memoirs as *A Flying Tiger's Diary*. He died in 2009. He was credited with 7 air-to-air victories, tying him as the eighth-ranked AVG ace, and was

himself shot down twice. His CAMCO bonus account credits him with an additional 2.77 enemy aircraft destroyed on the ground.
- 29 January 1942: 2 Ki-27 Nate fighters
- 25 February 1942: 3 Ki-27 Nate fighters
- 26 February 1942: 1 Ki-27 Nate fighter
- 4 May 1942: 1 Ki-21 Sally bomber

That last Sally belonged to the 98th Sentai based at Mingaladon airport near Rangoon. It crashed inside China, and some other planes in that formation also sustained damage from Bond's attacks.

Gregory Boyington was arguably the most famous and certainly the most colorful of Chennault's pilots. Reared in Okanogan, Washington, under his step-father' surname, he graduated from the state university, married, and went to work as a draftsman for Boeing Aircraft as Gregory Hallenbeck. When he discovered that his name was really Boyington, he took the opportunity to join the Marines as a flying cadet, an ambition for which marriage had previously disqualified him. When he heard that somebody was recruiting pilots for service in China, he seized that opportunity as well. In theory, only reserve officers were supposed to be released for the AVG, but evidently the Marines were glad to be rid of him. He was a drinker and a troublemaker, then and later, and of course he had lied about his marital status.

He came to hate Chennault, a sentiment that seems to have been reciprocated. The dispute extended to his combat record: Boyington claimed that he was entitled to six victories, but the AVG records credited him with only two, both Nakajima Nates shot down over Rangoon. (There's some evidence that he may indeed have accounted for another plane.) His CAMCO bonus account thus stands at 3.50, the two Nates plus a 1.5 share of the planes supposedly destroyed on a strafe of a Japanese airfield at Chiang Mai, Thailand.

Boyington resigned in April 1942, returned to the U.S., rejoined the Corps, and became the commander of the Black Sheep squadron, VMF-241, in the South Pacific. He was nicknamed "Pappy" by the younger pilots, a name that he later legally adopted. He was shot down and imprisoned at Rabaul, a fate which few Allied airmen survived, but he had the good fortune to be sent back to Japan where he endured the horrors of Omori prison camp. Meantime he was awarded the Medal of Honor. He emerged a hero at war's end, to live a tumultuous life thereafter, much as he had done before. He wrote a novel loosely based on the AVG, and a colorful but unreliable autobiography that became a television series in the 1970s. He died in California in 1988.

Gilpin (Gil) Bright from Pennsylvania divided his boyhood between Philadelphia and the family farm in Reading. He prepped at Phillips Exeter Academy before enrolling at Princeton, but dropped out of college after two years in order to become a Navy aviator. He was a flight instructor at Pensacola when he signed up for the AVG. Assigned to the 2nd Squadron, he was shot down during his first combat over Rangoon, belly-landing his P-40 in a rice field. He was later credited with a Kawasaki Ki-48 medium bomber and a Nakajima Ki-27 fighter over Rangoon and another Ki-27 over Baoshan, China. His CAMCO bonus account stands at 6 enemy aircraft, including 3 planes destroyed on the ground.

When the AVG disbanded, Bright accepted a commission as a major in the USAAF, assigned to Tex Hill's 75th Fighter Squadron. As an Army pilot, he was credited with two "Zero" fighters in China, thus becoming an ace; later, in North Africa, he was credited with at least one Italian and one German aircraft, which made him one of the few American pilots credited with victories over all three Axis air forces. (Ajax Baumler was another.) Postwar, he worked for a Philadelphia brokerage house, then became a self-employed ironworker. He died in 1973.

Robert Brouk was born 1917 in suburban Chicago, the son of an immigrant sign painter from what is now the Czech Republic. He grew up in Cicero and graduated from a local junior college before enrolling at Lewis Institute of Technology (now Illinois Tech). He dropped out to join the U.S. Army, completed flight training at Kelly Field, Texas, and was assigned to Mitchel Field, New York, where he was recruited for the AVG. As a wingman in the 3rd Squadron at Rangoon, he claimed a Mitsubishi Ki-21 Sally bomber on December 23 and a Nakajima Nate fighter on Christmas Day, 1941. In April 1942, he was credited with a Nakajima Hayabusa fighter and a half share in an observation plane, for a score of 3.5 victories. When the AVG disbanded in July, he returned to Cicero, fell in love, and rejoined the U.S. Army as a married man. On December 19, he was killed when another plane collided with his. A widow after three weeks of marriage, Virginia Brouk would follow his adventurous example, joining the Women's Army Corps and serving overseas in Egypt.

Carl Kice Brown Jr from Grand Rapids, Michigan, proved to be the last survivor of the Flying Tigers. I met him in 1990 at an AVG reunion in Ojai, California, where he shrugged off his year in Burma and China: "I never claimed to do very much," he said. Born in Michigan in 1917, he joined the U.S. Navy in 1939. He was assigned to a torpedo squadron aboard USS *Saratoga* when he was recruited for the AVG. Before sailing for Burma, he married a Michigan schoolteacher named Jean Buekema.

Assigned to the 1st Squadron, he took part in the Flying Tigers' first fight on December 20, a melee near Kunming in which 15 pilots were credited with shooting down four Kawasaki Ki-48 medium bombers, a tally confirmed in Japanese records. They had agreed to share the credit equally, so Brown like the others was credited with 0.27 enemy aircraft on his CAMCO bonus account. Sometime after this, he was apparently seconded to the CAF flight school, perhaps to replace the dead Marion Baugh. In time he returned to the combat squadrons when the flight school was closed down.

After the AVG was disbanded, Brown flew as a transport pilot for CNAC. Postwar, he went to medical school and became a doctor in 1951. After interning at Los Angeles County General Hospital, he flew for the newly formed Flying Tiger Line before beginning a medical career, specializing in neurology and anesthetics. At some point before 1962, he married for the second time, to Anne Heard, with whom he regularly attended CNAC/AVG reunions — by 1990 accompanied by no fewer than seventeen children, sons- and daughters-in law, and grandchildren. By this time, Dr. Brown was the physician at California's Corcoran State Penitentiary, where Charles Manson was among his patients. The last of the Flying Tigers pilots, he died at his Corcoran home in September 2015, three months before he would have celebrated his 100th birthday. What a life!

George Burgard was a native of Pennsylvania, born in 1915. He attended Bucknell and spent six years as a newspaperman before joining the U.S. Army. Trained in B-17s, he was serving as a Ferry

Command pilot when he joined the AVG. He was a flight leader in the 1st Squadron, awarded a Ten Star Wing Medal by the Chinese for his victories. (His CAMCO bonus account shows 10.79, with the fraction resulting from a strafe of a Japanese airfield while the Panda Bears were stationed at Rangoon.) Following his year in the AVG, Burgard flew for American Export Airlines; postwar, he ran a machine shop in his native Pennsylvania, where he died in 1978. The record shows him in a three-way tie as a double ace:

- 21 February 1942: 2 Ki-27 Nate fighters
- 25 February 1942: 1 bomber + 2 fighters
- 26 February 1942: 3 Ki-27 Nate fighters
- 12 June 1942: 1 Ki-45 Toryu fighter + 1 Ki-27 Nate fighter

The Kawasaki Ki-45 *Toryu* (Dragon Killer) was piloted by Sergeant Jiro Ieiri, commander of "Nagano Force" of about five of the new, twin-engine fighters, based at Canton. Ieiri was killed in the crash, but the radioman-gunner survived to have his picture taken with Burgard and other Flying Tigers. The Ki-45s fared so badly on this occasion that they were used thereafter only in ground support missions.

Herbert (Pat) Cavanah of New York City was a "Naval Aviation Pilot" in Patrol Squadron 12 when recruited for the AVG, meaning he was one of the last of the enlisted pilots in U.S. service. At 30 years of age, he was also one of the older AVG recruits. That plus his experience in the cockpit of a lumbering PBY Catalina flying boat was not good preparation for a P-40 Tomahawk; though assigned to the 3rd Squadron, he apparently never deployed with them to a combat area. He served to disbandment and was back in New York by August 1942, when he took a job as a ferry pilot for American Export Airlines. He may also have flown for CNAC in China, and in February 1945 he received an instrument rating as a lieutenant in the U.S. Navy. I have no idea what happened to him after that.

Allen Bert Christman was born 1915 in Fort Collins, Colorado. He got an engineering degree from what is now Colorado State University, moved to New York City, and worked as a comic-strip artist for the Associated Press, writing and drawing the "Scorchy Smith" series about an American pilot-adventurer. The work inspired him to take flying lessons and eventually to join the Navy as an aviation cadet in 1938. He served aboard USS *Ranger* with Tex Hill and Ed Rector, and with them signed up for the AVG. At the same time, he drew the "Three Aces" comic, featuring three pals who'd flown as mercenaries during the Spanish Civil War. That strip backed up the "Superman" adventures in *Action Comics* magazine.

In Burma, Christman famously drew caricatures of his mates in the 2nd Squadron, some of them actually painted on their P-40s. Sent down to Rangoon in January, he was shot down in his first aerial combat and again in his second. He survived the first misfortune but died in the second, on January 23, 1942, killed by machinegun fire as he floated down in his parachute. He was posthumously promoted to major in the Chinese Air Force.

Thomas Cole, born 1916 in Clayton, Missouri, was a PBY Catalina pilot recruited from Patrol Squadron 44 in San Diego. In his AVG identification photo, he seems older than most of his mates in the 2nd Squadron. For all that, he adapted well to the tricky P-40 Tomahawk, for he was the first "big boat" pilot to make the transition to fighters, and he went down to Rangoon with the rest of his squadron. Jim Howard remembered him as the "spark plug" of the Panda Bears' softball team.

Cole was credited with a Nakajima Ki-27 Nate fighter on January 24, 1942, but six days later was either shot down or flew into the ground on a strafing mission, trying to relieve the pressure on 17 Indian Division that was retreating from the Japanese advance. Tragically, the troops he tried to strafe were actually the Indians, so if he was indeed shot down, it was by friendly fire. Jim Howard was just ahead of him that day; he held his fire, and when he pulled out he glanced back in time to see Cole's Tomahawk disappear in a sheet of flame as it hit the ground. Like Bert Christman, he was posthumously promoted, to CAF captain in his case, and he was also awarded a Cloud Banner medal for "bravery and outstanding combat performance."

Edwin Conant was probably the most curious AVG volunteer. Born John Perry in San Diego, he dropped out of college to join the Army as an aviation cadet but washed out of the program. He then applied to the Navy under a friend's name and this time succeeded in his quest; in 1941 he too was flying a PBY Catalina off the California coast. Unlike Cole, he had a terrible time mastering the knack of landing a high-powered taildragger on an asphalt runway, smashing up three Tomahawks at the Toungoo training base. He didn't fly his first combat missions until the end of May 1942, over the Salween River and again down to Vietnam.

"Conant" served to disbandment, then rejoined the Navy and became an outstanding fighter pilot, to judge by three air-to-air victories over Japan and the award of a Silver Star for bravery. Postwar, he served as an early Navy helicopter pilot. He returned to civilian life under his borrowed name, but eventually he was outed by a sharp-eyed California highway department clerk who saw that two Edwin Conants — born in the same town on the same day! — were applying to renew their driver's licenses.

Elmer Cook from Santa Maria, California, was a fighter pilot with the Army's 8th Pursuit Group at Mitchel Field, New York, so should have been a good prospect for the AVG combat squadrons. However, he had crashed a P-40 in October 1940, and no sooner did he reach Burma than he submitted his resignation and went home, in September 1941. It was widely believed at the time that some men joined the AVG to get out of military service and become civilian airline pilots, and this may have been true of Cook.

Albert Criz, born 1917 in San Antonio, California, was another Army pilot with P-40 time, though with even less success: he crashed three fighters in the spring of 1941. He went to Burma but soon resigned. His discharge is dated three days before the Pearl Harbor attack, but he may actually have gone home earlier. A man with the same name helped design and build a "lifting body" glider for the U.S. Army in 1943. Whether that was the ex-AVG pilot or not, it does seem that Criz returned to Army service as a fighter pilot and made his way to China, for he crashed a North American P-51 at Tanchuk in July 1944. He died in 1997 in California.

John Croft from Trenton, New Jersey, was an Army pilot when he joined the AVG. He went down to Rangoon with the 1st Squadron, and served at other combat bases, but about the only recollection I can find of him is the day — February 6, 1942 — he tore off one landing gear at Mingaladon airport while landing from a fight. He served to disbandment and went to work as a test pilot for Republic

Aviation after he returned to the U.S.

James Cross from Huntsville, Missouri, was an Army ferry pilot and a friend of George Burgard and Charlie Bond. When they told him about the AVG, he eagerly signed up for duty in China. He was credited with a 0.27 share of a Kawasaki medium bomber shot down in that first great interception near Kunming on December 20, and he deployed to Rangoon and other combat outposts with the 1st Squadron. During the Salween River campaign, he was wounded in combat with a Nakajima Ki-27 Nate and was sent to India for treatment. He helped ferry Republic P-43 Lancer fighters from India to China and otherwise served with the group until it was disbanded in July 1942. He became a Pan American ferry pilot upon his return to the U.S.

John Dean from St. Peter, Minnesota, is a bit of a mystery, and I can't seem to find his branch of the military service when recruited for the AVG. He was assigned to the 1st Squadron when he arrived in Burma, flew up to Kunming with other pilots in December, and got that 0.27 victory credit during the group's first interception of a Japanese formation south of the city. His first actual shoot-down was at Rangoon on January 29, when he was credited with a Nakajima Ki-27 Nate fighter.

On June 12, over Guilin, China, he claimed another Nate and a twin-engine Kawasaki Ki-45 Toryu fighter, identified at the time as a bomber. He served to the AVG's disbandment, then joined CNAC as a ferry pilot, flying over the "Hump" of the Himalayas, equally at risk from Japanese fighters and collisions with the mountainous terrain. He and his crew perished on November 17, 1942, when their Douglas C-47 transport crashed en route to India. The wreck was located 70 years later on 13,500-foot Changshan Mountain near Dali city, but the crew's remains have not been recovered.

John Donovan from Montgomery, Alabama, was a Navy flight instructor at Pensacola when recruited for the AVG. To judge by his letters home, he was a rare Flying Tiger who enjoyed the food and accommodations in China; his major complaint was that he couldn't get enough flight time in a P-40 Tomahawk. He was assigned to the 3rd Squadron but did not deploy with them to Rangoon. Not until April did he see his first combat, when Nakajima Ki-43 Hayabusas of the 64th Sentai attacked the AVG's temporary base at Loiwing on the China-Burma border. He was credited with one Hayabusa shot down.

On May 12, 1942, Donovan took part in a raid on the Japanese airfield at Hanoi, northern Vietnam. Evidently he was flying one of the new P-40E Kittyhawks, for Link Laughlin recalled that Donovan and Tom Jones were "scudding down the runway unloading their fifty-calibers and dropping weed cutters [20-pound bombs] like they were going out of style." Donovan's plane was apparently hit by ground fire: "He goes straight into the runway and skids clear off the end in a big rolling ball of flame." His CAMCO bonus account also credited him with three planes destroyed on the ground on that occasion.

Parker Dupouy was born in Providence, Rhode Island, in 1917, and in 1939 he graduated from Brown University with an engineering degree. He was a P-40 pilot for the 8th Pursuit Group at Mitchel Field when Claude (Skip) Adair signed him up for the AVG. Flying for the 3rd Squadron, he deployed to Rangoon soon after the Pearl Harbor attack and led a six-man flight on December 23, when he was credited with damaging three Japanese aircraft. On Christmas Day he improbably claimed a Messerschmitt Bf-109, an identification that was confirmed by an English pilot.

As the Japanese pilots headed for home, Dupouy and Bill Reed chased two Hayabusas out over the Gulf of Martaban; Reed shot down the first and Dupouy went after the second, which was piloted by Lieutenant Okuyuma Hiroshi. Over-running his target, Dupouy's right wingtip sheared a wing off the lightly built Japanese fighter, which cartwheeled into the water. Dupouy successfully flew back to Mingaladon airfield and landed safely.

On March 21, 1942, over the fall-back base at Magwe, he was credited with another Hayabusa shot down. Later, over Loiwing on April 28, he and Tom Haywood were jointly credited with yet another Hayabusa, for a total of 3.5 air-to-air victories. Dupouy served with the AVG to its disbandment, and afterward went to work for Republic Aviation, testing P-47 Thunderbolts as they came off the assembly line. Married, with four children, he died in 1994.

John Farrell *of Kansas City, Missouri, was one of the Army flight instructors recruited as check pilots for the CAF. Like John Black-*

burn, he made an early transition to the P-40 and deployed to Rangoon with the AVG 1st Squadron in January 1942. He apparently had second thoughts. In his diary, Charlie Bond noted that Farrell was one of two pilots who declared "No more P-40 flying" and hoped to pilot the AVG Beechcraft transport instead.

Nevertheless, Farrell dutifully escorted Blenheim bombers over the Salween River on February 21 and engaged in a battle with Nakajima Ki-27 Nates that were also escorting bombers to the front. He took a bullet through his windscreen but was credited with shooting down one of the Japanese fighters. He was decorated with the Cloud Banner, served with the AVG to its disbandment, and returned to the U.S. Army. In the 1950s, he was apparently living in Chicago, but I can find nothing else about his life after the Flying Tigers.

William Fish of Newtonville, Mass., graduated from Maine's Bowdoin College in 1938. He joined the Navy, earned his wings, and in time signed up for the AVG. He qualified in the P-40 Tomahawk and was assigned to the 2nd Squadron, but evidently never deployed to a combat base. In May 1942, he received an honorable discharge for "tropical diseases," as he explained in an article for the *Philadelphia Inquirer*. "After a rest," he promised, "I'm going to report for further service." Evidently he did, because the article is attributed to *Lieutenant* Fish. I can find no other information about him.

Ben Foshee was born in 1915 in Red Level, Alabama, and graduated from Alabama Polytech (now Auburn University). He was a Navy aviator when recruited for the AVG. He qualified in the P-40 and was assigned to the 3rd Squadron, but evidently spent much of his time piloting the Beechcraft as one of Chennault's pilots. On May 4, 1942, he was caught on the ground by a Japanese bomber raid at Baoshan, China, as the Flying Tigers were falling back toward Kunming. He was badly wounded, as were an AVG ground crewman, a CAMCO employee, and several Chinese hostel workers. A Chinese doctor tried to amputate his leg, but Foshee insisted on waiting for the group surgeon. He died before Doc Richards could reach him.

Henry Fuller *was another of the army flight instructors who signed up as a check pilot for the CAF. Born in 1916, the son of a prominent Florida politician, he graduated from the University of*

Miami. He resigned from the CAF flight school shortly after the outbreak of hostilities and thus received a "dishonorable discharge" from Chennault. He flew for Pan American and the Air Transport Command. Postwar he graduated from Miami University Law School in 1950 and began practicing law. He was killed in a fishing accident in 1958.

Henry Geselbracht was born 1918 in Kansas City, Missouri, and had his first airplane flight when he was 16, at the Chicago World's Fair. He enrolled at Washington University in St. Louis, but transferred to the University of California at Los Angeles, graduating in 1939. As a Navy aviator, he flew one of the attack planes in the Hollywood epic *Dive Bomber*. He was himself a dive bomber pilot, posted to USS *Saratoga* with other AVG recruits including Bob Neale and Jim Howard. He was assigned to the 2nd Squadron and went down to Rangoon for the air superiority battles of January 1942. But it was not until the ill-fated raid on Japanese targets in Thailand on March 24 that he got his first victory credits.

"Gesel" was one of four pilots who strafed the railroad station at Chiang Mai and then some barracks and vehicles in the vicinity of Lamphun, where Jack Newkirk crashed and was killed. Supposedly 15 Japanese aircraft were destroyed on the ground at Chiang Mai by the other AVG flight, and as often happened when a pilot was killed, the survivors split the bonus money among everyone taking part in the mission, adding 1.50 to each man's CAMCO bonus account. Gesel was among those who volunteered two weeks' extra service with the AVG. He died in Los Angeles in 1969.

Henry Gilbert was the youngest Flying Tiger, and one of the first to fall in combat. A native of Bremerton, Washington, he was fresh out of Navy flight school at Pensacola when he volunteered to fly for China. (As the story is told, so many Pensacola aviators wanted to sign up that the commander tore the list in half.) He didn't reach Burma until the end of October, when he was assigned to the AVG 3rd Squadron. He went down to Rangoon with the other Hell's Angels soon after the outbreak of war, and he was among those who intercepted a "huge conglomeration" of Mitsubishi Ki-21 heavy bombers over the waterfront on December 23, 1941, in his and the squadron's first combat. Fate did not permit him to learn the rules of aerial survival, for he was caught in the crossfire from the bombers' defensive guns. An incendiary bullet must have hit the Tomahawk's fuel tank, for it exploded in flames and fell into the harbor. He had celebrated his 22nd birthday in October.

Edgar Goyette was born 1911 in Sebring, Florida. A Navy aviator, he was serving at the Norfolk base when he signed up with the AVG, by which time he was 30 years old, an age at which the zest for combat begins to fade. Though he qualified in the P-40 and was duly attached to the 2nd Squadron, Chennault evidently considered him more suitable as a staff officer. So, when the combat squadrons moved to Rangoon and Kunming after the Pearl Harbor attack, Goyette remained at the Toungoo training base, which was to serve as a repair and supply depot for the Americans stationed at Mingaladon airport outside Rangoon.

He later briefly served at Mingaladon as its maintenance and supply officer, then took an AVG convoy up the Burma Road to Kunming. Chennault assigned him first to the CAF flight school, then to the team ferrying Republic P-43 Lancer fighters from India to China for the CAF. (These substandard Army fighters had been released to China to equip the 3rd American Volunteer Group. The project was canceled with the outbreak of war, and in U.S. service the Lancer served mostly as a combat trainer and as the prototype for the P-47 Thunderbolt.) After surviving two wrecks, he returned to Kunming "and again started my training program with the Chinese pilots and around the 1st of July started back home as the AVG was disbanded." He apparently then joined the Army, and postwar flew for Eastern Airlines. He died in 2000.

Paul (P.J.) Greene from Clarendon, Texas, was born in 1917 and attended New Mexico Military Institute before becoming an aviation cadet at the Army's Randolph Field. He crashed a North American BT-9 trainer in March 1941 but evidently satisfied his superiors that he had the right stuff to be a flight instructor; he was serving at Randolph with R.T. Smith when they joined the AVG. Both were assigned to the 3rd Squadron and took part in its early combats at Rangoon in December 1941. "P.J." flew on Hank Gilbert's wing in that first combat on December 23. The same day, he was credited with shooting down a Nakajima Ki-27 fighter and was himself shot down.

As would happen later to Bert Christman, he bailed out and was strafed in his parachute, but was saved when an RAF pilot in a Brewster Buffalo drove the Nate away.

In the spring of 1942, P.J. helped ferry replacement P-40E Kittyhawk fighters to China, and on April 28 he was credited with shooting down a Nakajima Ki-41 Hayabusa fighter. Returning to the U.S. Army after the AVG was disbanded, he helped train pilots and as a lieutenant colonel deployed to Italy as commander of the 97th Fighter Squadron, flying Lockheed P-38 Lightnings. Postwar, he ran a salvage firm in Long Beach, California, and was involved in other business ventures, meanwhile building and flying his own home-built aircraft. He settled in Washington State. He died in Texas in 2005.

Clifford Groh, born 1917 in Wilmette, Illinois, was a Navy pilot when recruited for the AVG. Assigned to the 3rd Squadron, he was credited with his first victory — a Nakajima Ki-27 Nate — at Magwe, Burma, on March 21, 1942. This was evidently the fighter flown by Major Okabe Tadashi, commander of the Japanese army's 11th Sentai. On April 8, over Loiwing on the China-Burma border, he was credited with his second kill, a Nakajima Ki-43 Hayabusa of the 64th Sentai. From Japanese accounts of the air war in Southeast Asia, it seems clear that this was the fighter flown by Captain Anma Katsui, a squadron leader in the 64th Sentai who had been credited with destroying at least 12 enemy planes in China, Malaya, and the Dutch East Indies. His Hayabusa crashed in a paddy field two miles south of the Loiwing airstrip, with four AVG pilots — Groh, Wolf, Overend, and R.T. Smith — each claiming it as his own.

Groh served with the group until it was disbanded, and afterward was a transport pilot for CNAC. Postwar, he was one of the founding pilots of the Flying Tiger Line. He died in 1979.

Ralph Gunvordahl, born in 1919 in Burke, South Dakota, was a Navy aviator before joining the AVG. As a wingman with the 3rd Squadron Hell's Angels, he was credited with destroying a Mitsubishi Ki-21 heavy bomber during that December 23 battle over Rangoon. He resigned in January 1942 with a disaffected group of four AVG pilots, five ground crewmen, and two CAF check pilots, each of whom received a "dishonorable discharge" from Chennault. By April he was in Chicago and planning to visit his parents in South Dakota before going on a "secret mission," according to the *Chicago Tribune*. He evidently was killed in 1943 while flying as a test pilot, whether for the military or for an airframe company.

Lester (Joe) Hall *of Salina, Kansas, attended Kansas State College before joining the Army and becoming a flight instructor. Recruited for the CAF flight school, he volunteered for the combat squadrons when the school closed down in the spring of 1942. He was assigned to the 2nd Squadron and flew his first combat mission over the Salween River toward the end of May. He served two extra weeks after the AVG was disbanded on July 4. (Curiously, his discharge certificate does not show this additional service.) He later flew as a transport pilot for CNAC. On March 14, 1944, he lost an engine flying over the Hump and had to jettison millions of dollars worth of newly printed Chinese currency. In the 1950s he worked as an instrument-flying instructor for airline pilots in Denver.*

Maax Hammer was born 1916 in East St. Louis, Illinois. (The spelling of his first name was a family inheritance.) He attended Washington University in St. Louis, Missouri, across the Mississippi River from his home town. He later transferred to Louisiana State University, obtained a private pilot certificate, and joined the U.S. Army. After completing flight training at Kelly Field, Texas, he was assigned to fly P-40s on the East Coast, probably for the 8th Pursuit Group at Mitchel Field, where he was recruited for the AVG. Eight days after he reached Burma, he was killed in a training accident on September 22, 1941, when his P-40 got into an inverted spin. Buried at St. Luke's graveyard in Toungoo alongside Armstrong and Atkinson, and like them was transferred postwar to India and Hawaii, to be identified and brought home for burial in 2017.

David Harris was born in Mount Pleasant, Michigan, in 1917. He attended Governor Dummer Academy in Massachusetts and enrolled at Amherst College, dropping out after a year to become an Army pilot. He was assigned to the 8th Pursuit Group at Mitchel Field, New York, when he joined the AVG in the summer of 1941. At Toungoo, he qualified in the Curtiss P-40, but when his good friend Pete Atkinson died in a training accident, he requested and was given a staff job. (One of Chennault's talents as a commander was to make the best use of the material at hand. If he thought less of a pilot who didn't want to fly combat, he never seemed to show it.) Harris served to the group's disbandment and afterward was a test pilot for the Republic and Grumman companies. Postwar, he was a businessman, sailor, and glider pilot. He died in 2012 in Frankfort, Michigan.

Raymond Hastey was born about 1902 in Chipley, Georgia. An Army pilot, he would have been 39 when he joined the AVG — a bit old for combat flying in the 1940s. Nevertheless, he qualified in the Curtiss P-40, went down to Rangoon with the 2nd Squadron, and on January 24, 1942, was credited with a Mitsubishi Ki-21 heavy bomber in what appears to have been his first combat sortie. Four days later, his Tomahawk was crippled by a Japanese fighter; he bailed out. Remembering what happened to Bert Christman, he let himself fall free for "a mile" before pulling his ripcord.

As the story is told, the experience so unnerved him that he asked to be taken off flight status. Bob Neale obliged, making him the squadron's transportation officer, a lucrative position with its opportunities to send black-market goods to China. In May, at Kunming, he resigned and went home, receiving the customary dishonorable discharge. He returned to Army service and retired as a lieutenant colonel in 1962. He died in 1999 in California at the admirable age of 97.

Thomas Haywood was born 1917 in St. Paul, Minnesota, and studied aeronautical engineering at the state university before dropping out to become a Marine Corps aviator. He was flying a Grumman fighter for VMF-1 at Quantico, Virginia, when he joined the AVG. Assigned to the 3rd Squadron, he deployed to Rangoon with the Hell's Angels in December 1941 and was credited with shooting down three Mitsubishi Ki-21 heavy bombers during the Christmas campaign. On January 17, 1942, the squadron having returned to Kunming, he shared the credit for yet another Ki-21 intercepted near the China-Vietnam frontier. And on the great April 28 turkey shoot near Loiwing, he again claimed a one-half victory credit, this one against a Nakajima Ki-43 Hayabusa of the 64th Sentai.

Haywood served to the group's disbandment, and after returning to the U.S. he ferried Consolidated B-24 Liberator bombers for a military contractor. Postwar, he joined the Flying Tiger Line. When he died in 1979, the company gave his name to a newly delivered

Boeing 747 that would later crash upon landing at Singapore as a result of poor communication between the pilot and the airport control tower.

Robert (Duke) Hedman was the only Flying Tiger, and one of the few fighter pilots anywhere, to become an ace in a single firefight, on December 25, 1941. (The AVG record is confused because one of those victories was shifted to an earlier day, and again because he and his mates had agreed to share their bonus credits equally.) Born 1916 in Webster, South Dakota, he attended the University of North Dakota and was serving with the 1st Pursuit Group at Michigan's Selfridge Field when he joined the AVG. The Chinese awarded him a Six Star Wing Medal.

Hedman stayed on as a pilot for CNAC, making 350 flights over the Hump of the Himalayas between India and China. Postwar, he flew for the Flying Tiger Line until he retired in 1971. Though his CAMCO bonus account stands at only 4.83, he was actually credited with 6 victories, putting him in a three-way tie as the AVG's tenth-ranking ace. He died in Las Vegas in 1995.

- 25 December 1941: 4 Ki-21 Sally bombers + 1 Ki-43 Hayabusa fighter
- 10 April 1942: shared 1 Ki-43 Hayabusa fighter
- 20 April 1942: shared 1 Ki-15 Babs observation plane

The Hayabusa supposedly shot down on April 10 was flown by Sergeant Yasuda Yoshito of the 64th Sentai. Yasuda not only survived the encounter but managed to fly back to Chiang Mai — and to live through the war, later writing about this combat in terms that make it certain he was the pilot supposedly shot down by Older and Hedman.

John Hennessy was born 1916 in Brookline, Massachusetts. He became a pilot in the Navy and was probably a married man when he joined the AVG. Though attached to the 1st Squadron, I can find no evidence that he ever flew the Curtiss P-40; perhaps, like Dave Harris, he was unnerved by the fatal training accidents at Toungoo. Instead he became the primary pilot for the group's twin engine Beechcraft transport, a plane notorious for its mechanical failures. After one tricky forced landing, Charlie Bond lauded Hennessy in his diary as "one damn good pilot."

Hennessy famously broke into the post office at Lashio, Burma, to collect mail for the AVG just before the city fell to the advancing

Japanese army. He served with the group until its disbandment, then returned to the U.S., where a New York newsman photographed him in Flying Tiger uniform with Dick Rossi, Pat Cavanah, and Louise Hennessy, his wife. Evidently he then went to work a test pilot. Postwar, he flew for American Airlines. He died in Center Harbor, New Hampshire, in 1991.

David (Tex) Hill was born 1916 in Korea to a missionary father who later became chaplain to the Texas Rangers. He graduated from Austin College in 1938 and joined the Navy soon after, serving as a dive bomber pilot on USS *Saratoga* and *Ranger*. He replaced Jack Newkirk as commander of the 2nd Squadron Panda Bears in March 1942. With 10.25 air-to-air victories and another plane destroyed on the ground, he was decorated with the British Distinguished Flying Cross and the Chinese Nine Star Wing Medal. (It ought to have been a Ten Star Medal, but his final victory was credited after the AVG had officially gone out of business.)

Devoted to Chennault, Hill was one of just five Flying Tigers who accepted induction into the U.S. Army in July 1942. He was commissioned as a major and continued to lead the Panda Bears, now designated the USAAF 75th Fighter Squadron; and on his second combat tour in China, he commanded the parent 23rd Fighter Group. Meanwhile he scored six more air-to-air victories and became a triple ace. The young Army fighter pilots who served under him were fond of his laid-back briefings, which might consist of just three words: "Y'all follow me!"

Postwar, he served in the Texas Air National Guard and Air Force Reserve, retiring as a brigadier general. He died in San Antonio in 2007. His combat record with the Flying Tigers:
- 3 January 1942: 1 Ki-27 Nate fighter
- 23 January 1942: 2 Ki-27 Nate fighters
- 24 January 1942: 1 Ki-21 Sally bomber + 1 Ki-27 Nate fighter
- 29 January 1942: 1 Ki-27 Nate fighter
- 24 April 1942: shared 1 Ki-15 Babs observation plane
- 28 April 1942: 2 Ki-43 Hayabusa fighters
- 5 May 1942: 1 Ki-43 Hayabusa fighter
- 6 July 1942: 1 Ki-27 Nate fighter

Fred Hodges of Memphis, Tennessee, was an Army pilot with the

1st Pursuit Group at Selfridge Field in Michigan when he signed up for the AVG. As the story is told, he was nicknamed "Fearless" for his dread of the insects that populated the barrack at Toungoo. He was assigned to the 3rd Squadron and flew in combat during the Christmas battles over Rangoon. But it was not until the AVG fell back to Magwe that he was credited with a Nakajima Ki-43 Hayabusa of the 64th Sentai. He was most famous for his marriage to an Anglo-Burman girl, Helen Anderson, at the Loiwing factory toward the end of March, when the pilots elected the CAMCO manager as mayor on the theory that, like a ship's captain, he would then be able to officiate at a wedding. (Olga Greenlaw said that the marriage was later regularized by British Army chaplain.)

Hodges served with the group until it was disbanded, then flew at least briefly for CNAC. He must have left China after a year or so, because in 1944 Major Fred Hodges was serving with the USAAF 369th Fighter Squadron in England, flying a P-51 painted with the Flying Tiger shark face.

Louis (Cokey) Hoffman was born 1898 in Patterson, New Jersey, so was 43 when he joined the AVG as the oldest of its pilot-recruits. His family had moved to San Diego when he was a boy, and he joined the California National Guard at the outbreak of the First World War. As soon as he turned 17, he joined the Navy and served aboard the cruiser USS *Dale* in Asian waters.

Hoffman earned his wings as a Naval Aviation Pilot (an enlisted aviator, usually with the rank of chief petty officer) at the somewhat advanced age of 30. He flew almost every sort of Navy warplane, on floats and wheels, off battleship catapults and carrier decks. Among other assignments he was one of the "Flying Chiefs" of VF-2, flying a biplane fighter aboard USS *Langley*, the Navy's first aircraft carrier. However, a Navy aviator had to leave combat status after twenty years of service, so in 1935 Hoffman was sent to Pensacola as a flight instructor — an enlisted man teaching prospective officers how to fly, with all that that entailed in the status-conscious U.S. Navy.

I interviewed his widow in 1989 and came away with the understanding that by 1941 Hoffman had left the active-duty Navy and was a reservist on a refresher course at Pensacola when he signed up for the AVG. (He apparently got his nickname as a result of the quantities of Coca Cola he drank on shipboard, en route to Singapore and Rangoon.) As a member of the 1st Squadron, he was commended for his stubborn attack on Japanese bombers on December 20 near Kunming, pressing his attack until only one .30-caliber machinegun was firing; with the other pilots engaged that day, he got a 0.27 victory credit on his CAMCO bonus account. At the end of the year, he went down to Rangoon with the other "Adam & Eves," only to be shot down and killed in his first fighter-to-fighter combat on January 26, 1942.

Leo Houle was born 1914 in Worcester, Massachusetts. He was a Navy aviator when he joined the AVG but found himself in the same Catch-22 as some other late arrivals in Burma: he didn't have enough experience to qualify in the P-40, and without qualifying he couldn't serve with his squadron at Rangoon. He resigned with three other pilots in January 1942, returned to the U.S., and went back on active duty with the Navy. As a lieutenant, he served at Squantum Naval Air Station in Massachusetts, teaching WAVE (female volunteer) officers to fly.

James Howard was born 1913 in Canton, China, where his father was a medical missionary teaching eye surgery. In 1927 the family returned to Missouri, and he graduated from a St. Louis prep school. He went to Pomona College in California, intending to follow his father into medicine; soon after getting his bachelor's degree, however, he joined the Navy and earned his aviator's wings. In the summer of 1941 he was assigned to USS *Enterprise* at Pearl Harbor, but was on temporary duty on the West Coast aboard *Saratoga* when the AVG recruiter signed him up.

As a member of the 2nd Squadron, he earned the nickname (from Greg Boyington) of "the automatic pilot" for the methodical way he pressed his strafing attacks on Japanese airfields in Thailand. His CAMCO bonus account reached 6.33 aircraft, but four of those were on the ground. In air-to-air combat, he was credited with a one-third share of a Japanese reconnaissance plane on January 19, 1942; a Nakajima Ki-27 Nate fighter on January 24; and another Nate over China on July 4, the day the AVG was formally disbanded.

Like several other pilots, Howard served two extra weeks before returning home and joining the Army as a captain in the USAAF. In England, he commanded the 356th Fighter Squadron and again displayed his steadiness and resolve while escorting B-17 Flying Fortress bombers, credited with destroying three or more German fighters in a melee on January 11, 1944, a feat he shrugged off with the faux-hillbilly comment: "I seen my duty and I done it." He was awarded the Medal of Honor for his heroism on that occasion, making him the second Flying Tiger to be so honored. Postwar, he continued on active and reserve duty with the U.S. Air Force until retiring with the rank of brigadier general. He died in 1995 in Florida.

Lynn Hurst from Tulsa, Oklahoma, was another of the Navy aviators aboard USS *Saratoga* who volunteered for the AVG. He was given a medical discharge in February 1942, but I can find nothing else about him, whether during his AVG service or afterward.

Kenneth Jernstedt was born 1917 in Yamhill County, Oregon. He graduated from Oregon's Linfield College in 1939. He joined the Marines, earned his wings at Pensacola, and was stationed at Quantico, Virginia, making 17 carrier landings with Grumman fighters on USS *Wasp* and *Ranger*. He joined the AVG with Tom Haywood and Chuck Older, and sailed with them as part of the first large contingent of volunteers for the Chinese Air Force. Assigned to the 3rd Squadron, he deployed with his fellow Marines to Rangoon after the outbreak of hostilities and was credited with shooting down a Mitsubishi Ki-21 heavy bomber on December 23, 1941, and a Nakajima Ki-47 Hayabusa fighter on Christmas Day. Over Magwe on March 28, 1942, he was credited with another Hayabusa, for a total of three air-to-air victories.

While stationed at Magwe, Jernstedt ran his CAMCO bonus account up to 10.5 by a remarkably successful strafe (with Bill Reed) of two Japanese-occupied airfields near Rangoon. He served with the group to disbandment and afterward joined Republic Aviation as a test pilot. Postwar he returned to Oregon and ran a Coca Cola bottling company, meanwhile serving as mayor of Hood River and state legislator. He died in 2013.

Thomas Jones from Seattle, Washington, was a Navy dive bomber pilot on USS *Yorktown* when recruited for the AVG, and in the spring of 1942 he would help adapt the group's newly arrived P-40E Kittyhawks to that purpose. He was of course tapped for the 2nd Squadron with its preponderance of ex-Navy personnel, and he rose to vice squadron leader despite a comparative lack of combat activity in the group's early months. He was credited with shooting down a Nakajima Ki-43 Hayabusa in the great April 28 turkey shoot — his only air-to-air victory, though credited with destroying three planes on the ground at Hanoi in the strafing and bombing raid in which John Donovan was killed. He was also active in bombing Japanese troop formations on the Salween River.

On May 16, 1942, Jones was making practice runs at the Kunming bomb and gunnery range when "when he suddenly failed to pull out and crashed into the target area," as armorer Chuck Baisden recalled. "He was killed instantly. It appeared to be target fixation to me, but we will never know for sure."

Robert (Bus) Keeton from Manzanola, Colorado, was another Navy aviator and one of the "big boat" PBY Catalina pilots from Patrol Squadron 12, and he too was tapped for the 2nd Squadron. (He owed his nickname to the Hollywood comic Buster Keaton.) In February 1942, he was stationed at the former AVG training base at Toungoo as a test pilot, checking out P-40 Tomahawks as they were repaired from damage sustained at Rangoon. One day, six single-engine Mitsubishi Ki-30 light bombers attacked Kyedaw with an escort of Nakajima Ki-27 Nate fighters. Keeton was caught on the ground on that occasion, but in the afternoon the siren went off again, and this time he managed to take off before the enemy came in sight, flying one of the war-weary P-40s — without oxygen. He climbed to 20,000 feet, where his head began to hurt so badly that he descended to a lower altitude, just in time to attack what must have been a Kawasaki Ki-48 medium bomber returning from a raid upcountry. He was credited with the victory. After he moved back to China, he was credited with a Nakajima Ki-43 Hayabusa fighter on April 21. He served with the group until its disbandment, and served as a Pan American ferry pilot when he returned to the United States.

John Kelleher from Goldendale, Washington, was likely born in 1917. He was probably an Army pilot, and he must have rejoined the Army upon returning to the U.S., because his name would later appear in the USAAF "accidents and incidents" list. In any event, he quit the AVG soon after reaching Burma, with a discharge date of September 24, 1941.

Donald Knapp was born 1918 and gave his home town as San Diego, California, suggesting that he was a Navy aviator, perhaps a flying-boat captain. He was one of four AVG pilots who quit in January 1942 because they hadn't been able to qualify in the Curtiss P-40. He later served as a Grumman F4F Wildcat pilot in the Pacific theater. He died in New Mexico in 1996.

Matthew Kuykendall from San Saba, Texas, was born 1918 and obtained a private pilot certificate while an undergraduate at Texas A&M. He joined the Army, earned his wings, and was stationed at Barksdale Field, Louisiana, in January 1941 when he crashed a Seversky P-35 fighter. Later, on temporary duty at Eglin Field, Florida, he learned about the AVG from Ajax Baumler.

In Burma, he joined the 1st Squadron and deployed with it to Rangoon, where he was wounded in a battle over Mingaladon airport on January 29, 1942. (War correspondents were told not to mention pilots by name, and Kuykendall on that occasion was identified as "Kirk from San Saba.") But it was not until May 5, over the AVG fall-back base at Baoshan, China, that he was credited with his first and only victory, a Nakajima Ki-27 Nate of the 11th Sentai. He served to disbandment and afterward flew for American Export Airlines and worked for Consolidated Aircraft in Fort Worth, Texas. Postwar, he returned to San Saba and managed the family ranch until his death in 1974.

Chauncey (Link) Laughlin was born 1916 in Independence, Missouri, but grew up in Olathe, Kansas. He graduated from Westminster College in Fulton, Missouri, later famous as the site of Winston Churchill's 1946 "Iron Curtain" speech. He joined the Marines in 1940, earned his wings at Pensacola, and remained there as a flight instructor before joining the AVG and going to Burma in November 1941. He was assigned to the 3rd Squadron but remained at Kyedaw airfield in Toungoo when the Hell's Angels deployed to Rangoon in December. On Christmas Eve, he and Frank Adkins were tapped to replace the two pilots who had been killed the previous day at Mingaladon, but the squadron moved back to Kunming before they had a chance for aerial combat.

On April 8, over Lowing on the China-Burma border, Laughlin was credited with shooting down two Nakajima Ki-43 Hayabusa fighters of the 64th Sentai, and on April 25 he was one of five pilots who claimed a reconnaissance plane (probably a Mitsubishi Ki-51 Sonia) near Loiwing, to bring his air-to-air tally to 2.2 enemy aircraft. On May 12, he was also credited with three planes destroyed on the ground at Hanoi, northern Vietnam. After the AVG disbanded in July, he flew for CNAC until he went back to the U.S. in 1944. He then returned to the Marines — as a lowly second lieutenant, though he was soon promoted to major. Postwar, he flew for the Flying Tiger Line and became a businessman and journalist in Florida, where he died in 1995.

Frank (Whitey) Lawlor was born 1914 in Winston-Salem, North Carolina. He graduated from the state university and joined the Navy in 1938; he was a fighter pilot on USS *Saratoga* on the West Coast when he joined the AVG. He deployed to Rangoon with the 2nd Squadron, where he became an ace with five claims against Japanese fighters, all Nakajima Ki-27 Nates. He added two more in May, and was duly awarded a Seven Star Wing Medal by the Chinese. He returned to the Navy after completing his AVG tour, ending the war as a lieutenant commander. He died in 1973 and is buried at Arlington National Cemetery. He tied Charlie Bond and Jack Newkirk as the eighth-ranking AVG ace with 7 air-to-air victories:

- 23 January 1942: 4 Ki-27 Nate fighters
- 29 January 1942: 1 Ki-27 Nate fighter
- 5 May 1942: 2 Ki-27 Nate fighters

Robert Layher was born 1916 in Dallas, Oregon, but grew up in Otis, Colorado. He was yet another of the PBY Catalina pilots with Patrol Squadron 12 in San Diego who signed up for the AVG. Assigned to the 2nd Squadron, he went to Rangoon at the end of 1941 and was credited with a one-third share of a Japan reconnaissance plane plus a half share of a fighter destroyed on the ground. He served two extra weeks in China, then rejoined the Navy when he returned to the U.S. For the rest of the war, he flew a Sikorsky S-44 flying boat for American Export Airlines on the naval diplomatic run. In 1946 he returned to Colorado as a rancher, later settling in Kansas. He died in 2006.

Edward Leibolt from Camden, Ohio, was a P-40 pilot in the Army when he joined the AVG. On the ship coming over, he met a Canadian woman whom he continued to see when he was stationed at Toungoo (and later at Rangoon). Assigned to the 1st Squadron, he took part in the melee near Kunming on December 20, earning a 0.27 victory credit in his CAMCO bonus account. He then deployed to Rangoon with the other Adam & Eves.

In the afternoon of February 25, 1942, Leibolt took off from Mingaladon as flight leader to intercept a Japanese formation. His engine apparently began to falter, and at 6,000 feet he opened his canopy, whether to bail out or to improve his vision for a forced landing. Dick Rossi took over the leadership role, and Leibolt was never seen again, though over the next several days the Adam & Eves flew a grid search pattern over the rivers and paddy fields of South Burma. It would be pleasant to think that he walked off into the sunset with his Canadian friend, but more likely he died in the crash of his Tomahawk or at the hands of the Japanese who soon occupied South Burma.

Leibolt couldn't have flown his usual aircraft on February 25, because a P-40 Tomahawk bearing his name as pilot later served with the 23rd Fighter Group in Kunming. John Leibolt, the son of of the missing man, would later serve as a Flying Tiger Line pilot.

Robert Little came from Spokane, Washington. He was an Army pilot (probably with the 8th Pursuit Group at Mitchel Field, New York) when recruited for the AVG. He served with the 1st Squadron in Rangoon, where he was credited with no fewer than nine Nakajima Ki-27 Nate fighters in January and February 1942, as well as a Nakajima Ki-43 Hayabusa over Loiwing on April 8, putting him in a three-way tie with George Burgard and Chuck Older as the AVG's third-ranking ace. He was killed in action while bombing Japanese positions on the Salween River on May 22, 1942. His P-40E Kittyhawk was hit by anti-aircraft fire, which may have detonated one of the bombs he was carrying.

- 29 January 1942: 1 Ki-27 Nate fighter
- 6 February 1942: 2 Ki-27 Nate fighters
- 25 February 1942: 3 Ki-27 Nate fighters
- 26 February 1942: 3 Ki-27 Nate fighters
- 8 April 1942: 1 Ki-43 Hayabusa fighter

Ernest (Buster) Loane *was born in Presque Isle, Maine, in 1917. He graduated from Bowdoin College, joined the Army, earned his* wings, and was a flight instructor at Kelly Field, Texas, when he signed up as a Chinese Air Force check pilot. When the flight school closed down in the spring of 1942, he became a P-40 pilot in the AVG 1st Squadron, the Adam & Eves. He served two extra weeks with the group, to smooth the transition to the 23rd Fighter Group, then joined CNAC to fly transports over the Hump between India and China. He stayed with the Chinese airline until 1947, when he signed on with Chennault's Civilian Air Transport, on paramilitary flights until the Communist victory in 1949. He later flew for the Flying Tiger Line. He died in 1977.

William (Mac) McGarry from Los Angeles attended Loyola College before joining the Army and becoming a P-40 pilot with the 1st Pursuit Group at Selfridge Field. Some accounts say he designed the logo for the 1st Squadron Adam & Eves, showing a snake twined around a green apple. (The apple couldn't be red for fear it might be mistaken for the *hinomaru* sunburst on the wings and fuselage of Japanese warplanes.) He became an ace over Thailand and South Burma in January and February 1942, and on March 24 was one of Chennault's picked team that strafed Chiang Mai airfield.

Hit by anti-aircraft fire, McGarry struggled to retain altitude for the return flight, but finally bailed out over northern Thailand. Captured by Thai police, he was roughly interrogated by the Japanese but then returned to local authorities and the comparative comfort of a Thai jail. Freed in 1945, he earned his law degree from Loyola and followed a military and civilian practice until he retired to Desert Hot Springs, California. The record credits him with 8 air-to-air victories, making him the seventh-ranking AVG ace and the only one to have been taken prisoner:

- 26 January 1942: 1 Ki-27 Nate fighter
- 6 February 1942: 1 Ki-27 Nate fighter
- 25 February 1942: 4 Ki-27 Nate fighters
- 26 February 1942: 2 Ki-27 Nate fighters

With additional credit for planes destroyed on the ground (including the Chiang Mai strafe), McGarry's CAMCO bonus account stood at 10.29. He died in 1990, not long before the wreck of his P-40 Tomahawk — tail number P-8115 — was found in the rain forest and put on display at Chiang Mai airport. It was the discovery of those relics that prompted me to write *Remains: A Novel of the Flying*

Tigers, which begins and ends with the wreckage of a Tomahawk in the rain forest.

Maurice McGuire of San Jacinto, California, was a Navy pilot on USS *Saratoga* when he joined the AVG. Like several other recruits, no sooner did he reach Burma than he resigned and went home, with a discharge date of September 24, 1941. A test pilot for Ryan aircraft, he was killed in a crash in March 1945.

George McMillan was born 1916 in Winter Garden, Florida, and graduated from South Carolina's Citadel military college in 1938. He earned his wings the following year, serving first as a fighter pilot with the 20th Pursuit Group in California and then as a test pilot at Eglin Field, Florida, where he was recruited for the AVG. Assigned to the 3rd Squadron, he was credited with 3.5 bombers shot down over Rangoon during the Christmas campaign, and was himself shot down on Christmas Day, 1941. He added another on January 17, 1942, near the China-Vietnam border, for a total of 4.5 air-to-air victories. Because bonus payments were sometimes divided equally among pilots taking part in an interception, his CAMCO account was actually lower.

McMillan served to disbandment, rejoined the Army, and returned to China as a major to serve briefly with the Chinese-American Composite Wing before taking command of the 449th Fighter Squadron, flying the Lockheed P-38 Lightning. He was credited with four additional Japanese fighters before he was killed in action on June 24, 1944.

Lacy Mangleburg of Athens, Georgia, was an Army pilot with the 20th Pursuit Group at Hamilton Field, California, flying Curtiss P-36 and P-40 fighters. He joined the AVG, sailed for Burma, and trained with the mostly Navy pilots of the 2nd Squadron. In December 1941, he was picked by Erik Shilling as part of a team to test the suitability of three Curtiss-Wright CW-21 Demon fighters for the AVG. Based on a civilian sportplane, the Demon had an impressive rate of climb but was too lightly built to survive in combat, as Dutch pilots were discovering over Java. Chennault wanted them in Kunming, however, because they could easily out-climb the much heavier P-40 Tomahawk, giving the AVG a better chance to stop the occasional high-flying scout plane that flew over the city.

On Christmas Eve, therefore, the Demon pilots set out for Lashio, halfway up the Burma Road, a trip on which the engine of Shilling's plane kept misfiring. At Lashio a mechanic suggested refueling with lower-octane gasoline, which the three pilots did. They took off again, crossing into China at 5:30 p.m., by which time Shilling's engine was again misfiring. Sixty miles from Kunming, it quit altogether, and he made a successful forced landing. The Demons had no radios, and Shilling had the only map. After wandering aimlessly for some time, the other two pilots also made crash landings. Mangleburg first tried to land in a river, but powered off again and slammed into a terraced slope, where the fuel tanks ruptured and his airplane burst into flame. He died in the cockpit: December 24, 1941.

Neil Martin was born 1917 and grew up in Texarkana, Texas. Said to be a gifted athlete, he graduated from the University of Arkansas, joined the Army, and was flying for the 8th Pursuit Group at Mitchel Field, New York, when recruited for the AVG. Assigned to the 3rd Squadron, he was regarded as one of its more experienced pilots, and it was he who gave R.T. Smith his cockpit check on September 17. He went down to Rangoon with the Hell's Angels in mid-December and was the leader of a three-plane flight that intercepted the Mitsubishi Ki-21 heavy bombers of the 98th Sentai over the Rangoon waterfront on December 23, 1941.

"Martin broke away and scooted out in front," as a witness recalled, and was met with the massed fire of eighteen greenhouse guns. He then made a climbing turn, which was an even worse mistake. Even the Japanese would later recall the plane that "turned away, showing his belly to our gunners." Martin's Tomahawk went down in flames.

Kenneth Merritt of Arlington, Texas, was an Army pilot when he joined the AVG. Assigned to the 2nd Squadron, he was sent down to Rangoon soon after the Pearl Harbor attack to fly one of the Curtiss CW-21 Demon fighters back to Toungoo. With Erik Shilling and Lacy Mangleburg, he eventually made up the Demon flight, and on December 24 the three of them set out to ferry the interceptors to Kunming. The planes were lost after Shilling crashed and the other pilots did not know how to find Kunming; Merritt was injured in his crash landing, but found his way to Kunming and recovered well enough that he accompanied the Panda Bears when they relieved the Hell's Angels after the Christmas campaign.

On January 4, 1942, Merritt was credited with shooting down a Nakajima Ki-27 Nate. Four days later he died in a freak accident when Peter Wright, returning from an attempted night interception, suffered a hydraulic break while trying to land at Mingaladon. Blinded by a jet of hydraulic fluid, he ground-looped and skidded into an automobile driven by Ken Merritt, who in a misguided effort to be helpful had parked beside the runway with his headlights on.

Einar (Mickey) Mickelson, born 1915 in York, North Dakota, made his home in the wonderfully named town of Fergus Falls, across the state line in Minnesota. After graduating from high school, he took a train to New York City, a steamer across the North Atlantic, and trains again through much of Europe to attend the 4th Boy Scout Jamboree outside Budapest, camped in the royal forest with 25,791 other Scouts. (How many of those lads would die in the Second World War?)

Mickelson graduated from North Dakota State University in 1940, joined the Navy, and earned his wings at Pensacola. He qualified as a P-40 pilot with the AVG 1st Squadron and was credited with shooting down a Kawasaki Ki-48 Lily medium bomber in the group's first combat near Kunming on December 20, 1941 — one of three pilots credited with victories that day. (That would be reduced to 0.27 on his CAMCO account, when the bonus money was shared among 15 pilots.) The encounter must have affected him greatly, because he never again flew a combat mission. Instead, he joined John Hennessy as pilot or copilot for the Beechcraft transport, and when the group disbanded in July 1942 he joined CNAC to fly supply missions over the Hump.

During his stay-overs in India, Mickelson met, fell in love with, and married Natalie or Natalia Beloff, a young Russian whose family had fled after the Bolshevik Revolution, so that she grew up in Asia. On February 21, 1943, not long after the wedding, Mickelson was flying to China when his transport was attacked by a Japanese interceptor; he was seen to bank left into clouds from which he did not emerge. The remnants of his plane were spotted on a mountainside the following year, but the wreck has never been reached. His widow later worked in the CNAC office in Kunming and eventually married another American pilot, settling with him in Maine.

In 2008, Fergus Falls decided to honor its native son by choosing my Flying Tigers history for its community-wide "Big Read" and inviting me to talk about Mickey Mickelson, the AVG, and the Second World War. Over the years, my long obsession with the American Volunteer Group has taken me to many places in four countries and given me many fine moments, but that was one of the most memorable.

Robert (Moose) Moss was born 1918 in Poplar Arbor, Georgia, and grew up in a literal log cabin on a farm in nearby Moultrie. He graduated from Doerun high school and the University of Southern Georgia, where he played football (the first game he played was also the first football game he'd ever seen) and apparently was also a gymnast. He joined the Army, earned his wings, and became a fighter pilot with the 1st Pursuit Group at Selfridge Field, where he crashed a P-40 in March 1941. He was in the first large contingent of AVG pilots and crew that traveled to Asia on the *Jaegersfontein*, traveling on a passport that identified his profession as "acrobat."

Moss deployed to Rangoon with the 2nd Squadron at the end of 1941 and took part in strafing attacks on Japanese airfields in Thailand, during one of which he was credited with shooting down a Nakajima Ki-27 fighter, only to then lose a contest with two other Nates. He managed to keep his Tomahawk flying long enough to reach friendly territory, where he bailed out and hitched a ride in a bullock cart to an RAF advance field. He was shot down again on January 26, 1942, and this time had several teeth knocked out.

On March 15, attached to the 3rd Squadron at Magwe, he was credited with a second Nate. He served to the AVG's disbandment and afterward flew with CNAC on the India-China transport run. Postwar, back at the family farm, Moss and his wife built a diving pool, where after climbing down from his tractor at the end of the day he taught himself and his children to dive, and eventually coached children from all over. In 1993, shortly before his death, this evolved into Moultrie's Moose Moss Aquatic Center where six Olympic teams have since trained.

Charles Mott of Philadelphia was born 1914 and attended the University of Pennsylvania as a civil engineer. He enrolled in ROTC, then mandatory for young men at land-grant colleges, and graduated as a second lieutenant in the infantry. However, after a year working as a structural engineer, he resigned his reserve commission, joined the active duty Navy, and earned his wings at Pensacola.

Mott spent three years as a dive bomber pilot aboard USS *Ranger*, *Lexington*, and finally *Saratoga*, where he was recruited for the AVG in June 1941. A married man, and at 28 older than most of the pilots aboard *Jaegersfontein*, he did his best to enforce military discipline on the long sea voyage to Singapore, then coastwise to Rangoon. At Kyedaw airfield in Toungoo, he served first as assistant group adjutant and then as engineering officer, tasked with adapting the Army optical gunsight to the P-40 Tomahawk, whose windscreen had been fitted with thick British "armourglass" to protect the pilot, one of several modifications made to suit the Royal Air Force.

He deployed to Rangoon with the 2nd Squadron at the end of December 1941, and led the January 8 mission to strafe Mae Sot airfield in Thailand. In his first pass, he spotted two Japanese warplanes concealed in the rain forest; he lifted a wing and swung back to attack them. "There was a big boom up in the engine, and the thing quit cold," as he told me in 1988. "I was [about] thirty feet off the ground. I had quite a bit of speed, naturally, and I pulled up.... I rolled over — oh, I was 200 or 300 feet off the ground — and I kicked out."

His parachute opened just before he hit the ground, leaving him with cracked ribs and a broken arm, leg, and pelvis. The Japanese took him to a prison camp in Bangkok, where he taught himself to walk again. His reward was to be sent with British and Commonwealth prisoners to work on the "Death Railroad" made famous by the David Lean film, *Bridge on the River Kwai*. He escaped in 1945, made his way back to the U.S., and resumed his Navy career, retiring in 1963 with the rank of captain. He earned a master's degree from George Washington University and afterward worked as a consultant for the military services and for private industry. He died at his home in Vienna, Virginia, in 2004.

Robert Neale ended his AVG career in July 1942 as America's top-scoring fighter ace and acting commander of a U.S. Army unit — while still a civilian! Born 1914 in Vancouver, Canada, he grew up in Seattle and enrolled at the University of Washington, dropping out to join the Navy. He earned his wings in 1939 and became a dive bomber pilot on USS *Saratoga*. The flattop also numbered an enlisted armorer named Robert Neal among her crew, and when the AVG recruiters visited, both men signed up to go to Burma.

Neale was already an ace when he took over the 1st Squadron Adam & Eves at Rangoon after Sandy Sandell was killed, and he continued to accumulate victories thereafter. The British awarded him the Distinguished Service Order for his exploits in the defense of Burma, and the Chinese gave him a Ten Star Wing Medal. (He actually merited a higher honor, but probably the Chinese had never anticipated a 13-victory ace). He was one of the pilots who volunteered two weeks' additional service in China after the group was disbanded; during that interim, he commanded the 23rd Fighter Group pending the arrival of the designated commander, Colonel Robert Scott. After returning to the U.S., Neale served as a pilot for Pan American World Airways, ferrying planes and flying cargo. Postwar, he returned to Seattle and ran a fishing resort until his death in 1994. His CAMCO bonus account credited him with 15.55 enemy aircraft, including 13 air-to-air victories:

- 23 January 1942: 1 Ki-27 Nate fighter
- 24 January 1942: 2 Ki-21 Sally bombers
- 26 January 1942: 1 Ki-27 Nate fighter
- 6 February 1942: 1 Ki-27 Nate fighter
- 25 February 1942: 4 Ki-27 Nate fighters
- 26 February 1942: 3 Ki-27 Nate fighters
- 3 May 1942: 1 Ki-15 Babs observation plane

John (Jack) Newkirk was nicknamed "Scarsdale" by his family to distinguish him from a cousin with the same name. Born 1913, he received his Eagle Scout badge from no less a hero than the Antarctic explorer Richard Byrd. He learned to fly in a Curtiss Falcon biplane while a student at Rensselaer Polytechnic — until his money ran out. For three years he worked as a chemist in New York City, meanwhile taking night classes at Columbia and drilling with the National Guard. Then he returned to Rensselaer to complete the two years he needed to become an aviation cadet in the Navy. Thus he was 25 when he earned his wings and began to fly the biplane Grumman F3F and the Navy's hot new monoplane fighter, the Brewster F2A Buffalo.

Newkirk was assigned to USS *Yorktown*, flying the F4F Wildcat, when he volunteered for the AVG. At the age of 27, with his leadership training, he was already a dominant figure in the group when he arrived in Burma, and he was given command of the 2nd Squadron Panda Bears. By the time he led a mixed flight to Chiang Mai on March 23, 1942, he'd been credited with seven air-to-air victories, though some AVG veterans hinted that his claims were inflated. (It is certainly true that the squadron leaders, who had the primary and often only responsibility for signing off on victories, generally built up their scores more quickly than the other pilots.)

At Chiang Mai, Newkirk and his wingmen strafed the railroad station before going on to search for their assigned target at Lamphun. He was seen to crash in flames while attacking a target on the ground that has been variously identified as a Japanese armored car and a Thai bullock cart. His CAMCO bonus account totaled 10.5, of which 7 were air-to-air:

- 3 January 1942: 1 Ki-44 Shoki? fighter, 1 Ki-27 Nate fighter
- 20 January 1942: 2 Ki-27 Nate fighters
- 23 January 1942: 1 Ki-21 Sally? bomber, 2 Ki-27 Nate fighters

Charles Older was born 1917 in Hanford, California and graduated with honors from UCLA in 1939. He joined the Marines as a breather before law school, earned his wings at Pensacola, and was flying a Grumman fighter with VMF-1 when he joined the AVG. Assigned to the 3rd Squadron with the other Marine pilots, he deployed with the Hell's Angels to Rangoon, where he became an ace when credited with four heavy bombers and a retractable-gear fighter during the Christmas campaign. Awarded a Nine Star Wing Medal by the Chinese, he served with the AVG until it disbanded. Back in the U.S., he accepted a commission in the Army, returned to China to serve with the 23rd Fighter Group, and was credited with eight more air-to-air victories. He ended the war as a lieutenant colonel and finally earned that law degree from the University of Southern California.

Recalled to active duty in 1950, Older flew a Douglas B-26 Invader light bomber during the Korean War, making him probably the only Flying Tiger to serve as an Air Force pilot in a second conflict. Appointed to Los Angeles Superior Court in 1967, he presided most famously over the bizarre, ten-month trial of multiple murderer Charles Manson. Judge Older died in 2006.

The CAMCO bonus account credited Older with 10.08 enemy

aircraft, of which 10 were air-to-air victories. (See Duke Hedman's listing for more about the April 10 combat with Sergeant Yasuda's plane.)

- 23 December 1941: 2 Ki-21 Sally bombers
- 25 December 1941: 2 Ki-21 Sally bombers + 1 Ki-43 Hayabusa fighter
- 17 January 1942: 1 Ki-21 Sally bomber + 1 shared
- 29 March 1942: 1 Ki-46 Dinah observation plane
- 10 April 1942: shared 1 Ki-43 Hayabusa fighter
- 28 April 1942: 2 Ki-43 Hayabusa fighters

Arvid (Oley) Olson of Hollywood, California, was a P-40 pilot with the 8th Pursuit Group at Mitchel Field, New York, when he resigned to join the AVG. Soon after he reached the training base at Kyedaw airfield outside Toungoo, Burma, he was given command of the 3rd Squadron. Chennault apparently regarded him as the most promising squadron leader, because at the outbreak of war he appointed Olson "Group Commander in the Air." He took the Hell's Angels down to Rangoon on December 12, 1941, flying a Tomahawk with fuselage number 99.

Perhaps following the lead of the Royal Air Force commander at Mingaladon airport, he didn't go into combat during the Christmas campaign, unlike the squadron leaders who followed him at Rangoon. So it was not until January 24, 1942, back at Kunming, that he actually led a combat mission, escorting Chinese bombers on a raid into northern Vietnam. He later served at the AVG fall-back bases at Magwe in Burma and Loiwing across the border in China. Flying one of the new P-40E Kittyhawks, he was credited with his only air-to-air victory over Loiwing on April 8, a Nakajima Ki-43 Hayabusa of the 64th Sentai.

Olson served to the group's disbandment, returned to the U.S., and there rejoined the Army. He led the 1st Air Commando Group when it was activated in 1944, and he deployed with it to Burma as group operations officer, taking part in at least one glider mission to resupply British Chindit commandos behind Japanese lines. Postwar, he served a stint at the U.S. Military Academy at West Point, and evidently retired in 1953.

Edmund Overend of Coronado, California, was born in 1914. An honors graduate of San Diego State in 1939, he joined the Marines and served two years as a lieutenant in a machinegun company before earning his wings at Pensacola. Like most of the Marine pilots, he was assigned to the 3rd Squadron and served with the Hell's Angels at Rangoon during the Christmas campaign of 1941, when he was credited with three victories, each a Mitsubishi Ki-21 heavy bomber.

In April 1942, at Loiwing, Older became an ace shortly before his 28th birthday, and was duly awarded a Five Star Wing Medal by the Chinese. (With credit for ground strafing, his CAMCO bonus account stood at 5.83.) He was also active in the bombing campaign on the Salween River front. He served with the AVG until it disbanded in July, after which he rejoined the Marines to fly a Vought F4U Corsair fighter with VMF-321 in the Pacific Theater. He tallied 3.5 more combat victories and finished the war with the rank of major, decorated with both the British and the American Distinguished Flying Cross. For a time he headed the UNESCO mission on Taiwan. He died 1971 and was buried at sea.

- 23 December 1941: 1 Ki-21 Sally bomber
- 25 December 1941: 2 Ki-21 Sally bombers
- 8 April 1942: 1 Ki-43 Hayabusa fighter
- 28 April 1942: 1 Ki-43 Hayabusa fighter

George (Pappy) Paxton was born about 1902, making him one of the oldest Tigers, though I can't find a birth date for him. His home town is listed as Abiline, Texas, and he supposedly graduated from Yale and worked as a banker before joining the Navy. He flew for the short-lived Patrol Squadron 44 at San Diego before joining the AVG. Assigned to the 2nd Squadron, he was dubbed "Pappy" by the Panda Bears. (Though later overshadowed by the more famous Greg Boyington, Paxton was the only one with that nickname in the Flying Tigers. Boyington acquired it later, as a squadron commander in the South Pacific.) Paxton's only aerial combat was a traumatic one: on January 4, 1942, he took off from Mingaladon airport in a three-plane flight led by Bert Christman. Breaking out of the clouds at 11,000 feet, the Tomahawks were bounced by 31 Nakajima Nates of the 77th Sentai. Christman bailed out of his crippled fighter, but Paxton managed to ride his plane down to a crash landing at the airfield, though shot through the left shoulder and right side, with lesser wounds where a bullet hit a joint in his seat-back armor and fragmented.

He vowed never to fly another combat mission, a decision that Chennault respected. So Paxton became the group's paymaster and supply officer in Kunming, Calcutta, and New York City, where he worked at the CAMCO office in the summer of 1942 to wind down the group's financial affairs. He afterward worked for American Export Airlines at what is now LaGuardia Airport, meanwhile helping journalist Robert Hotz write one of the first Flying Tiger romances. Postwar, he remained active in AVG affairs, lobbying Congress to recognize the Tigers' military service, helping establish the Flying Tigers Association, and becoming co-author and chief character in a syndicated comic strip about his service in Burma. He died in 1979.

John (Pete) Petach was born 1918 and grew up in Perth Amboy, New Jersey. After graduating from New York University with a degree in chemical engineering, he joined the Navy and earned his wings at Pensacola. He was a dive bomber pilot for VS-42 aboard USS *Ranger* when he joined the AVG. Aboard *Jaegersfontein* en route to Singapore, he met the AVG nurse Emma Jane Foster, with whom he fell in love and whom he would marry in China. Assigned to the 2nd Squadron, he deployed with the Panda Bears to Rangoon and in January 1942 was credited with a share of a Japanese reconnaissance plane (probably a Ki-51 Sonia) over Mae Sot on the 19th, a Ki-30 Ann light bomber on the 23rd, and a Ki-27 Nate on the 28th.

In April, Petach shared in three further victories. He was among those who volunteered two extra weeks' service to ease the transition to the USAAF 23rd Fighter Group, with the result that he was credited with yet another Ki-27 Nate on July 6, for a total of 3.98 enemy aircraft destroyed. The cost was high: on July 10, 1942, on a mixed AVG-USAAF strike on Linchuan, he was shot down and killed. His widow went home without him, and their daughter Joan Claire Petach was born the following February.

Robert Power gave his home town as Staten Island, New York. He was a Navy aviator aboard USS *Saratoga* when he volunteered for the AVG, but was one of a cluster of recruits who quit almost as soon as they reached Burma, and who have a discharge date of September 24, 1941. He is otherwise a mystery, but probably he was the same Robert H. Power who in 1950 became a pilot for the Flying Tiger Line. If so, he was born 1913 and died 1968.

Robert Prescott was born in Fort Worth, Texas, in 1913, and therefore the oldest of the men who became fighter aces during their AVG service. He moved to California in 1934, attended junior college there, and enrolled in Loyola Law School in Los Angeles. He dropped out to join the Navy, serving as a flight instructor before he was recruited by the AVG. He was awarded a Five Star Wing Medal by the Chinese.

Returning to the U.S. when his tour with the AVG ended, he flew briefly for Trans World Airlines before heading back to China as a CNAC pilot. Postwar, he raised $160,000 and founded the Flying Tiger Line, the only "non-sched" established by Second World War veterans to survive and prosper, at least until it was absorbed by FedEx. (Until the FAA put a stop to it, he flew AVG veterans to their reunions without charge.) He died in 1978. The record shows him with 5.5 air-to-air victories, though his CAMCO bonus account was a bit smaller as a result of claims shared with fellow pilots.

- 29 January 1942: 1 Ki-27 Nate fighter
- 6 February 1942: 1 Ki-27 Nate fighter
- 25 February 1942: 3 Ki-27 Nate fighters
- 18 April 1942: shared 1 Ki-46 Dinah observation plane

Albert (Red) Probst from Waco, Texas, seems to have been born 1918 in the nearby village of Thrall. An Army pilot, he learned to fly at Randolph Field in San Antonio, where he crashed a BT-9 trainer in September 1940. He heard about the AVG as a second lieutenant at Maxwell Field, recruited by Skip Adair, who went there looking for Ajax Baumler. Like Greg Boyington, Probst was in debt, so the notion of a combat bonus appealed to him, and he figured as well that flying against Japanese pilots would be less hazardous than taking on the German Luftwaffe.

He sailed in *Jaegersfontein*, was assigned to the 1st Squadron, and deployed with the Adam & Eves to Rangoon early in 1942. On his first day at Mingaladon, he was involved in the disastrous air battle in which Cokey Hoffman was killed and Moose Moss shot down. He served two extra weeks with the AVG, returned to the U.S., and in September 1942 the *Chicago Tribune* reported that he was "en route to Washington to offer his services to the army air forces." Evidently the Army was happy to have him back, because in 1944 Probst crashed a Douglas A-26 attack plane attempting to land at Buffalo,

New York, at which time he was stationed at Love Field in Texas. I have no idea what happened to him after that, but he may have died in 1977.

Robert (Catfish) Raine was born 1918 in Palisades, Nevada, and attended 13 schools before graduating from Reno High — something of a record, surely! He went briefly to San Francisco State College, meanwhile learning to fly in nearby San Mateo, before he joined the Navy and earned his wings at Pensacola. He flew a Douglas TDB Devastator from USS *Saratoga* for Torpedo Squadron 3. A typographical error caused him to be recorded as Raines on his military records, and that was the name he carried into the AVG.

Arriving at Kyedaw airfield toward the end of October, he was assigned to the 3rd Squadron to make up for shortfalls in its roster. Not until April 25, 1942, was he noted in a combat report, for shooting down a Japanese scout plane and claiming a one-fifth share in another. These were fixed-gear Ki-51 Sonias. American and Japanese records agree that there were only two planes in the air that day, but mysteriously they became three in the CAMCO bonus account.

On June 22, flying a mixed AVG-USAAF mission, Raine was credited with a Nakajima Ki-27 Nate shot down, and on July 3, while escorting B-25 bombers, he was credited with another, giving him 3.20 air-to-air victories. He served two extra weeks in China and afterward joined CNAC, with 443 flights over the Himalayas. Returning to the U.S. toward the end of the war, he again served briefly in the Navy; postwar, he became one of the original investors and eventually one of the most experienced pilots of the Flying Tiger Line. With 32,000 hours in his logbooks over 38 years, he retired to Nevada in 1978 to raise horses. He died in Reno in 2005.

Edward Rector was born 1916 and grew up in Marshall, North Carolina. He graduated from Catawba College, joined the Navy, and became a carrier pilot with Scout Squadron 41 on USS *Ranger*, stationed at Norfolk, Virginia, and taking part in the Neutrality Patrol that guarded British convoys across the North Atlantic. Together with Tex Hill and Bert Christman, he was an early recruit to the AVG, and with them was assigned to the 2nd Squadron Panda Bears.

Rector was credited with shooting down a Kawasaki Ki-48 medium bomber near Kunming on December 20, 1941, though that became 0.27 on the CAMCO bonus account. Flying back to Kunming, he ran out of fuel and made a belly landing in a field, but managed to strip out the Tomahawk's guns and bring them back with him.

He went down to Rangoon with his squadron at the end of the year and was credited with shooting down a Mitsubishi Ki-21 heavy bomber and a Nakajima Ki-27 fighter on January 24, 1942. Two months later, he shared in the destruction of several Japanese aircraft on the ground at Chiang Mai, Thailand, and in April was given partial credit for downing a Mitsubishi Ki-51 and another unidentified plane during missions to support the retreating Chinese army. In May, he was in action over the Salween River, where the long retreat was finally halted, and on July 4 — the AVG's last day — he was credited with shooting down a Nakajima Ki-27 fighter, to bring his air-to-air victories to 4.75, just short of being an ace, while his CAMCO bonus account stood at 6.52.

Rector was one of five Flying Tigers to accept induction into the U.S. Army in July 1942, and he remained in China as a major commanding the 76th Fighter Squadron. He was credited with three more enemy aircraft during his Army service, for a total of 7.75 air-to-air victories. Postwar, he remained in the Air Force, retiring in 1962 as a colonel, and afterward worked as a consultant. He lived in Arlington, Virginia, a short walk from Arlington National Cemetery, where he was buried with military honors in 2001.

William Reed was born 1917 in Stone City, Iowa, but grew up in Marion. He studied economics at Loras College in Dubuque, graduating in 1939 with honors and as a varsity letterman. He joined the Army the following year. After earning his wings at Kelly Field, he became a flight instructor at Barksdale, Louisiana, where he was recruited for the AVG. As a pilot in the 3rd Squadron, he deployed with the Hell's Angels to Rangoon after war broke out and was credited with a Mitsubishi Ki-21 heavy bomber on December 23, 1941, and two Nakajima Ki-43 fighters on Christmas Day. The second Hayabusa went down in the same combat in which Parker Dupouy smashed into Lieutenant Okuyuma's fighter.

Reed did not score again during his AVG career, though he was credited with multiple Japanese planes destroyed on the ground during a highly successful strafing mission with Dupouy on March 18, 1942. His CAMCO bonus account therefore showed 10.5 enemy aircraft, including the 3 air-to-air victories. He served with the AVG to its disbandment, went home to Marion, and rejoined the Army in 1943 as a major. Back in China as part of the Chinese-American Composite Wing, he was credited with six more Japanese planes shot down, for a total of 9 aerial victories. Promoted to lieutenant colonel, he was given command of the 3rd Fighter Group, only to be killed when he had to bail out of his Curtiss P-40N fighter over Liangshan, China, on December 19, 1944. Evidently he was hit by the tail section, and his parachute did not open.

Freeman Ricketts of Walnut Creek, California, was a Navy aviator with 900 hours in his log books when he joined the AVG. Presumably he was one of the former PBY Catalina pilots, because he had great difficulty mastering the P-40: "Ricketts, one of the new group," wrote R.T. Smith in his diary in November 1941, "landed with his wheels only partway down, and they folded and he skidded along on his belly & washed out another ship. Stupidity!"

Assigned to the 2nd Squadron, Ricketts was scheduled to fly up to Kunming with the Panda Bears on December 19, but taxied into Chennault's Studebaker sedan and "chewed it up with his propeller," as Charlie Bond noted. Another contemporary account says that he damaged three Tomahawks during his training at Kyedaw airfield. On April 25, 1942, stationed at Loiwing on the China-Burma border, he shared in the credit for shooting down a Japanese scout plane, and on May 5, flying one of the new P-40E Kittyhawks, he claimed a "Zero" near the AVG fall-back base at Baoshan, giving him 1.20 air-to-air victories.

Ricketts volunteered two weeks' additional service in China when the AVG disbanded — which was unfortunate, really. On July 16, in a confusion of alarms, he took off from Hengyang and shot down a North American B-25 Mitchell bomber that he mistook for Japanese. The crew bailed out, and the pilot rode the bomber down to a crash landing. (In a nice illustration of the confusion and exaggeration of Second World War combat reports, he reported that his bomber been attacked and shot down "by two Zeros.") I have no idea what happened to Ricketts after that, but his signature appears in a collection of autographs from a Flying Tiger reunion in 1952.

Joseph Rosbert was born 1917 and grew up in Franklin, North

Carolina. He graduated from Villanova as a chemical engineer but soon joined the Navy, piloting a stately PBY Catalina for Patrol Squadron 44 in San Diego when recruited for the AVG. Reaching Burma at the end of October, 1941, he was assigned to the 1st Squadron, took part in the Adam & Eves' first air battle outside Kunming on December 20, and deployed to Rangoon early in 1942. Rosbert was another pilot whose CAMCO bonus account of 4.55 was actually lower than his air-to-air victory credits, because of bonus money shared with other pilots. He was awarded a Six Star Wing Medal by the Chinese.

He served two extra weeks during the transition to the 23rd Fighter Group, then joined CNAC as a transport pilot flying cargo over the Hump of the Himalayas. Postwar, he was one of the founders of the Flying Tiger Line before moving over to Chennault's Civil Air Transport, the predecessor of Air America. Later he owned a chain of "Flying Tiger Joe" restaurants. He died in Katy, Texas, in 2009. With six air-to-air victories, he tied with two others as the AVG's eleventh-ranking ace:

- 25 February 1942: 1 Ki-27 Nate fighter
- 26 February 1942: 3 Ki-27 Nate fighters
- 12 June 1942: 2 Ki-45 Toryu fighters

Richard Rossi was two years older than Rosbert but was otherwise very nearly his twin in AVG service. Born 1915, he grew up in Placerville and San Francisco. He attended the University of California at Berkeley, working betimes in the Merchant Marine, but finally dropping out in 1939 to join the Navy. He was a flight instructor at Pensacola when he joined the AVG. He too was assigned to the 1st Squadron and was awarded a Six Star Wing Medal by the Chinese.

When the AVG disbanded, he had 6.29 enemy aircraft on his CAMCO account, including six air-to-air victories. He remained in China as a CNAC pilot for the rest of the war, making 735 flights over the Hump. Postwar, he flew for the Flying Tiger Line until he retired in 1971. He was president of the Flying Tiger Association veterans's group for more than 50 years, until his death in 2008.

- 28 January 1942: 1 Ki-27 Nate fighter
- 25 February 1942: 1 Ki-27 Nate fighter
- 26 February 1942: 3 Ki-27 Nate fighters
- 12 June 1942: 1 Ki-27 Nate fighter

Edwin Rushton was born 1913 or 1914 in or around San Francisco. He was a Navy aviator aboard USS *Saratoga* when recruited for the AVG. He sailed to Burma, trained for a while at Kyedaw airfield, but apparently wasn't assigned to a squadron; he was discharged on October 24, 1941. He probably died in 2008, but I can find nothing about him for the years between.

Robert (Sandy) Sandell was born 1916 in Stroud, Oklahoma, and has also been identified as a native of St. Charles, Missouri. He joined the Army in 1933 and two years later was accepted for flight training, a process interrupted when he received an appointment to the U.S. Military Academy. He resigned from West Point in 1938 and returned to the Army Air Corps, earning his wings and becoming a flight instructor at Brooks Field outside San Antonio. He volunteered for the AVG, sailed on *Jaegersfontein*, and impressed the staff at Kyedaw airfield sufficiently that they gave him command of the 1st Squadron. The Adam & Eves did not particularly like him, if their memoirs are to be trusted: "a small fellow," as Charlie Bond described him, "with a mustache and a very cold manner."

But in his short combat career at Rangoon, he became one of the first of the AVG aces, with five air-to-air victories. (His bonus account read 5.23, reflecting his role in the December 20, 1941, melee near Kunming.) Forced down in his first combat on January 28, 1942, he made a dead-stick landing at Mingaladon airport, only to have a Japanese pilot dive on the Tomahawk and tear off its tail assembly.

He flew a different plane the following week, while line chief Harry Fox repaired Sandell's plane. On February 7, he took it up for a test flight, concluding with a barrel roll over the airport; he stalled and augured in. "The boys had to dig Sandy out," Fritz Wolf recalled, "and it wasn't pleasant." The Chinese promoted him to lieutenant colonel and gave him a Fifth Class Order of the Cloud and Banner, but did not award him the customary Five Star Wing Medal, suggesting that it was not awarded posthumously.

- 28 January 1942: 2 Ki-27 Nate fighters
- 29 January 1942: 3 Ki-27 Nate fighters

Charles Sawyer was born on a homestead in Emmett, Idaho, the year uncertain. He attended Idaho State University, became an Army fighter pilot, and was assigned to the 8th Pursuit Group at Mitchel

Field, New York, when recruited for the AVG. He took part in the group's first combat near Kunming on December 20, 1941, and got the 0.27 bonus like all the pilots in the interception. He deployed to Rangoon at the end of 1941 with the 1st Squadron, serving as the Adam & Eves' liaison officer with the RAF, and in the spring of 1942 helped ferry new P-40E fighters from India to China.

On June 22, flying one of the new P-40E Kittyhawks, he was credited with his first shoot-down, a Nakajima Ki-27 fighter near Hengyang. (The newly arrived Captain Ajax Baumler also scored that day.) Sawyer claimed another Nate on July 4, and on the same day joined the USAAF as a captain in the 76th Fighter Squadron, in which capacity he was credited with yet another of the fixed-gear Nakajima fighters.

He returned to the U.S. as a colonel in 1943, and after the war settled again in his home town, where he died in 1978. When his widow died in 2013, Sawyer's medals and other memorabilia were sold at auction for more than $125,000. Nobody seems quite sure who got the money, but apparently it was not his own family.

Frank Schiel was born 1917 in Phoenix, Arizona. He grew up in Prescott, attended the University of Arizona, and became an Army pilot at Kelly Field in Texas. He was stationed at the 23rd Proving Ground at Eglin Field, Florida, when recruited for the AVG. He sailed aboard *Bloemfontein* and at various times served with both the 1st and 2nd Squadrons. He was credited with shooting down a Nakajima Ki-27 Nate on January 24, 1942, at Rangoon, another on the 26th, a third on May 5 near Baoshan, China, and a fourth on June 22 near Hengyang, for a total of 4 air-to-air victories (7 on his CAMCO bonus account, reflecting three planes supposedly destroyed on the ground on May 12).

He was commissioned and given command of the USAAF 74th Fighter Squadron at Kunming, the former Hell's Angels. Major Schiel specialized in reconnaissance flights over Thailand and Vietnam; his work, wrote Colonel Robert Scott, involved "brains and camera instead of guns and bombs." He was decorated with a Silver Star for a flight over Hanoi, but was killed on a reconnaissance flight when his Lockheed Lightning photo plane crashed in December 1942, the day uncertain.

Arnold (Red) Shamblin from Commerce, Oklahoma, was one of the Army flight instructors recruited as check pilots for the CAF cadets. In a letter home, he told about arriving at Yunnan-yi on December 3, 1941, to find he would be one of the town's six white men, including Butch Carney, an AVG weatherman, a radio operator, "and we three: Van Shappard [sic], Buster Loane, and I. Everyone else is Chinese and a dirtier, unhealthier, bunch of people you've never seen."

Like Shapard and Loane, he joined the combat squadrons when the flight school closed down and volunteered to stay two weeks after the AVG disbanded. He flew his first combat sortie on May 25, 1942, bombing and strafing on the Salween front. Then, on July 10, he made the fourth pilot on a mixed AVG-USAAF mission from Hengyang to the walled city now known as Fuzhou. The Americans ran into anti-aircraft fire as they were diving to release their bombs; Pete Petach was shot down in flames, and Red Shamblin's Kittyhawk was also hit, though neither of the surviving pilots (Captain Ajax Baumler and Lieutenant Leonard Butsch) saw him go down.

He was therefore listed as "missing" in the AVG records. But in 1989, reading microfilm copies of the Japan Times & Advertiser, an English-language daily published in Tokyo throughout the war, I found a story published just five days after he went down. Shamblin, it said, bailed out of his crippled Kittyhawk, evaded capture for several hours, but finally was taken prisoner. He lived long enough to give his name, but there is no further mention of him in the record, and he did not emerge from prison camp at the end of the war. Like thousands of Anglo-American servicemen captured by the Japanese — 27 percent, in fact — he must have perished in captivity.

Evander (Van) Shapard was born 1917 and grew up in Columbia, Tennessee. He shared a name with two Tennessee heroes, who surely were related: a Confederate general in the Civil War and a Royal Flying Corps ace in the First World War. Van graduated from the local military academy and went to Alabama Polytechnic to study aeronautical engineering and drill with the ROTC. He evidently dropped out to join the Army and earn his wings, and thus became one of the flight instructors who went to Yunnan-yi to work for Butch Carney as check pilots. Like Shamblin, he was blooded *over the Salween River, flying a P-40E, and like him stayed on after the AVG was disbanded.*

In what was apparently his first air-to-air combat — July 4 over Hengyang — one wheel on his Kittyhawk failed to retract. An AVG crew chief recalled how, in his Tennessee drawl, Shapard radioed for help when beset by Japanese fighters: "Hey you guys, they's a Jap on my tail. What am I gonna do naow? Hey! He's still theah!" Then he burst into song: "When the roll is called up yonder ... I shore am gonna be there, somebody don't do nothin!" Shapard not only escaped but claimed a Nakajima Nate shot down, still with one wheel unretracted. He stayed in China as a CNAC pilot. He died in 1976.

Eriksen Shilling was born 1916 and listed Washington, D.C., as his home town when he joined the AVG. He was then a test pilot at the 23rd Proving Ground at Eglin Field, having flown every plane in the Army Air Corps inventory. At Kyedaw airfield outside Toungoo, he must have impressed Chennault, who chose him as the Flying Tiger champion in a mock combat with an RAF Brewster Buffalo, calculated to impress the American pilots with the superiority of their Curtiss P-40s. It worked: "Shilling had a dog fight with a Limey in a Brewster," one of the ground crew wrote in his diary, "and licked the pants off of him, so it should increase the confidence in our pilots quite a bit."

When war broke out, Shilling was picked to fly the AVG photo plane and to head up the ill-fated CW-21 Demon flight that ended so badly on Christmas Eve. (See the Mangleburg biography.) Shilling was fined and reduced in rank for that debacle, though Chennault soon forgave him. His only air-to-air combat seems to have been on that intercept near the China-Vietnam border on January 17, 1942, when the Flying Tigers claimed three Mitsubishi Ki-21 bombers shot down. They shared the bonus, giving Shilling 0.75 on his CAMCO account, but the actual credit went to others. He served with the group until it disbanded, then joined CNAC and flew 350 missions over the Hump.

Postwar, he signed on with Chennault's Civil Air Transport, flying cargo and passengers around war-torn China. Retreating with Chiang Kai-shek to Taiwan in 1949, CAT became an arm of the Central Intelligence Agency. Among other hazardous missions, Shilling dropped supplies to the surrounded French troops at Dien Bien Phu in 1954.

During the "American War" in Vietnam, he worked for another CIA contractor, Bird and Sons, flying unarmed bush planes in Laos, Cambodia, and Vietnam, a job that prompted me to call him "the last Flying Tiger" in my history of the AVG — a statement that made him uneasy. But he did, after all, take part in not one but four different wars!

When he left wartime flying in 1966, he became a captain for Swissair. He settled in California, wrote a memoir called *Destiny*, and lived long enough to sit in the cockpit of a restored Tomahawk at Planes of Fame in China, painted in Flying Tiger colors and bearing his name, as shown in Tom Cleaver's photograph below.

Erik died in 2002. I owe a particular debt to him. In the early 1990s, we both stumbled onto the internet, to a "news group" called rec.aviation.military. Like most AVG pilots, he was annoyed by my research on Japanese aircraft losses, which showed that (as any historian would have predicted, and as was the case in every theater of the Second World War), AVG combat claims were inflated. We regularly butted heads on this and other subjects, and when Erik could think of no better riposte, he would blow me off with something to this effect: "Ford isn't a pilot, so what does he know?" This annoyed me so much that I went down to a grass airfield on the New Hampshire seacoast and, after an embarrassing number of flight hours, checked out in a 1946 Piper J-3 Cub. I flew that pretty yellow bird for the next ten years, one of the most enjoyable activities I have ever undertaken. Erik also graciously helped me annotate the Royal Air Force pilot manual, one of those that accompanied the AVG Tomahawks when they were shipped to Rangoon. (See the section beginning on page 76.) Thank you, Erik, for those favors and for your service to the country!

Curtis Smith was another of the AVG's older volunteers. Born 1908 in Georgia, he attended the state university and joined the Army at 21, earning a commission and his wings but losing them both when Congress cut the number of Air Corps pilots to 250. He then became an enlisted Marine, but returned to the Army in 1933 as a sergeant-pilot to fly the airmail routes. Two years later he was commissioned in the Marine reserves, to be mobilized in 1940 as a flight instructor at Pensacola, where he joined the AVG at the age of 33.

As a member of the 3rd Squadron, he did not distinguish himself in his first combat at Rangoon; he went off flight status soon after, and for the rest of his tour served as the group adjutant. Back home in 1942, he returned to the Marines as a major. After another stint at Pensacola, he went to England as an observer, qualifying as an RAF pilot and marrying the Irish woman assigned as his driver. Toward the end of the war, he served in the Pacific as operations officer of Marine Air Group 14. Postwar, he helped run the family coffee business and served in the Marine Corps Reserve, including a stint at the atomic proving ground in Nevada. He retired with his family to Ireland, where he died in 1958.

Robert H. Smith was born 1918 and grew up in the wonderfully named Eagle River, Wisconsin. One of three Robert Smiths in the AVG (two pilots and a radioman), he attended Kansas State College and was an ROTC cadet before joining the Army and earning his wings. During his tour with the AVG, given the need to distinguish between one Bob Smith and another, he was often called "Snuffy," after a popular comic-strip character. Charlie Bond, in his diary, generally referred to him as "Smitty."

Under whatever nickname, he served with the 1st Squadron at

Rangoon as the Japanese were closing in, becoming an ace in a one-week period before the city was abandoned. Indeed, he and Bob Neale were the last Tigers to leave Rangoon, having spent an extra night at the airfield in hopes Ed Leibolt might walk in, as other missing pilots had done. Smith was awarded a Five Star Wing Medal by the Chinese. He rejoined the Army after his tour as a Flying Tiger, commanding the 12th Fighter Squadron in the Pacific, flying 83 missions, and ending the war as a major. Postwar, he operated a resort in Wisconsin before retiring to Florida, where he died in 1998.

- 21 February 1942: 1 Ki-27 Nate fighter
- 25 February 1942: 3 Ki-27 Nate fighters
- 26 February 1942: 1 Ki-48 Lily bomber

Robert (R.T.) Smith was born in York, Nebraska, in 1918 and grew up in Red Cloud. He enrolled at the University of Nebraska but dropped out in his senior year to join the Army. After earning his wings, he was assigned to Randolph Field as a flight instructor. With his buddy P.J. Greene he eagerly sought out the AVG recruiter and signed up to go to Burma, and with him became one of the 3rd Squadron Hell's Angels at Rangoon during the 1941 Christmas campaign, claiming three Mitsubishi Ki-21 heavy bombers, a share in another, and a Nakajima Ki-43 Hayabusa fighter. Over China in April 1942, he was credited with five more Hayabusas, plus a share in two observations planes. He was awarded a Nine Star Wing Medal by the Chinese.

R.T.'s facsimile diary, *Tale of a Tiger*, is one of the best of the AVG memoirs. He rejoined the U.S. Army when his tour was finished, serving with the 1st Air Commando in India and Burma and ending the war as a colonel. Postwar, he flew for Trans Word Airlines, wrote radio scripts and screenplays, co-owned a toy company, worked for Lockheed Aircraft and the Flying Tiger Line, served with the Air Force Reserve, and published his AVG diary under his own imprint. He died in 1995. His CAMCO bonus account shows 8.73 victories, but his actual credits were somewhat higher at 8.9:

- 23 December 1941: 1 Ki-21 Sally bomber + 1 shared
- 25 December 1941: 2 Ki-21 Sally bombers + 1 Ki-43 Hayabusa fighter
- 8 April 1942: 2 Ki-43 Hayabusa fighters
- 10 April 1942: 1 Ki-43 Hayabusa fighter

- 25 April 1942: shared 2 Ki-15 Babs observation planes
- 28 April 1942: 1 Ki-43 Hayabusa fighter

Those April 8 encounters are both echoed in Japanese accounts. The first Hayabusa was flown by Lieutenant Hinoki Yohei of the 64th Sentai; it was badly shot up but brought him home to Chiang Mai. (What R.T. thought was smoke from a burning plane was actually gasoline escaping from a punctured fuel tank and vaporizing in the cold air.) The second fighter belonged to Sergeant Goto Chikara, who was not so lucky: he crashed 30 or 40 miles south of Loiwing.

R.T. took a 35 mm Leica camera with him to Burma and with it captured some of the Flying Tigers' most memorable moments.

Gail Stubbs of Edwardsville, Missouri, was born in 1918. He went to the University of Missouri for three years, dropping out to earn his wings as an Army pilot. He signed up for the AVG, sailed for Burma, and at some point was reassigned to the CAF flight school at Yunnan-yi. Perhaps for that reason, he resigned toward the end of December and therefore got a "dishonorable discharge" from Chennault. That didn't harm his military career: he became an Army fighter pilot and a staff officer in the 10th Air Force in India, which must have annoyed Chennault if he knew about it. (For nearly a year, July 1942 to March 1943, Chennault's China Air Task Force was a stepchild of the 10th Air Force.) Stubbs stayed with the postwar U.S. Air Force as a colonel, retiring in 1969. He died in Florida in 2002.

Frank Swartz was born about 1916; he gave his hometown as Dunmore, Pennsylvania, when he joined the AVG. He'd flown a Douglas TBD Devastator for the Navy's Torpedo Squadron Five on USS *Yorktown*, based at Norfolk Naval Air Station. Assigned to the 2nd Squadron, Swartz deployed to Rangoon with the Panda Bears and was in combat on January 4, 1942, when Bert Christman, Pappy Paxton, and Gil Bright were shot down. He flew a war-weary Tomahawk back to Kunming in February, but was in action again at Magwe during the heavy Japanese raid on March 22.

Caught on the ground like several other Flying Tigers, he jumped from his slit trench to help crew chief John Fauth, who had been hit by a bullet from a strafing Japanese fighter. "One big bomb fell within fifteen feet of them," Fritz Wolf said later, "and both were wounded badly." Dick Rossi recalled that "Swartz had part of his hand blown off and a bad gash in his throat." (Rossi and Swartz had been cadets together at Pensacola.) John Fauth died during the night, but at noon next day Swartz and another wounded crewman were put onto a CNAC DC-3 going to Calcutta, where Swartz underwent surgery. He seemed to be recovering well when a hospital-borne infection carried him off on April 24, 1942.

Estes Swindle from Sunflower, Mississippi, must have been an Army pilot when he joined the AVG, for he returned to that service after leaving the group. He went home on leave in September 1941 but never returned; he evidently resigned in November and was dropped from the rolls in January 1942. As an Army captain, he died in a mid-air collision while piloting a Curtiss C-46 transport over Hsinching, China, on October 10, 1944.

Stanley Wallace of Tulsa, Oklahoma, was another Army pilot who joined the AVG but quit soon after reaching Burma. He was discharged on September 24, 1941, rejoined the Army, and as Major Wallace flew a C-47 transport into Lashio, Burma, soon after it was liberated from the Japanese in the spring of 1945. As he boasted to a reporter, he was delighted to return to the scene of his adventures as a Flying Tiger. This prompted his fellow pilots to compare him to Douglas ("I shall return") MacArthur, and it also earned a rebuke from General Chennault in China.

Robert Walroth of Richmond Hills, New York, was a P-40 pilot with the 8th Pursuit Group at Mitchel Field when he joined the AVG. He too went home in the fall of 1941. I can find nothing else about him.

Eugene Watson of Birmingham, Alabama, was an accident-prone Army pilot before and after his brief stint with the AVG. He crashed a Bell P-39 Airacobra while stationed at Selfridge Field in May 1941, and a Seversky P-35 the following month. He joined the AVG, went to Burma, and promptly turned around and went home again, discharged on September 30, 1941. As an Army bomber pilot in Africa, he crashed for the third time in North American B-25 Mitchell at Fort-Lamy (now Ndjamena, Chad) in April 1943.

And yet another! **Richard White** of Phoenix, Arizona, was a Navy pilot who went to Burma with the AVG; he was discharged on November 5, 1941.

Fritz Wolf was born 1916 and grew up in Shawano, Wisconsin. He attended Carroll College, where he became an all-conference fullback for three years in a row, graduating in 1938. "About this time," wrote his son Rick in an online biography, "he realized that if he was ever going to learn to fly, now was the time." He joined the Navy, earned his wings, and became a dive bomber pilot on USS *Saratoga* — and a stunt man, flying a Vought SB2U Vindicator for the 1941 film *Dive Bomber*. With several of his shipmates, he joined the AVG and sailed on *Jaegersfontein* to Southeast Asia. As one of the 1st Squadron Adam & Eves, he was credited in the AVG record with shooting down two of the four Kawasaki Ki-48 medium bombers destroyed in the group's first combat, near Kunming on December 20, 1941. (Thanks to the Chinese warning net, this was one of very few engagements in which AVG claims exactly matched Japanese reported losses: three Lilys were destroyed in the air, and a fourth when it crash-landed in northern Vietnam.) On his CAMCO bonus account, however, Wolf only received the 0.27 credit awarded to each pilot taking part.

Stationed at Loiwing on April 8, 1942, he claimed two Nakajima Ki-43 Hayabusa fighters, to bring his bonus account to 2.27 and his actual victory credits to 4. Returning home after the AVG disbanded, he wrote "It's Hell Over China!" for *Air Trails Pictorial*. Back in the Navy, he flew a Grumman F6F Hellcat off USS *Yorktown* in the Pacific Theater and became an ace on a raid over the Japanese home islands in 1945. Postwar he was Wisconsin's director of aeronautics and later the state transportation director. He died in 1997.

Allen Wright was born 1920 and grew up in Dyersburg, Tennessee. After two years of college, he joined the Army, earned his wings at Kelly Field, and became an instructor at Maxwell Field, Alabama. There he was recruited as a check pilot for the Chinese Air Force at Yunnan-yi. When the flight school closed down in the spring of 1942, he became a P-40 pilot in the 1st Squadron Adam & Eves. Forced down during a combat over Guilin in June, he sprained his back and wrecked the plane he was flying. He returned home in July, married a former Miss Dyersburg, and then returned to China as a CNAC pilot in the spring of 1943. Their daughter was born in Memphis that November. A few weeks later — December 18, 1943 — Captain Wright tried to land in the fog at Suifu, China, when he crashed into a mountain and was killed. He was 23 years old.

Peter Wright was born in 1917 and grew up in Abingdon and Pittsburg, Pennsylvania. He studied for two years at Yale but lost his scholarship and dropped out to become a Navy aviator, flying a Douglas TBD Devastator torpedo plane on USS *Ranger* out of Norfolk, Virginia. He volunteered for the AVG, was assigned to the mostly Navy 2nd Squadron Panda Bears, and deployed with them to Rangoon toward the end of 1941. His most notable achievement was a fruitless night interception which ended in a crash landing at Mingaladon airport when a hydraulic line burst, spraying his goggles and face with hot hydraulic fluid (and causing the death of Ken Merritt) on January 8, 1942. In April, he was credited with destroying a bomber on the ground and another in the air during a strafe of the old AVG training base at Kyedaw airfield, now occupied by the Japanese. The planes were probably Kawasaki Ki-48 Lilys of the 8th Sentai, though neither loss is confirmed in Japanese accounts.

Later in the month, Wright shared in the kills of three scout planes, probably ground cooperation aircraft attached to an infantry division. In May, he took part in the strafing of Lao Kay, Vietnam, in which Lew Bishop was lost. He volunteered two extra weeks in China, and on July 9, based at Hengyang, he scored his final victory, a twin-engine "reconnaissance bomber" that was probably a Ki-48 Lily of the 90th Sentai at Canton. That brought his air-to-air victories to 2.65 and his CAMCO bonus account to 3.65.

Returning to the U.S., Peter Wright became a flying boat captain for American Export Airlines at LaGuardia airport in New York. (The old seaplane base is now Terminal A.) He also worked as a test pilot for GM-built Wildcat fighters. Postwar, he first became a helicopter salesman and in 1953 he founded Keystone Helicopter in Philadelphia and built it into one of the country's largest rotorcraft service centers. The company was eventually acquired by Sikorsky Aircraft, with Wright as its chairman emeritus. He died in 2007 in Bryn Mawr, Pennsylvania.

About Those Combat Claims

IN THE END, the Flying Tigers were credited with 296 Japanese aircraft destroyed in the air and on the ground. (The American Volunteer Group was not part of the U.S. military, and its record keeping was often haphazard; other documents suggest the total may have been 294 or 298.) Of those, according to research by Dr. Frank Olynyk, 230 were credited as air-to-air victories: 98 Japanese planes downed by the 1st Squadron (Adam & Eves), 68 by the 2nd Squadron (Panda Bears), and 64 by the 3rd Squadron (Hell's Angels).

In the pilot biographies in this book, I often give two figures for those who were credited with a combat bonus (paid by CAMCO, the group's ostensible employer) and also with an air-to-air victory in the AVG record. These can differ for two reasons. In the spring of 1942 Madame Chiang Kai-shek, the dictator's wife and head of the Chinese Aeronautical Commission, decreed that a $500 bonus would be paid for each Japanese plane destroyed on the ground, as well as those shot down in aerial combat. Then too, in some combats, AVG pilots agreed to share the bonus money among all those taking part in a mission. This was especially common when someone was killed or went missing.

In the 1980s, Frank Olynyk published a series of monographs analyzing American combat claims in the two world wars. In the case of the American Volunteer Group, he went through the Chennault Papers (originals at Stanford University's Hoover Institution, microfilm copies at the Library of Congress in Washington), pilot memoirs, and other sources to determine the date, place, and circumstances of each combat claim, and to attribute each victory to the pilot or pilots who actually scored it. I found his figures impeccable, and I used them in the 2007 Harper Collins update of my history of the group.

But of course these "victories" are not graven in stone; they represent only the beliefs of the individuals involved, sometimes but not usually confirmed by independent observers. And in retrospect, those numbers were often inflated. A good example is the AVG's first combat, near Kunming on December 20, 1941. As customarily told in Flying Tiger romances like Robert Hotz's wartime account, *With General Chennault,* or in the yarns told by Tiger veterans, nine out of ten twin-engine Kawasaki Ki-48 bombers failed to return to Gia Lam airfield in Hanoi, northern Vietnam. Assessing the results, Chennault supposedly said: "Well, that's a good start, but next time, get 'em all." Indeed, *Next Time Get 'Em All* is the title of a popular bit of aviation art by William Phillips, showing Bob Neale and Bill Bartling diving on the Japanese formation.

Whether or not Chennault said any such thing, that's not how the day's work went into AVG and CAMCO records. During his years as an Army officer, Chennault had worked out the principles of what he called "defensive pursuit," which he believed would enable fighter pilots to intercept and destroy enemy bombers before they reached their target. Chief among those principles was a ground-based warning net, linked by radio and telephone to the fighter base. After Japan attacked Chiang Kai-shek's stronghold along the Yangtze River in 1937, he created just such a network of observers, and wherever he established himself thereafter, he replicated it.

Thus, when those 10 Kawasaki Ki-48s fled southward on December 20, they were tracked by watchers on the ground, who reported that they saw 3 bombers fall to earth. A few days later, presumably from a spy on the ground in Hanoi, came a report that a fourth had crashed trying to land at Gia Lam airport. The 15 pilots agreed to share the $2,000 bonus, so each got $133.33, representing roughly 0.27 of an enemy aircraft destroyed. In the AVG record, however, only three pilots were credited with a shoot-down, Fritz Wolf with two victories, Mickey Mickelson and Eddie Rector with one apiece.

And those bombers were flying straight and level, trusting to their speed and defensive guns to keep them safe. Fighter-to-fighter combat was very different, with both sides relying as much on maneuverability as on speed or firepower. Not for nothing is such an encounter called a "dogfight" or, even more evocatively, a "furball," suggesting that all an onlooker can see is the fur flying from the hide of the opponents. In such an encounter, a kill is seldom a sure thing.

The uncertainty compounds with the number of aircraft involved. Two or three pilots may fire at the same enemy plane and watch it spin away in flames, and each man will come away convinced he alone shot it down. And perhaps it did not really go down! What seems to be smoke may actually be escaping gasoline, vaporizing in cold air, as happened to R.T. Smith in his April 8 battle with Lieutenant Hinoki. Or a plane heading for a seemingly inevitable crash may actually be diving away, to recover at a lower altitude, which is probably what fooled Duke Hedman and Chuck Older in their contest with Sergeant Yasuda two days later.

In the case of the AVG, most of its early battles took place in Burma, where in theory the Flying Tigers reported to the local Royal Air Force commander, who was supposed to sign off on the Americans' combat claims. There's no evidence that this was ever done, or anyhow not effectively. Instead, it was the individual squadron leaders — Oley Olson, Jack Newkirk, and Sandy Sandell, and later Bob Neale and Tex Hill after the first two were killed — who decided how many Japanese planes were destroyed and who would get the credit for them. After Burma fell to the Japanese and the AVG moved back into China, more control could be exercised by Chennault and the headquarters staff, and independent confirmation was sometimes provided by the Chinese warning net.

Thus we know that, at Loiwing on April 8, AVG ground crewmen found the wrecks of only three retractable gear Nakajima Ki-43 Hayabusas in the vicinity of the airport — something of a mystery, given that the pilots were claiming 12 "Zeros" shot down. But a close look at the combat reports shows that most describe a victory in one of those same three places, plus a few some distance to the south as the Japanese fled toward their home base at Chiang Mai in Thailand. This fits neatly with Japanese accounts of this battle, recalling three planes lost over the enemy airfield and another shot down as it was going home.

That fourth pilot was Captain Anma Katsui of the 64th Sentai, who crashed in a paddy field south of the Loiwing airfield, a circumstance that suggests that his was the Hayabusa claimed by Cliff Groh, Fritz Wolf, Eddie Overend, and R.T. Smith. (That wreck wasn't found by the Americans.) Multiple claims were similarly made against each of the three Hayabusas shot down close to the airport.

Of course it's possible that one or more wrecks were overlooked, but Loiwing was located in open country — and who could have flown those planes? We know the name of every 64th Sentai pilot. If one were lost, we know who he was and when it happened, and usually we know something about the circumstances. (A few pilots simply disappeared, much as Ed Leibolt disappeared at Rangoon. But even in those cases, we know who they were.) The 64th Sentai is, after all, as famous in Japan as the Flying Tigers are in the United States. Both groups were the subject of a wartime feature film celebrating its exploits, and many books were written about it during and after the war. For the record, the other pilots who died at Loiwing on April 8 were Sergeant Wada Haruto and Lieutenant Okumura Muneyuki — both combat veterans — along with a replacement named Kuroki Tadao.

In 1989-1990, I had a Verville fellowship at the National Air & Space Museum that allowed me to spend a year translating Japanese accounts of the air war in Southeast Asia. My NASM mentors were Robert Mikesh and Donald Lopez, the latter a veteran of Chennault's 23rd Fighter Group. (As it happens, Don had replicated Parker Dupouy's feat, ramming a Nakajima Hayabusa in the air, destroying the Japanese fighter while he himself nursed his P-40 back to his home field.) My translator was Miyuki Rogers, the Japanese wife of an American graduate student. I borrowed the books from the superlative Asian collection of the Library of Congress, and with Miyuki I worked out what Japanese historians and combat veterans had written about those months when Japan seemed unstoppable and the western Allies were more or less in continual and humiliating retreat. As an illustration of the fame of the 64th Sentai, when Miyuki went home that Christmas and told her family what she had been doing, her mother stood up and sang the group's regimental song, buried in memory for nearly half a century.

We found that, of the AVG's claim of 296 enemy aircraft destroyed, in the air and on the ground, perhaps 115 could be matched to actual Japanese losses. Not surprisingly, the largest discrepancies were in aircraft supposedly destroyed on the ground, and especially in the AVG raids upon enemy airfields at Chiang Mai in Thailand on March 24, 1942, and near Hanoi on May 12.

When the book was published, Flying Tiger veterans were of course outraged. ("Bullshit," was R.T. Smith's verdict in *Air Classics* magazine.) Yet it shouldn't have surprised anyone. As the British aviation historian Christopher Shores wrote in 2007: "over-claiming, albeit in the best of good faith in most cases, certainly seems to have been endemic in aerial combat. It happened on every front and with every air force.... Fighter pilots by and large were young, aggressive and optimistic men who knew what they should be seeing and wanted to see." There is scarcely a Second World War air force or theater of war that wasn't the subject of one or several volumes by Chris Shores, often in collaboration with one or two nationals of the subject country, the better to study the archives in the national language. As a rule of thumb, he and other researchers have found that fighter pilots of the 1940s over-claimed by three to one, with the German *Luftwaffe* and Finnish *Ilmavoimat* faring a bit better as a result of combat conditions and more stringent reporting requirements.

Before the first edition of *Flying Tigers* was published by Smithsonian Institution Press in 1991, only one American researcher had compared U.S. combat claims and the Japanese records. That was John Lundstrom in his studies of U.S. Navy fighter pilots in the first year of the Pacific War. His findings were very similar to mine: like the Flying Tigers, the Navy's "First Team" over-claimed by about 2.5 to 1 — which is to say, more modestly than in many air forces, notably including Japan's.

Alas, I'm afraid this didn't much console AVG veterans in 1991, nor does it seem to comfort those who uphold their legacy today. They much prefer the "official" number, and even to multiply it to "upwards of a thousand aircraft which could not be confirmed officially, but which pilots recounted having watched disappear into the mountains or sea."

100 Hawks for China: The Story of the Shark-Nosed P-40 That Shocked the Japanese in the Opening Months of the Pacific War

How the Planes Reached China

PARTIALLY DEAF, suffering from chronic bronchitis, and ostracized professionally for his belief that bombers were vulnerable to intercepting fighters, Captain Claire Lee Chennault retired from the U.S. Army Air Corps on April 30, 1937. Eight days later he embarked for China, to serve as a flight instructor for the Nationalist government.

With the outbreak of the Sino-Japanese War in the summer of 1937, Chennault became aviation advisor to the Nationalist Chinese Air Force under Generalissimo Chiang Kai-shek. He followed the Nationalist government as it retreated inland, from Nanjing to Hankow to Chongqing. Safe from invasion but not from aerial attack, Chongqing became the ghastly exemplar of the results of "strategic bombing" as it would be practiced in World War II.

His own fighter force destroyed by nimble Japanese planes, Chiang played a wild card. In November 1940 he sent Chennault to Washington, D.C., to buy U.S. fighters for the defense of Chongqing. Chennault had convinced the Generalissimo that a small force of highly trained men, flying aggressively, could take the offensive against the Japanese.

Given a choice, Chennault would not have picked the Curtiss P-40 — or any other airplane with a liquid-cooled engine — to equip his American Volunteer Group in China. Yet in a way he had been present at its creation. As a captain in the Army Air Corps in 1934, he had helped draw up the specifications for America's first modem fighter, or "pursuit," as the airplane was called at the time: a low-wing, all-metal aircraft that could fly level at a then-impressive 300 mph. To enter in the resulting competition, Curtiss-Wright developed the Hawk 75, which the Army Air Corps would later adopt under the designation P-36. But the airplane was slow and under-armed compared with the warplanes being produced in Europe. Because its Pratt & Whitney engine was air-cooled, the Hawk 75 had a large frontal surface area, which gave the fighter a stubby, no-nonsense look but did nothing for its aerodynamic efficiency. So Curtiss began to experiment with a liquid-cooled Allison engine manufactured by General Motors. The marriage of Hawk 75 airframe and Allison engine produced the Hawk 81.

In spite of the components it shared with its predecessor — virtually everything except the snout, which was elongated to house the new, narrower engine — the Hawk 81 had a radically different appearance. Like the British Spitfire and the German Messerschmitt Bf-109, it had a sinister look. Unlike them, however, it also seemed to have a *face*, the result of moving the radiator air scoop to the front of the aircraft, just below the propeller. If the Hawk 81's conical spinner suggested a nose, the air scoop suggested, irresistibly, a mouth. It was inevitable that combat pilots would decorate it with the teeth and staring eyes of a shark.

Claire Chennault cared little for appearances, and even less for liquid-cooled engines. To him they were an abomination, the product of engineers who had never been forced to contend with combat. Under wartime conditions, he believed, radiators and coolant tanks would be vulnerable to bullets or shrapnel, and the complicated fuel system would be fouled with dust and grime. But Curtiss-Wright was convinced that the Allison engine was the only one available that would give its craft the speed to compete with European fighters. Despite its extra weight, the liquid-cooled engine could boost the streamlined Hawk 81 to a top speed of about 350 mph. The airplane won the Army Air Corps fighter competition in 1939 and was designated the P-40.

The original P-40 had two .50-caliber machineguns that fired half-inch bullets at a rate synchronized to the turning of its constant-speed propeller; it also had a .30-caliber machinegun for each wing. Curtiss produced 342 of these airplanes in the summer and fall of 1940. Some were also ordered by France, which fell to the German army before the planes arrived. They were taken over by the British Royal Air Force, which put them into service with the designation of

Tomahawk Mark I, in deference to its American origins. They were used to train U.S. volunteers assigned to RAF "Eagle" squadrons.

By October 1940, the lessons learned by British and French pilots in the opening months of the European war led to modifications. The P-40B was kitted out with pilot armor, a second pair of wing-mounted guns, and externally sealed fuel tanks. The RAF adopted it as the Tomahawk II and used it to equip British Commonwealth squadrons in North Africa.

This model was in turn replaced by the P-40C, which had a more effective internal sealing membrane for its fuel tanks, along with a better radio and shackles for an external fuel tank. Some of the C models were sent to Hawaii and the Philippines, where they would mostly be destroyed on the ground by the Japanese onslaught of December 7-8, 1941. To the Royal Air Force this was the Tomahawk IIB, and like its predecessor it went to equip squadrons in North Africa.

With the escalating war threatening even the United States, Franklin D. Roosevelt's "arsenal of democracy" had set out to build 6,000 military aircraft in 1940, 18,000 in 1941, and 50,000 in 1942 — more than in all other nations of the world combined. The Hawk 81 was the first U.S. fighter produced in significant quantities. Because it was based on an existing airframe, Curtiss could rush it into production a full year ahead of competing manufacturers. By November 1940, Allison-powered Hawks were pouring out of a newly built factory in Buffalo, New York, at the then-unprecedented rate of 10 per day.

China, though, had scant chance of obtaining this or any other U.S. fighter. Warplanes were allocated on a priority basis. First in line came the Royal Air Force, which was rebuilding its fighter fleet after the Battle of Britain the previous summer, when the RAF and the Luftwaffe had all but destroyed each other over England. Next was the U.S. Army Air Corps, then beginning its own expansion program. Any leftover airplanes were sorely needed by other European nations, by British Commonwealth forces in the Pacific, by the Netherlands East Indies. . . But China? There was no priority for China. In American eyes, the Sino-Japanese War was still a sideshow. If the Chinese had any illusions on this score, they had only to look at the composition of the Joint Allocation Committee, which had been set up in September 1940 to parcel out war materiel. The committee was staffed by representatives of the Army Air Corps, the Navy's Bureau of Aeronautics — and the British Purchasing Commission.

T.V. Soong, Chiang Kai-shek's brother-in-law, had been in Washington since June 26, 1940, lubricating the wheels of diplomacy. On July 9, the wily and genial Soong lunched with treasury secretary Henry Morgenthau. Three days later he sent Morgenthau a note suggesting that the United States loan China $50 million to support its currency, $20 million to improve the Burma Road — the 2,100-mile supply line from Rangoon, on the Burmese coast, to the Nationalist capital at Chongqing — and $70 million to buy military supplies, including "300 pursuits [and] 100 light bombers with spare parts."

Soong also cultivated such power brokers as Lauchlin Currie, Thomas Corcoran, and Joseph Alsop. The first was a presidential aide, the second had been, and the third was a newspaper columnist who was related to both the president and the president's wife. These were important credentials. Washington still had a small-town power structure, and major deals were transacted through a network of friends.

In November, Soong's one-man China lobby was reinforced by Claire Chennault; General Mao Pang Chu, the plump and handsome chief of the Chinese Air Force; and Arthur Young, a financial advisor to Chiang Kai-shek's government. They met in the economist's apartment, with Mrs. Young banished to another room to preserve secrecy. She heard all, nevertheless: the men had to speak spoke loudly in deference to Chennault, whose hearing had been impaired by years of open-cockpit flying.

Young was dismayed by Chennault and Mao's description of the CAF. "China had only 37 fighter planes," he wrote later, "and none that could cope with Japan's Zeros. The only bombers available were 31 of slow Russian types with difficult flying characteristics, that could not be used at night and could be used in daytime only with fighter escort. Anti-aircraft equipment was inadequate and badly worn.... In contrast they stated that Japan had 968 planes in China exclusive of Manchuria, and 120 in Indochina. These included late type fighters and bombers, fast and well-armed."

They worked out "an aviation program," as Young described it, "aimed at protection of Chungking and of the Burma Road." The program was both more ambitious and more specific than Soong's proposal of July 12, calling for 100 of the new Curtiss fighters, 250 radial engine Navy fighters (at Chennault's insistence, one suspects), 100 twin-engine bombers, 10 DC-3 cargo planes, and 150 trainers. It also requested spare parts, anti-aircraft guns, gasoline and ammunition for a year of combat, the machinery to build 136 new landing fields, and 350 U.S. flight instructors and technicians.

Soong presented his revised shopping list (along with a request that the United States equip 30 Chinese divisions at a cost of $1 million each) to the White House on November 25. The next day he and the Chinese ambassador called upon Secretary of State Cordell Hull to cultivate his support and to deliver a letter, probably drafted by Chennault, from the Generalissimo to FDR. In it, Chiang suggested that a few hundred U.S. bombers and fighters would enable the CAF to take the offensive against Japanese-occupied Taiwan and Hainan, and even Japan itself.

While his brother-in-law made the rounds in Washington, in effect playing the good cop, Chiang Kai-shek stayed in Chongqing and played the bad cop. His most effective bargaining chip was the threat posed by the Reorganized National Government in Nanjing. Disregarding its ubiquitous regional warlords, China at the end of 1940 had three rival governments: the Nationalists in Chongqing, the Communists in Yenan, and a Japanese puppet regime in Nanjing under the leadership of Wang Ching-wei.

If he emerged as the major force in China, Wang Ching-wei would of course lift a great burden from Japan, which had 750,000 men tied down in fitful combat with Chiang Kai-shek's Nationalist (Kuomintang) army and Communist guerrillas. Chiang Kai-shek sent regular bulletins to Roosevelt about the progress of Wang's government, Japanese peace overtures, and German offers to guarantee Japan's peace terms. With China pacified, Japan would be free to move south, obtaining rubber from Indochina and oil from the Netherlands East Indies and possibly joining hands with Germany and Italy across the Indian subcontinent.

Duly alarmed by these reports, FDR had told his advisors to work up a loan agreement to be announced as soon as his re-election was out of the way in November. He also dispatched advisor Lauchlin

Currie to see Tommy Corcoran in his office on K Street, four blocks from the White House.

Corcoran's profession was an honorable one at the time, although it later fell into disrepute: he made deals for a fee. He cheerfully exploited his White House connections, and in return he did small favors such as the one Currie now asked of him: "Based on my understanding of the [U.S. Congress] I had to predict how much trouble there would be if the president sent modest aid to China [in violation of the Neutrality Acts] just to forestall Chiang's surrender," Corcoran wrote in an unpublished manuscript that was shown to me by Claire Chennault's widow. "I reported back to Currie: there'd be very little trouble as things then stood and were likely to stand in the near future.

"Acting for the president," Corcoran continued, "Currie then suggested that as a private individual I start the paperwork and charter a Delaware corporation to be known as China Defense Supplies. Frederick Delano, the president's elderly uncle who'd spent a lifetime in the China trade, was a co-chairman of the board [with T.V. Soong]. My brother David took a leave of absence from Sterling Drug to become president. I remained nominally only the organizer of the firm. By design I took no title, and only earned a modest $5,000 fee for putting the company together." Corcoran's stipend would be worth about $100,000 today.

While China Defense Supplies was being prepared as a conduit for military aid, the lobbying went forward to fund it. On November 29, Morgenthau called a staff conference. "The president just called me up," he noted, "and told me in strictest confidence ... that he is sending part of the fleet to the southern part of the Philippines. He is worried about something going on between Wang and Chiang, and he wants me to make a stabilization loan of $50 million to the Chinese in the next 24 hours." The loan would be repaid with shipments of raw materials and agricultural materials, including hog bristles wanted by the U.S. Navy for paint brushes.

Next day, on cue, Soong was sitting in Morgenthau's office, blinking benignly through his round spectacles—the good cop. Morgenthau recorded the conversation in his diary, as he did almost every day. Soong said that Chiang "asked for between $200 million and $300 million, that is what he asked for."

"What will you take?" asked the pragmatic Morgenthau.

"Well, we are not choosers, Mr. Secretary."

"I see," Morgenthau responded. "But as to take care of the immediate situation, say for six months —"

"I should imagine $100 million."

"I see.... Who else in Washington have you told this to, I mean officially?"

"Of course, I saw the secretary of state," Soong said. "I handed him a memorandum to be presented to the president."

"... Approximately what is in it?"

"Well, just two things in it. One is for airplanes and the second is for [currency] stabilization."

"Well now, was there any time factor in there?" asked Morgenthau.

"It is very urgent because of the Japanese recognition of Wang Ching-wei."

Morgenthau did not forget the bad cop back in Chongqing: the Generalissimo could settle with Wang if the United States dragged its feet or came back with a demeaning counter-offer. The treasury secretary had reached the bottom line, and he knew it: "What would you call a minimum that might be helpful?" he asked.

"I should say $100 million," Soong replied.

So it was settled, except for the problem of finding the airplanes. But not even this was outside Morgenthau's province, and a solution began to emerge at a meeting at his home the following Sunday. Curtiss-Wright had just begun to build a huge block of Hawk 81-A2s — the Tomahawk IIB with its improved fuel tanks and other modifications — for the Royal Air Force. The RAF began receiving the first of its 630-airplane order in November, and deliveries were scheduled to continue until March 1941. Curtiss happened to have enough parts on hand to build a few hundred extra Tomahawks before changing the production lines to manufacture the Kittyhawk (P-40D in U.S. service), which had a different profile, a larger engine, and four .50-caliber wing guns. Morgenthau thought that China's needs could be met by extending the Tomahawk production run.

Other countries wanted fighters, too, and on Monday, December 23, a good portion of FDR's cabinet met to work out a formula for allocating the extra airplanes. Cordell Hull convened the meeting in his office. Present were three other cabinet members — Morgenthau, Frank Knox of the Navy Department, and Secretary of War Henry L. Stimson — and assorted military and civilian advisors, including General George C. Marshall, the Army chief of staff.

Morgenthau opened the discussion. In the spring of 1941, he said, Curtiss-Wright could turn out 300 fighters beyond its commitments to the RAF and the Army Air Corps. How should they be spread around? Like boys choosing sides in a sandlot baseball game, the great men began to argue, their words paraphrased by a stenographer:

"Secretary Hull suggested that as the President had promised 30 planes to the Greeks that the 300 P-40's should be divided 150 to China, 120 to South America, and 30 for the Greeks.

"General Marshall said that he had a list of the various South American countries showing how the War Department thought planes should be allocated in that area. Secretary Knox stated that 150 would have to go to the British. To which Secretary Stimson added that the war was in Europe and the Far East, not in South America; therefore the planes [should] go to the British and the Chinese....

"Secretary Hull said that he thought the planes should go to China, and Stimson added that he thought China should get pursuit ships before she got bombers. Secretary Morgenthau inquired as to whether there were any other pursuit ships available that the Air Corps did not like. Major [Patrick] Timberlake said that the Republic P-43 was not particularly well liked by the army as it had no armor and no leak-proof tanks.... Admiral [Harold] Stark asked if leak-proof tanks could not be put in those planes, but Major Timberlake said it could not be done.

"Coming back to the P-40, Admiral Stark stated that he thought part of the planes should go to South America. The South American idea, however, was turned down emphatically, and it was resolved that the 300 P-40's should be divided equally between the British and the Chinese.... After a good deal of discussion, however, it was decided that if the British gave up current deliveries to the Chinese, then the British should receive planes on a two for one basis. In other words, the British would give up to the Chinese 50 in January, 25 in February, and 25 in March, making a total of 100, but she would get back 300 later in the spring, giving her a net gain of 200. Secretary

Morgenthau said he would get in touch with the British right away and ask them to place the order."

On January 10 the British agreed to this proposition. The RAF would give up 100 of their Tomahawk IIBs during the first three months of 1941, and in return would get all the planes to be built at the end of the scheduled production run.

Also in early January, Chennault laid the groundwork for the recruitment of the First American Volunteer Group, the men who would fly and maintain the fighters. AVG pilots and technicians — given FDR's special dispensation to resign from the U.S. armed forces — set out for Southeast Asia in the summer and fall of 1941.

Diverted as they were from a British allocation, Chennault's fighters were painted in RAF "sand and spinach" camouflage — alternating bands of tan and green — except for their undersides, which were pale blue to blend with the sky. (The U.S. Army P-40s were painted olive drab above, light gray below.) More significantly, the British infantry rifle of the day, the bolt-action Enfield, took a cartridge differing in small but important details from that used by the U.S. Army. The RAF had specified that the Tomahawk wing guns be built to handle the Enfield rounds, and 64 of the airplanes diverted to China were thus equipped. The others, for reasons now impossible to fathom, were delivered without any armament whatever; these had to be fitted with machineguns scrounged up in the Far East. As a result, Chennault's Volunteers would go into combat with four different ammunition requirements: .303-inch British, .30-inch U.S., and .317-inch Chinese rounds for their wing guns, plus the .50-inch rounds for the nose guns.

The RAF and the Army Air Corps also used different radio frequencies. The British had therefore ordered their fighters without communications equipment, planning to install their own sets. But China Defense Supplies could obtain neither RAF nor Air Corps equipment, and instead shipped 100 RCA radios designed for light civilian sport planes. As a result, AVG pilots often went into combat unable to talk to the control tower or to one another.

T.V. Soong used $4.5 million of his recently acquired funds to pay for these "bastard aircraft," as Joseph Alsop described them to me in an interview at his Georgetown home. As each of the 36 Tomahawks made for China in January came off the production line, it was fitted into two huge crates, one for fuselage and engine, the other for wing assembly, propeller, and empennage. The crates were loaded onto flatcars and sent by rail to New York, where they were transferred to a Norwegian freighter. The ship sailed at the end of February, headed for Burma by way of South Africa and the Indian Ocean. Unknown to Chennault, his little air force was about to be reduced by one: during unloading at Rangoon, a wing crate fell into harbor. It was hoisted out and left to sit on the dock with the rest, while saltwater corrosion ruined the aluminum covering.

The easterly route required two extra weeks, and in early March Soong petitioned the State Department for the remaining shipments to be sent westward in U.S. freighters through the Panama Canal and across the Pacific. Impossible, said State. Burma was a British colony, Britain was at war, and the Neutrality Acts forbade U.S. vessels from carrying war materiel to the port of any belligerent. So the planes were loaded into a Norwegian freighter. The second lot of Tomahawks — 32 of them — was shipped late in March via the same tedious route and under the same impartial flag.

At this juncture, an entrepreneur named William Pawley turned up in Washington with a 1933 Curtiss-Wright contract assuring him a commission on any of its airplanes sold in China. He demanded his contractual 10 percent, as if he had personally brokered the sale. Curtiss refused to pay, whereupon Pawley threatened to embargo the airplanes still in New York. An exasperated Henry Morgenthau called a meeting in his office on April 1, during which Pawley agreed to waive his claim in return for a $150,000 contract to assemble the airplanes in Burma. Morgenthau decided to capitulate: if you can't beat him, hire him.

All obstacles cleared at last, the final lot of 32 Hawks left New York toward the end of April.

In July Roosevelt approved a bomber group and a second fighter group for China, but because the airplanes were not shipped before the Japanese attack on Pearl Harbor in December, the Volunteers fought with only the airplanes sent in early 1941. A dozen were wrecked in training, and dozens more were sidelined for lack of replacement parts. Some replacement Kittyhawks (P-40E models) arrived in the spring of 1942, but at no time did Chennault have more than 55 combat-worthy fighters.

The wider war transformed the mission of the AVG. With his tiny force, Chennault had to defend the Burma Road from December 8, 1941, to July 4, 1942, by which time Burma was lost and the Volunteers inducted into the U.S. Army Air Forces. His gallant mercenaries — known to the world as the Flying Tigers — had compiled an astonishing record against a far superior force, claiming 296 Japanese aircraft destroyed in the air and on the ground. (Japanese records indicate that the tally was much exaggerated, while AVG veterans swore that it is conservative.) For their part, the Flying Tigers lost most of their Tomahawks and 23 of their men, all but one of them fliers. Three other pilots were captured by the Japanese but survived the war.

RAF Pilot's Manual

THIS MANUAL PROBABLY accompanied the China-bound Tomahawks to Rangoon, or may have been separately acquired by CAMCO. It was typed up, mimeographed, and published as a spiral-bound booklet by the British Air Ministry, and the title page says "Tomahawk I," referring to the bare-bones P-40 built for France and taken over as a combat trainer by the Royal Air Force. However, internal evidence (especially the engine designation and occasional references to the RAF blocks from which the Chinese allot-ments were taken) ties it to the Curtiss Tomahawk IIB fighters sent to Burma for the American Volunteer Group. There is also some internal evidence, including references to French instrumentation, suggesting that the text was not brought entirely up to date. For that reason, I sent a copy to Erik Shilling, an AVG veteran with a background as a test pilot, to see how it compared to the planes he had flown in Burma and China. His notes are a valuable corrective.

I copied the manual in 1989 at the National Air & Space Museum, which in turn had copied it from Larry Pistole's large collection of AVG memorabilia. Mr. Pistole's collection was later acquired by the Flying Tigers Association, and NASM's copies somehow went missing, so mine is the only version known to be accessible.

In transcribing the manual, I followed the original as exactly as possible, including its spelling and typography. Words in brackets [like this] have been added. Similarly, my comments and Erik's are bracketed and set off from the main text. Erik's comments strongly support the argument that the planes sent to China had components of older aircraft installed, no doubt so Curtiss could use up its inventory of parts, and that the hybrid planes more closely resembled IIA models than the IIBs shown in Curtiss records (or in U.S. Army terms, P-40Bs rather than P-40Cs as I had originally believed.)

I should say that, after studying the manual and especially the section on Handling and Flying Notes, I am astounded at the information those fighter pilots of the Second World War had to fix in their minds. It was all I could do to manage the Piper Cub with its five-instrument array and its similarly elemental flight controls. Really, one could fly the Cub at a steady 60 miles per hour — take-off, cruise, and landing speed — all at 60 mph. (I did vary the speed, of course, but it wasn't absolutely necessary.) How in the world did Erik and his mates fly their Tomahawks in combat, at night, in the tropics, at sea level and over high mountains? Their minds must have been organized very differently from mine. Here's to them, and to the fabulous plane they flew!

The three-view drawing on the following page is by Richard Ferriere and is a good representation of the Tomahawks that went to Rangoon in the spring of 1941. My thanks to Richard for permission to include it here. — *Daniel Ford, March 2022*

Curtiss P-40B
Tomahawk

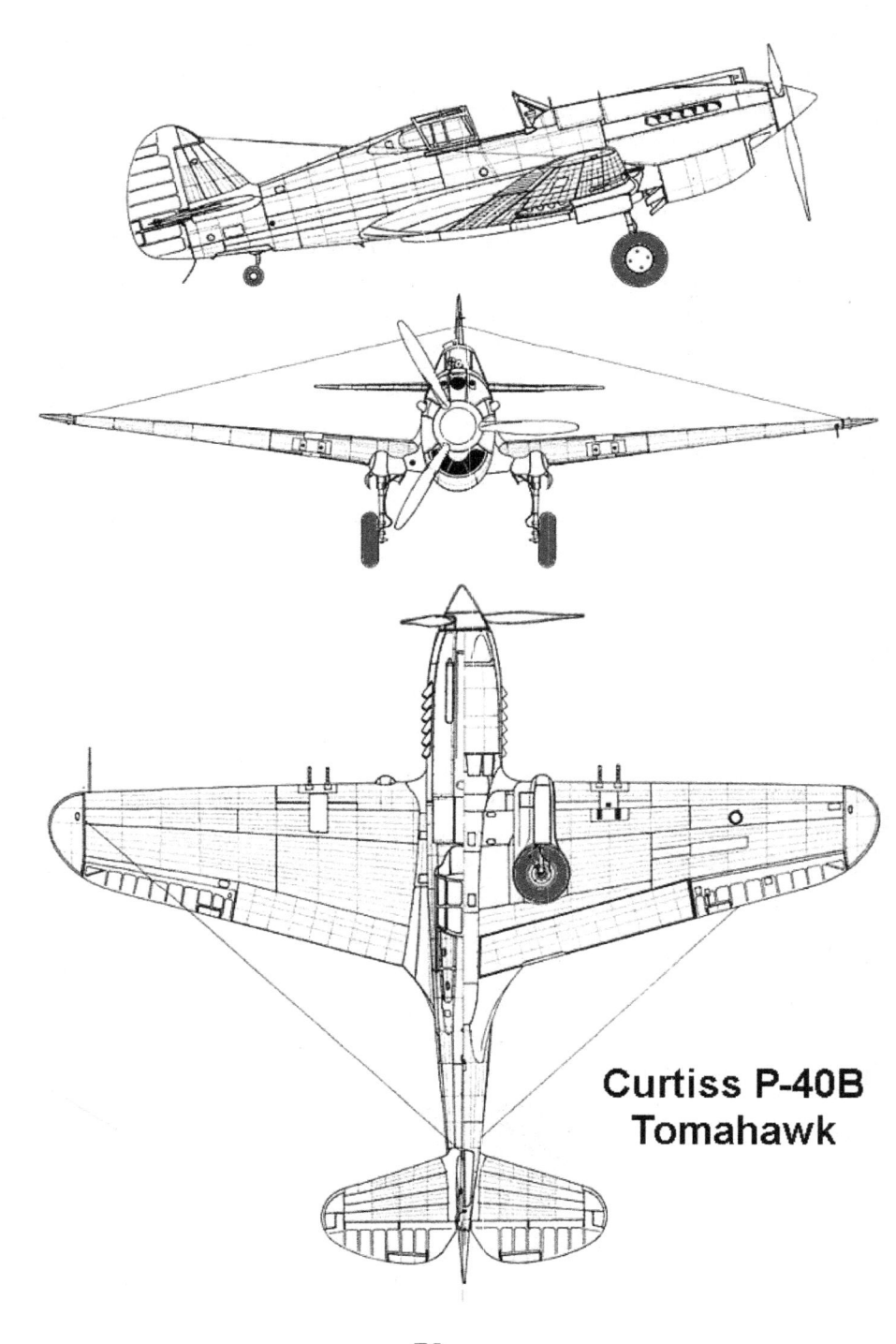

FOR OFFICIAL USE ONLY

AIR PUBLICATION 2013A

Pilot's Notes

PILOT'S NOTES

TOMAHAWK I

ALLISON V-1710-C15 ENGINE

AIR PUBLICATION 2013A

Pilot's Notes

INTRODUCTION

1. The Tomahawk I is a single-seater, low wing, monoplane with retractable landing gear and enclosed cockpit, powered with an Allison V-1710-C15 engine, which drives a Curtiss multi-position, constant speed, electrically operated, tractor propeller. The following are the main dimensions:

Span 37 ft., 3 1/2 in., Overall length 31 ft. 8-9/16 in.

Overall height with tail down 9 ft., 7 in.

2. The cockpit is totally enclosed. The windscreen is in three sections of laminated glass and behind the windscreen there is a section of 1-1/2 inch glass for protection from gunfire. The transparent cabin cover slides fore and after for entry and exit purposes. An emergency release is provided by which the entire sliding section has an emergency exit on the port side, for use in event of turnover. The structure behind the pilot is of

sufficient strength to withstand a turnover landing. Three pieces of armor plate are provided; one piece 7 mm. thick ahead of the pilot from the windscreen line down to the top of the engine, a piece 7 mm. thick behind the pilot's back, and 9 mm. thick behind his head.

[*Daniel Ford:* The British "Armourglass" proved incompatible with the U.S. Army optical gunsight, forcing the AVG to make do with iron ring sights or a vulnerable jury rig made locally. The reference to pilot armor is further proof that the manual has been at least partly updated for the Tomahawk IIA or IIB.]

   3. The main plane is a cantilever multi-spar, skin stressed type built in two pieces and joined at the centerline of the airplane. The wing tips are detachable. The joint where the two wing sections are connected will serve as a skid in case of an emergency landing with the wheels retracted.

   The ailerons are both dynamically and aerodynamically balanced. They are operated by the conventional stick control. A fixed type trimming tab, adjustable on the ground is provided on each aileron. The ailerons have a stressed metal skin leading edge and are fabric covered.

   The flaps are of the split trailing edge type, extending from the aileron to near the centerline of the airplane and are operated hydraulically by an electrically driven pump or by an emergency hand pump. An indicator on the instrument boards shows the position of the flaps at all times when the battery switch is on.

   4. Cooling system - Air passing through prestone radiators and oil cooler and exhausting into a common exit duct. Airflow through this duct is controlled by cowl flaps operated by a lever on the starboard side of the cockpit with a locking device incorporated.

5. **Wing Guns** - Two rifle caliber guns may be carried in each panel. Wing gun charging handles are located on the centerline of the airplane beneath the instrument panel. Ammunition boxes hold 500 rounds per gun. The trigger switch is located on the stick.

6. **Fuel Tanks** - The fuel is carried in three tanks two in the center of the wing and one in the fuselage aft of the pilot. The total capacity of the three tanks is 132.6 imperial gallons. (See fuel system diagram.) All fuel tanks have "Superflexit" covering.

[*Daniel Ford:* See Erik's comments in Part II about the AVG fuel tanks. The reference to a Superflexit "covering" suggests that the Tomahawk IIB had an exterior sealant rather than the more effective internal membrane that should have been installed at this point in the production run. (A rubber coating inside the tank would tend to close itself from the weight of the gasoline, while a bullet hole in the exterior coat would tend to be held open.) At first I regarded this statement as a carry-over from an earlier version of the manual, but it tracks with Erik's recollection and goes to support the argument that Curtiss used left-over P-40B components when assembling the Hawks for shipment to China.]

Oil Tank - Oil is carried in a 12.7 imperial gallon tank in the fuselage behind and above the fuselage fuel tank. Climbs up to 60° and dives up to 90° should be performed only with not less than 1/3 of the maximum oil capacity. The tank should be refilled to 9.6 imperial gallons maximum service capacity at all times.

Coolant Tank - The coolant expansion tank is forward of the firewall and has a capacity of two imperial gallons.

7. **The fuselage** is of semi-monocoque, skin stressed construction, and has a motor mount of welded steel tube and steel forged links. The

fuselage access door is on the port side of the fuselage near the tail.

8. Fuselage Guns - Two synchronized guns may be carried just ahead of the pilot. These are .50 caliber Colt guns, and are charged directly through an opening on each side of the instrument panel. Electrically operated rounds indicator are mounted near the instrument board on the upper longeron. The gun triggers are electrically operated by a selector switch located above the port longeron, and the trigger switch is located on the stick. Ammunition boxes hold 380 rounds per gun.

9. Battery - A 34 ampere hour capacity, 24 volt battery is carried in the airplane and is accessible through the fuselage access door.

10. Landing Gear - The landing gear is equipped with oleo-pneumatic shock struts which are hydraulically retracted to rotating backward about a trunion at the top of the strut. During retraction the strut is rotated 90° about its longitudinal axis by gears, so that the wheel lies flush in the wing. The gear is locked in both the up and down positions by hydraulically operated mechanical locks. The upper half of the strut has members attached to take side and drag loads and is attached to the lower half of strut through a scissors to take torque. The landing gear is equipped with 30 inch diameter smooth contour tires and wheels with 12 x 2 1/4 inch hydraulic brakes. An indicator on the instrument panel shows the position of the landing gear at all times when main battery switch is turned on.

11. Tail Wheel - The tail wheel assembly consists of a standard steerable knuckle unit and a 12 1/2 inch wheel with earth conducting tire. The steering mechanism disengages at approximately 35°

deflection from the longitudinal axis and when disengaged will swivel through 360°. The tail wheel is fully retractable and operates "clam shell" doors which enclose it completely after retraction. An indicator on the instrument board shows the position of the tail wheel at all times when the battery switch is turned on.

12. Fixed Tail Surface - The tail plane and fin are of all metal constructions attached in fixed alignment to the fuselage.

13. Control surfaces - The rudder and elevators are aluminum alloy construction, fabric covered. They are dynamically balanced and are equipped with trim tabs controlled from the cockpit. Rudder and elevators are controlled by the conventional pedals and stick.

14. Additional Equipment - In addition to the armament, the airplane is equipped with parachute flares, landing light, recognition device, oxygen, life preserver, radio, map case, engine and cockpit covers, navigation, formation, identification and cockpit lights. (See Section 1.)

15. Tie Down Rings are located inboard of the wing tips on the underside of the wing and marked "Tie Down".

16. Tool Box - A tool box for carrying the airplane and engine tool kit as an overload is provided in the fuselage and is accessible through the fuselage access door.

17. First Aid Kit - is located on the port side of fuselage being accessible through fuselage service door.

18. Propeller - The propeller is a Curtiss multi-position and/or constant speed type. The propeller is operated electrically from the

airplane electrical supply thru brushes mounted in a housing, attached on the engine section, to slip rings mounted on the rear boss of the propeller hub, and thence to the pitch changing motor.

Automatic electric cutout switches limit the pitch range for ordinary operation and give high and low pitch settings.

Two types of control, manual selective and automatic, are available for selection by the pilot. The change from one to the other is made by a toggle switch located on the propeller control panel. (See Section 1, para. 11).

SECTION 1

Pilot's Controls and Equipment

Introduction

This section gives the location and, where necessary, explains the function of the controls and equipment in the pilot's cockpit.

NOTE: On aircraft Nos. A.H. 741 to A.H. 970 inclusive certain of the electrical switches are "on" when in the "Up" position and care should be taken to identify these. All switches are clearly marked "Off" and "On".

1. Cockpit - The cockpit is fully equipped and has the normal stick and rudder pedal controls which are dealt with individually in the following paragraphs. The sliding hood can be pushed right back from the cockpit and is operated by a crank mounted on the upper right longeron. A pin on the crank engages holes in the drum and locks the cabin in the full back, full forward and intermediate positions.

An emergency hood release is also fitted and is

a lever painted red, located at the top forward frame of the cabin roof. In case of an emergency, while in flight, the entire enclosure may be released from the fuselage by pulling on this lever. In the event of turnover on the ground, pull the panel release handle and push open the emergency exit on the left hand side of the cabin enclosure. This emergency exit may be operated from the outside by means of a handle located on the lower rear left hand cabin frame.

An emergency release which disengages the catches from the crank is located at the top of the windshield and consists of a turnbuckle and wire painted red. This eliminates winding the crank for rapid opening but the enclosure must then be pushed back by hand.

A ventilator for the cockpit is operated by a push-pull control located below the instrument board on the port side. When the control is pulled out hot air is admitted to two vents,: one permitting hot air to enter directly into the cockpit, the other deflects the hot air between the windscreen and bulletproof safety glass, acting as a defroster, before passing into the cockpit.

2. The seat is adjusted vertically by a lever on the starboard side of the seat. The lever is moved upward and to the rear permitting the seat to be raised manually. A release lever controlling the position of the pilot's harness belt is provided at the port side of the seat. To operate, push button on top of lever and move lever to rear locking position. This permits free movement of the pilot in a fore and aft direction. A pilot's relief tube is suspended from the bottom of the seat.

3. Control Column - The control column is of the conventional design. The control column hand grip

has two switches; the one on the top of the grip is a push button and operates the landing gear; the other is a trigger switch and operates the firing of the guns.

[*Erik Shilling*: Ours did not have the top button. The hydraulic switch was a light weight switch just below the pistol type control handle, and operated by the little finger.]

4. **Rudder Pedals** - The rudder pedals are of conventional design and they are adjustable for leg reach by releasing a pin by means of the lever on the inboard side of the pedal, and moving forward or aft as required.

5. **Brakes** - Brakes are operated by toe pedals and the parking brake lever is located below the instrument board and may be engaged by being pulled back when the pedals are depressed. It is automatically disengaged when the pedals are depressed.

6. **Trim Tabs** - The adjustable trim tabs for the rudder and elevators [sic] controls are located at the port side of the cockpit near the pilot's seat, and work in the same plane as the controls concerned. The elevator wheel has a crank handle for rapid adjustment. Dials at the hand wheels indicate the positions of the tabs.

[*Erik Shilling*: the ailerons [also had] a cockpit trim control which was located in front and just below the rudder trim vertical to the rudder trim.]

7. **Retractable Landing Gear** - The retractable landing gear is operated hydraulically by either the emergency hand pump or the electric pump. An operating instructions plate is located on the left hand side of the cockpit. On aircraft Nos. A.H. 741 to A.H. 999 and A.K. 100 to A.K. 155 inclusive, a selector lever extends forward along the port side

of the cockpit and has a push button on the end which must be depressed to move the handle from neutral. (The handle may be returned to neutral without depressing the button.)

To retract the landing gear depress the button on the end of the handle, and raise the handle to the "Up" position. Then operate the electrical pump by pressing the switch button on the top of the control column. <u>As a precaution the gun selector switch should be "Off" in case the trigger switch is squeezed by mistake.</u> The switch must be held "On" during the period required for the retraction of the landing gear. To lower landing gear move handle to down position and operate switch button as before.

[*Daniel Ford:* Note what Erik says above, that on the AVG Tomahawks the button on top of the stick was replaced by a toggle below the pistol grip.]

NOTE: - On aircraft A.K. 156 and onwards the push button on the undercarriage selector lever is replaced by a safety latch bolt which must be pulled forward before the lever can be moved.

To ensure positive engagements [sic] of the locks, the switch should be held on for a few seconds after the indicator and the warning horn show that they are down. As a final check the pilot should try and move the hand pump lever on the right hand side of the cockpit. If this lever cannot be moved, except by a high load which brings the hydraulic bypass valve into operation, the pilot can be sure that the landing gear is locked down. <u>The selector lever should then be raised to its neutral position. This hydraulic valve control lever should be in neutral when taking off or landing.</u>

An indicator on the instrument board indicates

the position of the landing gear whenever the battery switch is turned "On." A warning klaxon which operates when the throttle is closed with the wheels retracted, is only connected to the locks and consequently will sound when the wheels are down if the locks are not engaged.

This klaxon circuit is controlled through a toggle switch which is mounted just ahead of the throttle quadrant and is actuated by a cam mounted on the throttle rod. This cam may be pulled out to turn the klaxon off temporarily during a throttled dive with the wheels retracted. It engages automatically when the throttle is opened to the stop.

<u>Emergency operation</u>: In the event of the electrical system failing, select the required position for the undercarriage on the selector lever and operate hand pump on right hand side of the cockpit.

<u>Warning</u> - Never operate pump with selector lever in "Up" position when airplane is resting on its wheels.

[*Erik Shilling*: In the event of electric failure the gear was dropped by operating the emergency hydraulic hand pump. In the event of a hydraulic failure, the handle was removed from its normal position, and placed on a second position outboard of the normal position. In this position, would direct pressure to the main gear and lower the mains, but it would not lower the tail wheel which was left retracted.]

Before starting engine or taxiing, check landing gear lock by shifting selector to "down" position and operating the hand pump until it is solid to fore and aft movement. <u>Return valve lever to neutral position</u>.

8. <u>Wing Flaps</u> - The wing flaps are operated hydraulically by either the hand pump or an

electrically operated pump. The selector handle is located on the port side of the cockpit beside the pilot's seat and moves fore and aft; - forward for "Down" and aft for "Up" and neutral for "Off". The hand operated hydraulic pump (see para. 7) may be worked back and forth to raise or lower the flaps after the up or down position has been selected on the handle. The flaps may be operated manually in order that partial setting may be obtained more easily. With air loads on the flaps they will close automatically as soon as the selector switch is moved to the "Up" position.

[*Erik Shilling*: our flap control lever had a push button on the end which had to be depressed in order to move the flap handle out of the neutral position. When placed in the up position, the little finger was used to turn on the electric hydraulic pump. The same switch was used to actuate the hydraulic pump both for the Flaps and Gear.]

NOTE: - Flap selector lever cannot be set to "Up" position until undercarriage lever has been returned to neutral.

[*Erik Shilling*: We did not have this type of flap control.]

9. **Undercarriage and Flap Position Indicator** - The position indicator is located on the lower port side of the instrument board. The wheel and flap images simulate the actual position of the landing wheels, tail wheel and flaps. The images disappear from view when the electrical power is off, thereby indicating failure of the instrument, or open battery or generator circuit. The battery switch must be "On" to maintain operation of the indicator. The battery switch should be "Off" before leaving the airplane.

Engine Controls

10. **Throttle Quadrant** - The throttle, automatic mixture and propeller controls are located on the

throttle quadrant. The mixture control locates the automatic rich and automatic lean positions. Approximately the last 10° movement of the "lean" mixture on the quadrant is the engine "idle cut-off" position. There is a spring stop included to prevent mixture control from entering the "idle cut-off" position when normal pressure is applied.

11. <u>Airscrew [Propeller] Operating</u> - This may be either "Automatic or "Manual Selective". When on <u>automatic</u> control, a selected engine speed is held constant by an engine driven governor. Speed selection is accomplished by adjustment of the propeller control on the throttle quadrant, and the toggle switch on the propeller control panel is in the "down" or "on" position.

When on <u>manual selective</u> control, that is with switch in "Hand control" position, the propeller acts as a controllable pitch propeller by the operation of the "Increase R.P.M.", or "Decrease R.P.M." switch. Circuits are independent of the governor so that if the governor fails the propeller can be used as a multi-position controllable propeller.

Since the markings on the propeller control are for approximate settings, the tachometer should be relied up to obtain the desired R.P.M.

<u>General Operation: Automatic Control</u> - Set toggle safety switch which is of the circuit breaker type to "On" (Down) (automatic control) position at all times that constant speed control by C.P. lever on throttle quadrant is desired. (If the switch throws out it may be reset by turning to "Off" then to "On". Successive throwing out will probably be an indication of short circuit or overload and the switch should be left off, in this event, the pitch should be changed only if

absolutely necessary.)

The desired R.P.M. can then be obtained by moving the constant speed control lever on the throttle quadrant.

Manual Control - Set switch from "on" (automatic control) to "Hand Control". **The throttle quadrant lever is then cut out** and any change in R.P.M. must be made by operating the manual switch over to "Increase" or "Decrease" until the desired changed in engine revs has been made.

[*Erik Shilling*: The propeller control was a four position toggle switch. Up was automatic, down and left was manual decrease, down to the right was increase rpm, and center was off.]

12. **The Fuel Cock** is located on the port side of the cockpit below the hand fuel pump and marked to show the tanks and capacities.

13. **Fuel Quantity Gauge** for the auxiliary tank is located on the instrument board and the front and rear main tanks on the floor of the cockpit.

[*Erik Shilling*: The fuel selector had five positions. 1. Res. 2. Main. 3. Aux. 4. Fuse. 5. Off. The reserve and main tanks were one and the same . The main tank was feed by a stand pipe in the main tank and the reserve fed from the bottom of the same main tank. The reserve was used for all take offs and landings. When reserve was selected, fuel was taken from the bottom of the main tank and fed fuel to the engine. In other words the stand pipe used all of the fuel in the main tank, but when the main was selected, it used all, except I believe, a positive amount of fuel giving 20 minutes at METO power. This was a positive indication of exactly how much fuel remained, eliminating the pilot having to rely upon a fuel gage which at best was an unreliable.] [METO is the maximum power that can be applied except during take-off.]

14. **Carburetor Air Heat Control** - is located on the same bracket as the rounds indicator on the starboard side. The carburetor air intake is a

scoop built into the top of the engine cowl. A butterfly valve, controlled from the cockpit, is located immediately above the carburetor air screen and permits either cold or warm air or a mixture of both to enter. Warm air for the carburetor is taken from inside the engine compartment. The carburetor air screen is installed to prevent the passage of any foreign matter into the carburetor. The carburetor air control should always be in the cold position when starting the engine.

15. <u>The Engine Primer</u> is located on the starboard side of the cockpit, just below the instrument panel.

16. <u>Starter</u> - A foot operated electric inertia starter is provided. A foot treadle on the cockpit floor is pushed back to operate a starter switch which allows a direct flow of current from the battery to the starter motor. When the starter has reached the desired speed, the foot treadle is pushed forward actuating a starter meshing solenoid and a booster coil; also by the same movement of the foot treadle the start switch contact is broken. The first few impulses of the engine in starting will automatically disengage the starter. On aircraft A.H. 971 and subsequent the foot operated starter is replaced by a two way toggle switch located on the switch panel on the port side of the cockpit. This is depressed to energize the starter and raised to engage it, and the switch automatically returns to the off position when released.

[*Erik Shilling:* Starter had the foot treadle starter.]

[*Daniel Ford:* This strikes me as particularly significant. All AVG aircraft were taken from blocks higher than AH and therefore should have had the toggle switch. I don't see how Erik could possibly be wrong on this, which leaves only two possibilities: that the manual is in error, or that the planes diverted to China were not equipped the same as those sent to North Africa for the RAF. I would bet on the second possibility.]

In case of battery failure, the starter may be cranked by hand with crank and extension provided for this purpose, both being located in rear access compartment. The starter is operated by turning the crank handle which is inserted in the spiral slot provided in the end of the crank extension, on right hand side of engine cowl. Turn the crank with gradually increasing speed until a fairly good rate of speed is obtained. Remove the crank handle and extension. The engagement of the starter will then be accomplished by a pull on the hand starter button located immediately above the crank. Caution: <u>Starter crank and extension must be removed immediately after cranking and before actuating starter pull</u>.

17. <u>Oil Dilution Control</u> is located on the switch panel on the port side of the cockpit.

(a) Before stopping the engine when a cold weather start is anticipated, hold the oil dilution control switch "On" for approximately four minutes at 800 RPM and stop the engine with the ignition switch, continuing to hold the dilution control switch "On" until the engine stops. Then turn the standard fuel cock to the off position.

(b) In starting the engine a normal start should be made. After starting the engine, if a heavy viscous oil is indicated by oil pressure that is too high or by oil pressure that fluctuates or falls back when the engine RPM is increased, the dilution valve should be held "On" to dilute the oil and correct this condition. Over dilution will result in a steady low oil pressure and should be avoided if possible.

(c) If the engine heat is excessive when operating the oil dilution control, the heat may evaporate the fuel out of the oil and leave the normal high viscosity oil in the engine. When this condition is encountered, the engine should first be shut off and allowed to cool for fifteen minutes, then re-started and the instructions outlined in paragraph "a" followed in preparing the engine for cold weather starting.

(d) Take-off may be made four minutes after starting the engine if there has been enough rise in oil temperature (40°c. minimum), if the engine holds its oil pressure and if the engine runs smoothly, or, the take-off may be made as soon after four minutes as these conditions are obtained.

18. <u>Hand Fuel Pump Control</u> is located on the port side of the cockpit forward of the throttle quadrant.

19. <u>Radiator Flap Control</u> is located on the starboard side of the cockpit near the floor. It consists of a long lever and a rack. The latter is provided with a stop at each end and may be set for "full open" (handle fully down), "Full closed" (handle fully up), or any intermediate position.

NOTE: Filling points for:

Wing fuel tanks through left hand wing fillet.

Fuselage fuel tanks through rear vision glass, left hand side, forward.

Oil tanks through rear vision glass, left hand side, aft.

Coolant tank through inspection door, top of engine cowl.

<u>Operational Equipment</u>

20. <u>Gun Firing Switch</u> - See Section 1, paragraph 1 [sic; should be para. 3]

21. <u>Switches and Rheostats</u> are located on panel on the left, below the throttle quadrant. Care must be taken to insure that all rheostats are in the extreme "Off" position when not in use, as they are equipped with integral switches.

22. <u>Oxygen</u> - Two oxygen bottles are carried in supports in the aft part of the fuselage, and accessible through the fuselage access door. The oxygen regulator and bayonet outlet are located on the starboard side of the cockpit. (Aircraft Nos. A.H. 741 to A.H. 990 have one bottle only)

[*Erik Shilling*: We did not have the oxygen as shown since it was a high pressure system, not the low pressure demand system.]

23. <u>Aircraft Flares</u> - Two M-8 type flares are carried in the flush type built-in wing flare racks. Flare release handles are located on the starboard side of the pilot's seat.

24. <u>Recognition Device</u> - A bracket for mounting the damped rate control is provided on the starboard side of the cockpit which actuates the recognition device mounted on brackets near the top of fuselage accessible through fuselage access door.

25. <u>Landing Lamp</u> - A landing light is fitted to the underside of the port wing and is operated by a switch on the main switch box.

26. <u>Formation Lights</u> - for lighting the upper surface of the wing are located in the fuselage aft of the cockpit. These are controlled through a rheostat on the port side electrical boxes. (Aircraft A.H. 971 onwards)

27. <u>Identification Lights</u> - Provisions are made

in top of the fuselage aft of cockpit enclosure and starboard rear wing fillet for upward and downward identification lights. The identification light switch box is located on starboard side of cockpit.

28. **Wireless Controls** - [Text omitted; the AVG Tomahawks had after-market civilian radios]

Miscellaneous Equipment

29. **Dalton Computer** - Provision is made for the Dalton computer to be inserted in a stowage on the port side of the cockpit.

[*Erik Shilling*: no Dalton computer.]

30. **Shield** - An instrument light shield is provided to prevent reflections on the windshield.

31. **Fire Extinguisher** - is located in brackets on port side of cockpit floor.

32. **Map Case** - is fastened to the starboard side of the cockpit.

33. **Life Preserver** - The back cushion of the pilot's seat may be used as a life preserver.

[*Erik Shilling*: no life preserver.]

SECTION 2

HANDLING AND FLYING NOTES FOR PILOT

INTRODUCTORY NOTES

Note: - These notes should be read in conjunction with the Flying Training Manual, Part 1, Chapter III, which sets forth in detail the technique which is only outlined here.

1. Full details of the equipment of the aircraft are given in Section 1, and pilots should be

acquainted with these details, which are only mentioned hereafter when there is some particular point to which attention should be drawn.

(i) <u>Hydraulic system</u>:- The hydraulic system operates the undercarriage, tail wheel and flaps, and a diagram of the complete system is given at the end of Section 1.

[*Daniel Ford:* Unfortunately the reproductions are so poor that I must omit them, here and elsewhere.]

(ii) <u>Undercarriage</u>:- See Section 1.

(iii) <u>Flaps</u>:- The operation of the flaps is dealt with in Section 1. In the event of flaps being required for take-off, it is advisable to operate them manually in order to obtain more easily the partial setting required. This setting should be 20°. When flaps are down, caution should be exercised not to re-set the selector to the "up" position when there is any possibility that the resultant loss of lift might prove dangerous. Flaps should not be lowered at over 140 m.p.h. and should be raised for taxiing.

(iv) <u>Wheel brakes</u>:- These are toe-operated. They are satisfactory in operation and may be applied reasonably hard to restrict the landing run, but the good taxiing qualities of the aircraft do not necessitate their use under normal taxiing conditions.

(v) <u>Gun firing system</u>:- As the guns are fired electrically through a trigger switch on the stick, great care must be taken that this is not depressed accidentally or when operating the undercarriage and flap switch.

(vi) <u>Trimming tabs</u>:- The elevator trimming tab is efficient and not unduly powerful for small movements of the trimmer wheel. The rudder trim is powerful and must be used at all times whenever speed of the aircraft is varied, particularly when the cockpit hood is open.

(vii) **Air screw [Propeller]**:- See Section 1, para. 11, for main operating instructions. When it is necessary to check the engine revs on the magneto switches, the propeller switch must first be put to the "Hand Control" position, when any fluctuations of revs will show on the rev counter. Care must be taken to see that the switch is returned to the "On" position, i.e., automatic position, so that C.P. lever on the throttle quadrant is again in operation, before taking off.

(viii) **Cockpit hood emergency release**: - See Section 1, para. 1.

(ix) **Fuel, Oil and cooling systems**:- Diagrams of these are given at the end of Section 1 [omitted]

Note:- On aircraft Nos. A.H. 741 to A.H. 970 inclusive, certain of the electrical switches are "On" when in the "Up" position and care should be taken to identify these. All switches are clearly marked "Off" and "On".

<u>FITNESS OF AIRCRAFT FOR FLIGHT</u>

2. Ensure that the total weight and distribution of the load are in accordance with the weight sheet summary and ascertain that the aeroplane is in all other respects fit for flight.

<u>PRELIMINARIES</u>

3. Before starting the engine, check the following:

(i) That the ignition switches are OFF;

(ii) That undercarriage, tail wheel, and flap selectors are in NEUTRAL;

(iii) That constant speed toggle switch on control panel is ON; i.e., in "Automatic Control".

(iv) That wheel brakes are ON

(v) Switch on main battery switch and check undercarriage, tail wheel and flap indicator

(vi) Turn on fuel and check fuel tanks for contents

(vii) Check controls for free movement.

STARTING ENGINE AND WARMING UP

Note: For main engine details see Handbooks and paragraph 27 of these Notes.

4. (i) If engine has been standing, turn over by hand.

(ii) Turn carburetor air to "COLD", radiator shutters to "SHUT".

(iii) C.P. control to 2800 r.p.m.

(iv) Throttle to give approximately 800 r.p.m.

(v) Mixture control to idle cut-off. (See note)

(vi) Wobble pump to 4 lbs. pressure.

(vii) Prime engine with two to four strokes

(viii) Mixture control to FULL RICH

(ix) Switch ON

(x) Push heel on starter pedal to energize starter.

(xi) When starter has reached sufficient speed, push down toe of starter pedal to engage.

Note:- Do not increase fuel pressure above 4 lbs. with the mixture control out of the idle cut-out position. If necessary, prime the engine to keep it from stalling, as pumping the throttle does not prime the engine.

TESTING ENGINE AND INSTALLATION

5. (i) Warm up at 800 to 1000 r.p.m.

(ii) Minimum oil temperature before running up over 40°C. - Maximum 85°C.

(iii) Oil pressure - 60 to 80 lbs.

(iv) Radiator temperature for running up - 80°C.

(v) Whilst warming up the engine, check the operation of the flaps.

(vi) Set propeller switch to "manual selective".

(vii) Check the functioning of the engine and magnetos at 2200 r.p.m. and 26 in. Hg. (65 Cm.Hg.)

Note:- Care must be taken to see that the tail does not lift when 1800 r.p.m. is exceeded, and it is advisable to have somebody holding this down whilst running up.

(viii) Reset propeller switch to "automatic" position and check C.P. controls.

TAXIING

6. Owing to the steerable tail wheel, brakes are not necessary in normal circumstances. The view ahead is average and the machine is readily controllable.

If the engine is kept ticking over for any period of time, it should be cleared by being run up against the brakes prior to take-off.

ACTIONS PRIOR TO TAKE-OFF

7. Prior to actual take-off, check the following points by means of some suitable reminder, such as "T" - "M" - "P" "FLAPS" - "RADIATOR"

(i) "T" - trimming tab controls for rudder and

elevator should both be in neutral as shown by the marks on the indicators.

(ii) "M" - mixture control should be at full rich.

Note:- It should be at auto-rich if aeroplane is above 3500 feet.

(iii) "P" - constant speed control should be set to give 3000 revs, and check that toggle switch is in the UP (automatic) position.

(iv) "FLAPS" - may be used up to 20° for take-off if required, although the advantage of so doing is very small. See paragraph 1 (iii).

(v) "RADIATOR" - position for this will be dependent on the outside air temperature.

<u>TAKE-OFF</u>

8. The aircraft is very easy to take-off and shows scarcely any inclination to swing, although a little right rudder may be needed. As the Allison engine has a particularly quick pick-up, the opening of the throttle must be done slowly and care must be taken to ensure that the specified maximum manifold pressure of 41 in. Hg (104 Cm.Hg. on French instruments) is not exceeded. See para. 27 for full engine take-off limitations.

<u>ACTIONS AFTER TAKE-OFF</u>

9. (i) Once clear of the ground, raise the undercarriage and tail wheel by pressing the release knob on the end of the undercarriage selector lever, bringing the lever up to the undercarriage "UP" position, and pressing the thumb operating switch on the top of the control column [toggle switch below the pistol grip, on the AVG Tomahawks].

[*Daniel Ford:* Erik says that on the AVG Tomahawks the button on top of the stick was replaced by a toggle below the pistol grip.]

This operation is rather slow and whilst the undercarriage is going up -

(ii) reduce the boost pressure to 35 in. Hg. and reduce revs to 2600, and

(iii) maintain a flying speed of approximately 140 m.p.h.

(iv) When the indicator shows that the undercarriage and tail wheel are finally up, check that they are locked into position by operating the emergency hand pump, and if it is solid then the undercarriage and tail wheel are full retracted. Return undercarriage selector lever to neutral position, and

(v) If lowered, raise the flaps by selecting the "Up" position on the flap selector lever, and press the thumb operating switch on the control column. When the flaps are up return the lever to neutral.

(vi) Set mixture control to automatic rich.

ENGINE FAILURE DURING TAKE-OFF

10. If the engine should fail during take-off, put the nose of the machine down and maintain flying speed. See that the undercarriage has commenced to come up and, if possible, select the "DOWN" position on the flap lever and give any possible assistance with the hand pump.

(i) Switch off and land straight ahead.

CLIMBING

11. Whilst climbing away, check cockpit instruments systematically.

(i) Best climbing speed up to 14,000 feet is approximately 150 m.p.h.

(ii) R.P.M. and boost as given in para. 27.

(iii) Mixture in automatic rich.

(iv) Radiator control adjusted to keep coolant temperature between 85°C minimum and 125°C maximum.

CRUISING

12. For high speed cruising the r.p.m. may be 2600, with manifold pressure at 35 in. Hg. and mixture control in automatic rich.

For normal cruising the r.p.m. should be 2280 with manifold pressure at 27.9 in. Hg. and mixture control in Automatic Rich.

For most economical cruising, set revolutions to 2190 and manifold pressure to 25.2 in. Hg. Switch propeller control from Automatic to Manual and weaken mixture on mixture control until engine shows a drop in revs of 40 to 50 r.p.m. Switch propeller control back to Automatic. Provided no change is made [in] altitude or cruising conditions this will be most economical condition.

GENERAL FLYING

13. Whilst this aircraft has a good view and is very maneuvreable [maneuverable], it is directionally unstable, and this instability most pronounced with the cockpit hood in the fully open position. It is necessary to use the rudder on all turns and it is also necessary to readjust the rudder bias for all changes of speed. As speed is increased the aircraft tends to yaw to the right, and left rudder bias must be applied. (See para. 14)

The controls themselves are powerful at all speeds. It is possible to obtain high acceleration loadings by coarse use of the elevators. Trimmer tabs are effective.

INSTRUMENT FLYING

14. Owing to the directional instability of this aircraft with the hood open, it is essential that the hood be shut before any blind flying is attempted. It will be necessary to fly with the feet on the rudder bar, and particular care must be taken to avoid yaw. It would be advisable to lower the seat in order to obtain a better view of the instruments, which are somewhat masked by the reflector sight bracket.

[*Daniel Ford:* The AVG Tomahawks used a jury-rigged optical sight, and some had none at all, so this caution did not apply.]

STALLING

15. The stalling characteristics of this aircraft are good. At minimum speed the stall is gentle and there is some buffeting and pitching before the wing, generally the right, drops gently, followed by the nose.

At high speed the machine can be stalled as a result of the coarse use of the elevators producing high acceleration loadings, but due warning is received, particularly on the high speed turn, by a shuddering of the aircraft, and loads of over 5g. can be applied to [from?] 180 to 200 m.p.h. without the aircraft stalling.

The stalling speeds of the aircraft at normal operational loads, were as follows:

Undercarriage up and flaps up - 80 I.A.S. [80 mph Indicated Air Speed]

Undercarriage down, flaps up - 82 I.A.S.

Undercarriage up, flaps down - 73 I.A.S.

Undercarriage down, flaps down - 75 I.A.S.

SPINNING

16. This aircraft has been spun up to 5 turns and recovery was normal. The commencement of the spin is erratic and the aircraft tends to come out unless held in the spin. As soon as the standard actions for recovery are taken the spin ceases.

GLIDING

17. This machine handles quite normally on the glide both with flaps up and flaps down.

(i) The glide with flaps up is flat and the view ahead is restricted.

(ii) With flaps and undercarriage down, the glide is steep and a good view is obtainable ahead. The lowering of the flaps makes the aircraft slightly nose heavy. Gliding turns with flaps and undercarriage down should be done at 105 to 110 m.p.h. at normal loadings.

(iii) The engine assisted glide is considerably flatter and should be done at 100 m.p.h., but the view forward is rather restricted by the high angle of the nose.

SIDE-SLIPPING

18. The aircraft can be side-slipped, although it is only just possible to hold the nose up and prevent the speed increasing unduly.

DIVING

19. The maximum permissible diving speed is 470 m.p.h. indicated.

[*Erik Shilling*: An indicated speed of 470 mph at 20,000 feet was a true airspeed of 658 mph ... or well into compressibility. A speed at which the controls became useless, and the plane could not recover from the dive.... This is what happened to Pete Atkinson over Toungoo.]

(i) Before commencing a dive propeller should be

put into coarse pitch to prevent over revving and the throttle should be left slightly open.

(ii) Flaps must never be used in an attempt to reduce diving speed.

(iii) As speed increases the aircraft tends to yaw to the right, this must be counteracted by the application of left rudder tab. With the hood open this tendency to yaw to the right is considerably worse than when the hood is shut.

(iv) As speed increases there is a tendency for the aircraft to become left wing low and roll to the left, which must be counteracted by the ailerons.

(v) Rate of descent is extremely rapid and speed is picked up very quickly.

(vi) Recovery is normal but elevators are powerful and considerable acceleration loads will result if too much force is used during recovery.

AEROBATICS

20. Subject to any current restrictions, normal aerobatics may be carried out on this aircraft. Due to the controls being powerful and moderately light the aerobatic qualities are good, but great care must be exercised to see that all aerobatics are carried out at sufficient height to enable the pilot to recover from a dive without exerting excessive loads on the aircraft. Care should also be taken to ensure that speed is maintained during aerobatics in the looping plane.

APPROACH AND LANDING (GENERAL)

21. This aircraft is very easy to land, but the following features should be noted:

(i) Landing must always be made with flaps down.

(ii) The angle of descent with flaps and wheels down and engine off is steep.

(iii) If an engine assisted approach is made with too much engine, the view ahead is apt to be restricted owing to the high position of the nose relative to the horizon.

(iv) When in the tail-down landing position this aircraft is at a considerable angle of attack so that if a 3-point landing is desired, some excess speed must be held in order to give sufficient elevator control to change the attitude of the machine from the steep gliding angle to the landing attitude, and to overcome any tendency to stall when making this change.

PRELIMINARY APPROACH

22. Reduce speed during the initial circuit of the aerodrome and -

(i) Open hood,

(ii) Ensure mixture control is in full rich,

(iii) Carry out the following vital actions in good time prior to the final approach, as the undercarriage takes some time to come down,

(iv) "U" - undercarriage and tail wheel down; depress button on the undercarriage selector lever and select "Down" position and press the operating switch on the top of the control column [toggle switch below the pistol grip]. Check that the undercarriage and tail wheel are locked down by operating the emergency hand pump. Undercarriage and tail wheel are fully down when this is solid. When down, return selector lever to neutral.

Note: Do not lower undercarriage above 175 m.p.h.

(v) "P" - pitch. Set constant speed control to give 3000 r.p.m., and check that the toggle switch on control panel is "ON" (in the down position).

(vi) "F" - flaps. When in the correct position for the final approach, select "flaps down" on the flap selector lever (lever forward), and press the thumb switch [toggle switch] on the control column until flaps are fully down. Do not lower flaps at over 140 m.p.h.

Note:- In the event of failure of the electric motor, undercarriage and tail wheel and flaps may be operated by selecting the required position on the selector levers and operating the emergency hand pump.

(vii) Radiator closed as necessary.

FINAL APPROACH

23. The final approach should be done at the following speeds under normal load conditions:

(i) For the engine off approach, a speed of 95 to 100 m.p.h. should be maintained. This will give a steep angle of glide and a good view will be obtained of the landing area. Control at these speeds is good.

(ii) An engine assisted approach should be carried out at approximately 90 to 95 m.p.h. For this, very little engine is required and if too much engine is used, whilst serving to reduce the approach speed slightly, the angle of approach is too flat for the pilot to obtain a satisfactory view of the landing area.

LANDING

24. (i) The landing itself is easy, but if a 3-point landing is made, the angle of attack as the aircraft settles on to the ground is high, and if

the flattening out process has been commenced too soon it might be possible to stall the aircraft and drop a wing, and this point should be watched.

(ii) Normally there is no tendency for this aircraft either to drop a wing or to swing after landing.

(iii) Brakes may be applied to reduce the landing run.

(iv) Flaps should be raised as soon as the run is finished and before taxiing in, but care must be exercised to see that the undercarriage and tail wheel selector lever is not moved instead of the flap lever.

Note:- If this mistake is made, the tail wheel will retract first before the undercarriage, so that the pilot should have warning that he has made a mistake and should cease to press the thumb operating switch [toggle switch] immediately.

<u>FORCED LANDING</u>

25. In the event of a forced landing, the pilot must decide whether or not it is advisable to lower the undercarriage or whether the landing should be carried out with the undercarriage retracted.

(i) If in doubt, decide to land with the undercarriage up;

(ii) Turn off the petrol and switch off engine; open hood.

(iii) Lower the flaps to reduce forward speed.

(iv) In the event of a forced landing on water, undercarriage, tail wheel <u>and flaps</u> should be UP. Hood must be open and harness done up.

NOTE:- FOR FURTHER DETAILS OF THE LATEST TECHNIQUE IN CONNECTION WITH ALL THE FOREGOING

NOTES, PILOTS SHOULD REFER TO FLYING TRAINING MANUAL, PART 1, CHAPTER III.

POSITION ERROR TABLE

26. The corrections for position error are as follows:

At 60 mph I.A.S. reading subtract 2.5 mph

At 80 mph I.A.S. reading subtract 2.5 mph

At 100 mph I.A.S. reading subtract 0.5 mph

At 120 mph I.A.S. reading add 1.0 mph

At 140 mph I.A.S. reading add 3.5 mph

At 160 mph I.A.S. reading add 5.0 mph

At 180 mph I.A.S. reading add 6.0 mph

At 200 mph I.A.S. reading add 8.0 mph

At 220 mph I.A.S. reading add 8.5 mph

At 240 mph I.A.S. reading add 9.0 mph

At 260 mph I.A.S. reading add 10.5 mph

NOTES ON THE ALLISON V-1710-C15 ENGINE

(Using 100 Octane Fuel)

27. The following should be carefully noted:

(i) Limited operational conditions

Take-off *

Maximum r.p.m. 3000

Maximum boost at S.L. 41.0 in.Hg.

Maximum boost above 2600 ft. 38.9 in.Hg.

Mixture control below 3500 ft. "Full-rich"

Mixture control above 3500 ft. "Auto-rich"

Climb *

Maximum r.p.m. 2600

Maximum boost 35.0 in.Hg.

Note: - For take-off and climbs of short duration (not exceeding 5 min.) from sea level, the throttle should be adjusted to give 41 in.Hg. and left in this position until the boost falls to 38.9 in.Hg. This boost should then be maintained by adjustment of the throttle. For climbs of longer duration the boost should be adjusted to 35 in.Hg.

Maximum cruising (mixture control "Auto-rich") *

Maximum r.p.m. 2600

Maximum boost 35 in.Hg.

Maximum cruising (mixture control "Auto-rich" or weakened) *

Maximum r.p.m. 2280

Maximum boost 29.2. in.Hg.

Maximum level (5 minute limit) *

Maximum r.p.m. 3000

Maximum boost 38.9 in.Hg.

Maximum dive *

Maximum r.p.m. 3120

Maximum 38.9 in.Hg.

(ii) **Oil Pressures**

Normal 60-65 lb./sq.in

Minimum 50 lb./sq.in

(iii) **Oil inlet temperatures**

Minimum for take-off 40°C

Normal 70-80°C

Maximum 85°C

(iv) <u>Coolant temperature</u>

Maximum 125°C

Minimum for take-off or flight 85°C

FUEL CAPACITY AND CONSUMPTIONS

28. Note the following:

(i) Fuel capacity (in gallons)

Main tank 50 gallons [62.5 US]

Fuselage tank 47 gallons [58.75 US]

Reserve tank 33 gallons [41.25 US]

Total 130 gallons [162.5 US]

(ii) <u>Fuel consumptions (in gallons per hour)</u>:

Approximate consumptions at 12,000 feet are as follows:

Climbing:

at 2600 r.p.m. and 35 in.Hg. boost ... 84 [105 US]

Cruising (mixture control "auto-rich"):

at 2600 r.p.m. and 35 in.Hg. boost ... 84 [105 US]

at 2280 r.p.m. and 29.2 in.Hg. boost ... 52 [65 US]

at 2280 r.p.m. and 27.9 in.Hg. boost ... 50 [63 US]

at 2190 r.p.m. and 25.2 in.Hg. boost ... 42 [53 US]

Note: It is possible to improve on the last cruising consumption by weakening the mixture as described in para. 11.

Tye Lett's Allison Engine Notes

ALLISON ENGINE

FIELD SERVICE MEMORANDUM

FAR EAST NO. 2

RANGOON, BURMA

September 26, 1941

To: Col. C. T. Chien.

From: Tye M. Lett, Jr.

SUBJECT; STARTING PROCEDURE, ALLISON MODEL V 1710 C 15 ENGINES

1. The Starting procedure described below is the latest as recommended by Allison for the V 1710 C 15 Engine.

2. It is observed that several methods of starting subject engine are in use at various points.

3. To provide specific instructions regarding procedure it is suggested that this information be relayed to all pilots and ground personnel concerned with the operation of Allison Engines.

I

PROPER STARTING PROCEDURE

The priming system on all Allison engines is independent of the carburetor, and pumping the carburetor throttle will not discharge fuel into the engine, as all fuel is injected by the fuel discharge nozzle to the supercharger inlet, where it is mixed with the air passed through the carburetor throttle openings.

(a) Set propellor to manual low pitch.

(b) Carburetor Heat Control should be in the OFF position.

(c) Set throttle at position corresponding to 1000-1200 R.P.M.

(d) Set carburetor manual mixture control in IDLE-CUT-OFF POSITION, and operate the wobble pump to maintain a fuel pressure of 4 lbs./sq in.

(e) Energize starter.

(f) Prime a COLD engine with not over two strokes for a large size primer, or four for a small size primer. For a WARM engine, one stroke with large primer; or two with a small size primer is sufficient. [The primer squirts raw gasoline into the carburetor.]

(g) Turn on ignition switch and engage starter. When propellor turns, maintain fuel pressure by wobbling; and as engine starts firing, move the carburetor manual mixture control to Automatic-Rich position.

Should engine stop, return the manual mixture control to IDLE-CUT-OFF position to avoid flooding the engine with fuel, as the fuel pressure will build up to normal operating pressure (12-14 lbs./sq in.) when engine starts firing. Another start can be made using the same procedure, and using priming charge only if necessary, and the engine is not over-primed.

(h) IF OIL PRESSURE is not established within 15 seconds after starting, stop engine by setting manual mixture control in IDLE-CUT-OFF and investigate oil pressure failure. If oil pressure is established at start, continue to warm engine up at 900-1000 R.P.M. as too low idling and warm-up speeds will result in oil and fuel load fouling of the spark plugs.

Warm-up speed can be increased up to 1400 R.P.M. as oil and coolant temperatures rise, and oil pressure is stabilized.

2

STARTING

(a) With Ignition Switch "OFF" pull engine through several revolutions, turning propellor by hand, with throttle open.

(b) Carburetor Heat in "OFF" or "COLD" position.

(c) Radiator flap position as required.

(d) Throttle 1/10 open, or 1000-1200 R.P.M.

(e) Mixture control in "IDLE-CUT-OFF".

(f) Electric and Propellor switches "ON".

(g) Propellor in Manual "Low Pitch".

(h) Fuel tank selector on "Reserve".

(i) Pump up, and maintain 4 lb fuel pressure.

(j) Start energizing starter.

(k) Prime "COLD" engine 3 strokes - "WARM", 1 stroke--close and lock primer.

(l) Turn ignition switch to "BOTH ON" position.

(m) Engage starter, and when engine starts firing, move mixture control to Automatic-Rich position.

(n) After engine starts, IDLE at 600 R.P.M. and if oil pressure is not established within 15 seconds, stop engine and investigate oil pressure failure.

(o) Start warming-up by operating the engine at 900-1000 R.P.M. gradually increasing to 1400 R.P.M. as the temperatures rise, and oil pressure stabilizes.

With throttle closed the Klaxon horn will be silent, if landing gear is locked down.

3

UNDERPRIMING AND OVERPRIMING

(a) Underpriming is sometimes caused by leaking primer lines and connections, or defective primer pump packing. The fuel supply to the primer, wobble or electric fuel supply pump, if so equipped, should be checked.

(b) Overpriming is first indicated by very weak combustion, followed by black smoke discharge from the exhaust. Excessive priming is evidence[d] by wet spark plugs and fuel appearing at the exhaust stacks.

(c) As the prime fuel is injected directly into the intake manifolds of each cylinder, excess fuel will not be carried off by the supercharge scroll drain which relieves the scroll housing of excess fuel delivered only by the discharge nozzle which has opened, either by too high fuel pressure being wobbled with carburetor manual mixture control out of IDLE-CUT-OFF position, or by leakage of the discharge nozzle. Check nozzle for leakage, or holding open due to dirt or foreign material.

(d) Overprining [overpriming] constitutes a dangerous fire hazard, as well as a detriment to the oil film lubrication of the pistons, rings, and cylinder walls of the engine.

(e) Extreme CAUTION should be taken to aboid [avoid] overpriming on either a HOT or COLD engine.

(f) To relieve overpriming, crank engine several revolutions, with switch in OFF position, throttle wide-open, and carburetor manual mixture control in

IDLE-CUT-OFF position. This can also be accomplished by turning propellor by hand in direction of rotation.

(g) Loss of compression (check by rotating propellor by hand in direction of rotation) due to over priming may require lubrication of pistons, rings, and cylinder walls with oil through the valve ports or spark plug holes.

<u>NOTE</u>: IT IS RECOMMENDED THAT ALL PERSONNEL BECOME FAMILIAR WITH THE SUGGESTIONS ON "GROUND TEST" AND "GROUND CHECK" AS DESCRIBED IN ALLISON TROUBLE SHOOTING AND MAINTENANCE MANUAL RECENTLY RELEASED.

/s/ TYE M. LETT, JR.

Far Eastern Representative

ALLISON DIVISION

P-8101 got its tail number because it was the first Tomahawk uncrated by the Indian, Chinese, and American workers at Mingaladon airport outside Rangoon. It was found to be incomplete, however, and was put aside until it could be made whole by parts from the plane whose wing had been damaged by salt water. As a result, it was the last plane assembled at Mingaladon airport, so the jubilant staff painted 99th on its flank. At Toungoo, it would be given fuselage number 92.

What We Know About the Hawks

CURTISS-WRIGHT gave a distinct factory model number to the China-bound Hawks: H81-A3. These planes were taken at random from a line assembling H81-A2 fighters for Britain and therefore should have been indistinguishable from the RAF Tomahawk IIB. However, there is convincing evidence that Curtiss-Wright fitted some or all the China-bound fighters with parts intended for the Tomahawk IIA. For aviation buffs, what this means in practice is that the AVG Tomahawks more closely resembled the U.S. Army's P-40B than the improved P-40C model developed as a result of British experience with earlier models of the Tomahawk.

As each plane was uncrated at Mingaladon airport, it was given a Chinese Air Force tail number beginning with **P** (for Pursuit) followed by **81** (for Hawk 81), and ending with a two-digit lot number from **01** to **99**. (Tail number P-8200 was assembled in Loiwing.)

In the lists that follow, each CAF tail number is further identified by its Curtiss serial number, its RAF block number, and the fuselage number given to it as it was assigned to the squadrons training at Toungoo. Numbers 1-33 went to the 1st Squadron Adam & Eves, 34-66 to the 2nd Squadron Panda Bears, and 67-99 to the 3rd Squadron Hell's Angels, for a total of 99 aircraft. When the CAMCO operation left Mingaladon after the Christmas raids, the final fuselage was loaded onto a truck and taken to the CAMCO factory at Loiwing, just over the border in China, where it was eventually mated with the wing from a crash-landed Tomahawk and put into service.

January allotment

Taken from a block with RAF serials AK100/570. Other aircraft in this series went to No. 73, 112, and 250 squadrons in North Africa, and some went to Russia (including three returned to the U.S. after the dissolution of the Soviet Union). No machineguns were supplied with this shipment, which arrived at Rangoon in May 1941.

P-8101 (Curtiss 15337, RAF AK466, fuselage no. 92) Flown by Hedman. Though the first to be uncrated, this was the last Tomahawk assembled in Rangoon, and it was delivered to Toungoo with "99" painted on on its flank, as shown on the facing page.

P-8102 (Curtiss 15338, RAF AK467, fuselage no. 13) Flown by Cross.

P-8103 (Curtiss 15339, RAF AK468, fuselage no. 3). Flown by Rossi and Bartling. Abandoned at Rangoon in February 1942.

P-8104 (Curtiss 15423, RAF AK471, fuselage no. 5 or 9 or 24) Flown by Bond and perhaps Burgard.

P-8105 (Curtiss 15424, RAF AK472, fuselage no. 67) Flown by Hodges. Wrecked in training accident, 23 Oct 1941.

P-8106 (Curtiss 15425, RAF AK473, fuselage no. 11?) May have been flown by Sandell. This was the first aircraft completed at Mingaladon and probably the first delivered to Toungoo.

P-8107 (Curtiss 15430, RAF AK478, fuselage no. unknown) Flown by Schiel. Destroyed in a training accident at Toungoo.

P-8108 (Curtiss 15431, RAF AK479, fuselage no. 37). Flown by Ricketts.

P-8109 (Curtiss 15432, RAF AK480, fuselage no. 68. Flown by Older. Damaged in a forced landing near Lashio, March 1942. This is the plane in the foreground of R.T. Smith's iconic photo of Tomahawks on patrol in China in the spring of 1942.

P-8110 (Curtiss 15433, RAF AK481, fuselage no. 42) Flown by Fish, a pilot who quit the AVG before the outbreak of war.

P-8111 (Curtiss 15438, RAF AK486, fuselage no. unknown) This was the first Tomahawk to be equipped with a thrust bearing sump.

P-8112 (Curtiss 15439, RAF AK487, fuselage no. unknown) Flown by Armstrong and destroyed in the training accident that killed him.

P-8113 (Curtiss 15444, RAF AK492, fuselage no. unknown)

P-8114 (Curtiss 15445, RAF AK493, fuselage no. 11?). This may have been the plane crashed-landed at Mingaladon by Sandell, its tail damaged by a Japanese suicide pilot, which probably led to Sandell's accidental death on 7 Feb 42.

P-8115 (Curtiss 15452, RAF AK500, fuselage no. 69) Flown by Bishop, Martin, and McGarry. Shot down over Thailand, 24 Mar 42, and McGarry taken prisoner. The wreckage of this aircraft is on display at Chiang Mai Air Force Base in Thailand.

P-8116 (Curtiss 15453, RAF AK501, fuselage no. 89?) Destroyed in a crash at Rangoon, 23 Jan 42.

P-8117 (Curtiss 15459, RAF AK507, fuselage no. unknown) Flown by

Bright and destroyed in a crash after his collision with Armstrong's Tomahawk near Toungoo.

P-8118 (Curtiss 15460, RAF AK508, fuselage no. 70) Flown by Olson.

P-8119 (Curtiss 15466, RAF AK514, fuselage no. 71) Flown by Overend, Curtis Smith, and Shilling.

P-8120 (Curtiss 15467, RAF AK515, fuselage no. 43) Flown by Keeton.

P-8121 (Curtiss 15473, RAF AK521, fuselage no. 88) Flown by Jernstedt.

P-8122 (Curtiss 15474, RAF AK522, fuselage no. unknown)

P-8123 (Curtiss 15480, RAF AK528, fuselage no. 36) Flown by Rector.

P-8124 (Curtiss 15481, RAF AK529, fuselage no. unknown). Plagued by leaky thrust bearing.

P-8125 (Curtiss 15487, RAF AK535, fuselage no. 1) Flown by Atkinson and destroyed in his fatal crash at Toungoo, 22 Sep 1941.

P-8126 (Curtiss 15488, RAF AK536, fuselage no. unknown) Flown by Hammer and destroyed in his fatal crash at Toungoo, 25 Oct 1941.

P-8127 (Curtiss 15494, RAF AK542, fuselage no. 47) Flown by Petach, R.T. Smith, and Layher? Crashed in China. The engine from this Tomahawk was reported to be on display at Torrence airport in California in the 1990s.

P-8128 (Curtiss 15495, RAF AK543, fuselage no. 54) May have been the aircraft destroyed when Christman was shot down at Rangoon.

P-8129 (Curtiss 15501, RAF AK549, fuselage no. unknown)

P-8130 (Curtiss 15502, RAF AK550, fuselage no. unknown)

P-8131 (Curtiss 15508, RAF AK556, fuselage no. 35 or 27) Reported flown by Blackburn and Prescott.

P-8132 (Curtiss 15509, RAF AK557, fuselage no. 15) Flown by Martin and probably destroyed when he was shot down at Rangoon, 23 Dec 1941.

P-8133 (Curtiss 15514, RAF AK562, fuselage no. 49) Flown by Swartz and Haywood.

P-8134 (Curtiss 15515, RAF AK563, fuselage no. 48) Flown by Hill.

P-8135 (Curtiss 15521, RAF AK569, fuselage no. 79) Flown by Hedman and Reed.

P-8136 (Curtiss 15522, RAF AK570, fuselage no. 40) Flown by Cole.

February allotment

Taken from a block with RAF serials AM370/519; arrived at Rangoon June 1941. Other Tomahawks in this series went to No. 73 and 112 squadrons in North Africa, and one RAF source lists AM598 (shown here as P-8160) as among those serving in North Africa; another says that AM460 (P-8161) did. The plane that went to China in its stead may have been AM498 (Curtiss serial 15951).

P-8137 (Curtiss 15828, RAF AM375, fuselage no. unknown)

P-8138 (Curtiss 15834, RAF AM381, fuselage no. 57) Flown by Howard.

P-8139 (Curtiss 15841, RAF AM388, fuselage no. 99) Flown by Olson.

P-8140 (Curtiss 15848, RAF AM395, fuselage no. 96)

P-8141 (Curtiss 15855, RAF AM402, fuselage no. unknown)

P-8142 (Curtiss 15862, RAF AM409, fuselage no. 41) Flown by Paxton, Merritt, Bacon, and Boyington.

P-8143 (Curtiss 15869, RAF AM416, fuselage no. 10) Flown by Farrell. Crashed Rangoon 23 Jan 1941.

P-8144 (Curtiss 15876, RAF AM423, fuselage no. 25) Flown by Mickelson.

P-8145 (Curtiss 15882, RAF AM429, fuselage no. unknown)

P-8146 (Curtiss 15884, RAF AM431, fuselage no. 7?) Perhaps flown by Neale.

P-8147 (Curtiss 15886, RAF AM433, fuselage no. 52) Flown by Shilling, Martin, and Hill. This has been identified as the AVG photo plane.

P-8148 (Curtiss 15888, RAF AM435, fuselage no. 86 or 98?) Flown by McMillan.

P-8149 (Curtiss 15890, RAF AM437, fuselage no. 58) Flown by Shapard and Houle.

P-8150 (Curtiss 15892, RAF AM439, fuselage no. 91) Flown by McMillan.

P-8151 (Curtiss 15894, RAF AM441, fuselage no. 33) Flown by Little.

P-8152 (Curtiss 15896, RAF AM443, fuselage no. 56) Flown by Bright.

P-8153 (Curtiss 15898, RAF AM445, fuselage no. 71 or 78?) Flown by Shilling and also identified as the AVG photo plane.

P-8154 (Curtiss 15900, RAF AM447, fuselage no. 97) Flown by Foshee and Moss.

P-8155 (Curtiss 15902, RAF AM449, fuselage no. 8?) Crashed Rangoon 23 Jan 1942.

P-8156 (Curtiss 15904, RAF AM451, fuselage no. 46) Flown by Lawlor.

P-8157 (Curtiss 15906, RAF AM453, fuselage no. 100) The 100th Tomahawk, assembled at Loiwing in March 1942 from a fuselage trucked up from Rangoon, the wings from a crashed aircraft, and instruments from other wrecks. Because it lacked critical instruments, it had been set aside and its own wings used to complete P-8194; see below.

P-8158 (Curtiss 15908, RAF AM455, fuselage no. 5?) Perhaps flown by Bond.

P-8159 (Curtiss 15910, RAF AM457, fuselage no. unknown)

P-8160 (Curtiss 15911?, RAF AM458?, fuselage no. unknown). Listed among RAF Tomahawks in North Africa.

P-8161 (Curtiss 15913?, RAF AM460?, fuselage no. 59) Also listed among RAF Tomahawks in North Africa. Flown by Bacon.

P-8162 (Curtiss 15915, RAF AM462, fuselage no. 94) Flown by Haywood, Neale, and Groh.

P-8163 (Curtiss 15916 RAF AM463, fuselage no. unknown)

P-8164 (Curtiss 15918, RAF AM465, fuselage no. 11?) Like P-8114, this is a candidate for the plane flown by Sandell and crashed at Rangoon.

P-8165 (Curtiss 15920, RAF AM467, fuselage no. 45) Flown by Bartelt and Moss. Made a forced landing near Lashio, March 1942.

P-8166 (Curtiss 15921, RAF AM468, fuselage no. unknown)

P-8167 (Curtiss 15923, RAF AM470, fuselage no. unknown)

P-8168 (Curtiss 15925, RAF AM472, fuselage no. 85) Flown by

Brouk, Hurst, and Greene. Shot down 23 Dec 1941.

P-8169 (Curtiss 15926, RAF AM473, fuselage no. 43) Flown by Keeton.

March allotment

Taken from the same block as February allotment. Arrived Rangoon July 1941. As a rule, the later arrivals were also assembled toward the end of 1941, and less is known about them.

P-8170 (Curtiss 15928, RAF AM475, fuselage no. 13) Flown by Layher, Little, and Hill.

P-8171 (Curtiss 15930, RAF AM477, fuselage no. 50?) Reporterd flown by Ricketts and Hill.

P-8172 (Curtiss 15931, RAF AM478, fuselage no. 50 or 7) Flown by Ricketts and Neale.

P-8173 (Curtiss 15933, RAF AM480, fuselage no. 77) This was R. T. Smith's Lucky Sevens, which I used as a leading character in my novel, *Remains: A Story of the Flying Tigers*. Wrecked by Rossi in a belly landing at Magwe.

P-8174 (Curtiss 15935, RAF AM482, fuselage no. unknown)

P-8175 (Curtiss 15937, RAF AM484, fuselage no. unknown)

P-8176 (Curtiss 15939, RAF AM486, fuselage no. unknown)

P-8177 (Curtiss 15940, RAF AM487, fuselage no. 38) Flown by Geselbracht.

P-8178 (Curtiss 15942, RAF AM489, fuselage no. 76 or 5?) Perhaps flown by McMillan or Bond.

P-8179 (Curtiss 15944, RAF AM491, fuselage no. unknown)

P-8180 (Curtiss 15945, RAF AM492, fuselage no. unknown)

P-8181 (Curtiss 15947, RAF AM494, fuselage no. 51) Flown by Cole.

P-8182 (Curtiss 15949, RAF AM496 fuselage no. 21) Flown by Boyington and Schiel.

P-8183 (Curtiss 15950, RAF AM497, fuselage no. 83) Flown by Hodges.

P-8184 (Curtiss 15952, RAF AM499, fuselage no. 44) Flown by Laughlin and Peter Wright.

P-8185 (Curtiss 15954, RAF AM501, fuselage no. 13?) Possibly flown by Cross.

P-8186 (Curtiss 15955, RAF AM502, fuselage no. 75) Flown by Reed. Some have said that this Tomahawk had RAF roundels.

P-8187 (Curtiss 15957, RAF AM504, fuselage no. 6) Flown by Dean. Made a belly landing.

P-8188 (Curtiss 15959, RAF AM506, fuselage no. 23 or 45?) Possibly flown by McGarry, Jones, and Bartelt.

P-8189 (Curtiss 15961, RAF AM508, fuselage no. unknown)

P-8190 (Curtiss 15962, RAF AM509, fuselage no. 16 or 6?) Flown by Dean.

P-8191 (Curtiss 15963, RAF AM510, fuselage no. 90) Flown by Dupouy.

P-8192 (Curtiss 15964, RAF AM511, fuselage no. unknown) This war-weary was inherited by the 23rd Fighter Squadron in July 1942 and was flown the following year by Pete Atkinson's brother, Lt. Ed Atkinson USAAF.

P-8193 (Curtiss 15965, RAF AM512, fuselage no. 74) Flown by Conant; destroyed in a belly landing 31 Oct 1941.

P-8194 (Curtiss 15966, RAF AM513, fuselage no. 7?) Flown by Sawyer and Neale? This was the Tomahawk whose wing assembly was ruined by salt-water corrosion when dropped into Rangoon harbor. It was made whole by the wing assembly from P-8157.

P-8195 (Curtiss 15967, RAF AM514, fuselage no. 84) Flown by Greene and probably crashed at Rangoon, 23 Dec 1941.

P-8196 (Curtiss 15968, RAF AM515, fuselage no. 34) Flown by Newkirk; destroyed when he was shot down or accidently crashed in Thailand, 24 Mar 1942.

P-8197 (Curtiss 15969, RAF AM516, fuselage no. 18) Flown by Kuykendall.

P-8198 (Curtiss 15970, RAF AM517, fuselage no. 5?) This may have been Bond's aircraft, destroyed when he was shot down at Baoshan, 4 May 1942.

P-8199 (Curtiss 15971, RAF AM518, fuselage no. unknown) Flown by Neale.

P-8200 (Curtiss 15972, RAF AM519, fuselage no. 39) The 100th Tomahawk inevitably got an out-of-sequence tail number. Flown by Moss.

First Blood for the Flying Tigers: Twelve Days After Pearl Harbor, They Took Their Revenge on the Empire of Japan

Why Doesn't He Blow Up?

WHEN JAPANESE PLANES laid waste to Pearl Harbor on the morning of December 7, 1941, the United States had exactly one air combat unit on the continent of Asia. That was the 1st American Volunteer Group – a covert operation, run out of the White House, equipped and paid by American money, but officially part of the Chinese Air Force. That made its pilots mercenaries, if you take a harsh view of such operations. AVG veterans preferred to think of themselves as America's first irregular military operation, the model for its secret air campaign in Laos during the Vietnam War or the Green Beret horsemen who helped topple the Taliban in Afghanistan in November 2001.

An American fighter group of the 1940s comprised three squadrons, each with about twenty planes and pilots – subject of course to "wastage" from combat, accidents, and general wear and tear. The AVG would never again be as strong as it was on December 7, when it was training at a British airfield in Burma, some 170 miles north of Rangoon. The idea was that the American irregulars would there be safe from Japanese attack. The quid pro quo – a side agreement between the British and the Chinese, apparently unknown to the Americans – was that if the Japanese ever attacked Burma, "a portion, or the whole" of the AVG would help the Royal Air Force defend Rangoon, whose port brought in war supplies for China, and whose airfield was equally important to British forces in Malaya and Singapore. At Rangoon's Mingaladon Airport, the only combat force was RAF 67 Squadron, equipped with obsolescent Brewster Buffalo fighters and staffed mostly by half-trained sergeant-pilots from New Zealand.

The AVG squadrons were therefore split, one sent down to reinforce the RAF at Rangoon, the other two flown back to a new station at Kunming in China's Yunnan province, where they arrived piecemeal on Thursday, December 18. Some of their ground crews had flown up on a DC-2 airliner belonging to the Chinese national airline; others were strung out along the Burma Road, China's lifeline, a thousand miles by truck, train, and riverboat: "Can't you 'ear their paddles clunkin' from Rangoon to Mandalay?" Paddlewheel steamers still plied the Irrawaddy River in 1941, and Eddie Rector had volunteered for the AVG out of love for Rudyard Kipling's poem. He probably wasn't the only one.

Rector was also one of the pilots who flew up to Kunming on December 18, finding the city a shambles from a Japanese bombing raid. "The streets were strewn with bodies," recalled another pilot, Fritz Wolf, writing not long afterward for a popular magazine. "The Chinese ... walked about the streets and picked up the bodies, placing them in neat piles." With two planes disabled, taking off for Kunming, the squadrons had thirty-four aircraft between them: Curtiss P-40s, liquid-cooled fighters diverted from a British order, and almost as out-of-date as those Buffaloes at Mingaladon Airport. The "Tomahawk," as it was known to the RAF, boasted two fifty-caliber (half inch) machineguns over the cowling, firing through the propeller arc, and four thirty-caliber guns in the wings. European air forces were already turning to more and larger guns; but Japan, and especially the army squadrons fighting on the mainland, still trusted to lighter armament. In the battles to come, the doughty old P-40 would prove faster, more robust, and more heavily armed than anything the Empire of Japan threw against it.

THE AVG'S COMMANDER was Claire Chennault, encouraged to retire from the U.S. Army Air Corps in 1937 with the rank of captain. He was hard of hearing, afflicted with bronchitis, and immensely unpopular with the Army brass as a result of his heretical notion that "pursuit" pilots could intercept and shoot down attacking bombers, provided only that the defenders had adequate warning, took the high perch, and worked as a team. He spent the next three years in China – training its pilots, advising Generalissimo Chiang Kai-shek, and perhaps flying the odd combat mission, though this has always been a matter of dispute. (Chennault's American admirers accepted his combat sorties as fact; his Chinese colleagues denied that they ever took place.) In 1940 he returned to the U.S. to oversee the recruitment of the American Volunteer Group.

Now, four years after he had first tried to build squadrons to defend China from Japanese attack, he finally had them: thirty-four Tomahawks, the pilots to fly them, and a warning net he had strung around Kunming and other major cities. In 1986 I talked to Lee Cheng-yuan, who had served as Chennault's radioman in the early years. He characterized the warning net as "the spider in the web" – a radioman linked by telephone to a dozen or so outlying watchers, who would call in reports of Japanese formations as they came over. Each "spider" then collated his set of reports and radioed them to the airport defending the city, where a commander would map the coming raid and calculate when and where to dispatch his interceptors.

Whether or not he ever fired a shot in anger, Chennault had *seen* a lot of aerial combat since 1937, and he probably understood it better than any other American group commander. He had coached Chinese pilots and foreign mercenaries; he'd studied the Russian squadrons sent by the Soviet Union to spoil the Japanese game in China; and he was bombed himself on more than one occasion. From this experience he drew two precepts: first, that if the Japanese attacked today, they'd follow with another attack tomorrow; and second, that if they suffered ten percent casualties, they would give up, at least for the present.

Chennault therefore kept one squadron on alert at Wu Chia Ba airport outside Kunming, with the other on standby. Friday passed without incident, however. So it came down to Saturday, December 20, by which time the Japanese triumph at Pearl Harbor had been followed by equal or greater success in Malaya, Singapore, the Philippines, and the Dutch East Indies (now Indonesia).

THE FIRST REPORT came in at 9:30 a.m.: ten Japanese bombers had crossed into China. A yellow warning flag was raised, and Chennault hurried to his command post in a graveyard near the airport, where he could hear the reports as they came in. "I watched Chennault's face," recalled radioman Don Whelpley, "as reports from the Chinese air radio net came in, tracing the progress of the attackers. *Heavy engine noise at Kaiyuan.* The lines tightened around his mouth as he pulled a pipe from the pocket of his khaki jacket [and] crammed tobacco into it. *Unknown aircraft over Hwaning, headed northwest."*

The attackers were Kawasaki Ki-48 medium bombers from the 21st Hikotai of the Japanese Army Air Force. A JAAF hikotai was a mixed unit, in this case one squadron of bombers and another of fighter planes. It was based in Hanoi, capital of what was then French Indochina and now is Vietnam, which had been occupied by the Japanese with the express purpose of stopping military supplies from reaching China, and also as a springboard from which to attack Kunming and the Chinese portion of the Burma Road. The Ki-48 – later known as "Lily" to Allied pilots – was light and fast, carrying 880 pounds of bombs and defended by three machineguns, roughly equivalent to the thirty-caliber guns on the P-40. The same planes had bombed defenseless Kunming on Thursday. Now they were outnumbered, by fighters with more and heavier armament.

They had one great advantage, however: the JAAF had been at war for more than four years, against the best pilots that China and the Soviet Union could bring against them. (In addition to providing the main air strength of China from 1938 to 1940, the Russians had fought a brief but bloody border war against the Japanese in Manchuria in the summer of 1939.)

Oddly, the 21st Hikotai's fighters – a dozen or so Nakajima Ki-27s, fixed-undercarriage "peashooters" armed with two rifle-caliber guns – should have escorted the bombers. That was, after all, the whole purpose of a hikotai, mixing two kinds of aircraft in order to exploit the strengths of each. But the Nates (as they would be known to Allied pilots) never showed up. They may have missed connections, or the bomber commander, Captain Fuji Tatsujiro, may have been fooled by the easy pickings over Kunming on Thursday. Another theory was advanced by Suzuki Goichi, interviewed by a television crew in 1992. The bombers, he recalled, had been designated a *suteishi butai* or "sacrifice squadron," intended to lure up enemy fighters and destroy them. This notion seems far-fetched, given the carefree way in which the Kawasakis advanced on Kunming, as Suzuki himself recalled:

"The Chinese air force had almost never showed up. There might have been some planes, but they had never appeared. So we did not even worry about them.... We left Hanoi at 10:20 [Tokyo time] on

[December] 20th. Altitude was 6,000 [meters]. It was fine day but there were some clouds. We came to near Kunming in about two hours."

In Chennault's theory of "defensive pursuit," the leading fighter pilot was supported by his wingman. In the same way, one flight of four aircraft would be supported by another, and the squadrons were similarly assigned to assault and supporting roles. On December 20, the "assault echelon" was Robert (Sandy) Sandell's 1st Squadron, known as the Adam & Eves in tribute to their role as "first pursuit." Jack Newkirk's 2nd Squadron, with the mild nickname of Panda Bears, was in reserve. (The 3rd Squadron pilots, down in Rangoon with the British, called themselves the Hell's Angels.)

So when the red flag was hoisted at Wu Chia Ba, it was Sandy Sandell and thirteen other Adam & Eves who rolled down the crushed-stone runway and took off to defend Kunming. They patrolled the railroad track leading southeast to Iliang, a logical route for the Japanese to follow. Meanwhile, eight Panda Bears served as backup, half of them patrolling over the airport while the others climbed to the northwest in case the Japanese circled around and approached from the unexpected side – which is just what they did. These four Panda Bears, who included squadron leader Jack Newkirk, were thus the first to spot the Kawasakis, arranged in a loose "vee of vees," three groups of three with the tenth plane tagging along with one of them.

The Americans couldn't believe their eyes: *"That can't be the Japs,"* cried one disbelieving Panda Bear. They then made the mistake common to green warriors, opening fire while still out of range. Alerted by the red tracer bullets from the Americans' guns, the Japanese pilots turned east and fled.

"Just before we reached to Kunming," as Lieutenant Suzuki told the story, "American airplanes came up in four units, each of which had six fighter airplanes." In reality, there were two separate attacks, with this first one involving only four Tomahawks. "We kept going on for a while. Then, American P-40s started to attack us all at once. Our squadron turned direction to left. I guess our leader thought none of us would survive if we kept going to the destination. We bombed a town below because we need to make our airplanes lighter by losing bombs."

Suzuki and his fellow pilots also tightened the formation, so their gunners could put out a crisscross fire. Now lightened, the Lilys had a top speed of 300 mph. The Tomahawks were faster, but not by much, and a stern chase is a long chase. So Newkirk waggled his wings and led his Panda Bears back toward Wu Chia Ba. "We lost a bit of face on that deal," one of them later confessed in a letter home.

For their part, the Japanese circled around Kunming, intending to pick up the railroad track that would lead them back to Hanoi. Instead they ran into the Adam & Eves. Following Chennault's doctrine, Sandy Sandell had likewise split his forces, putting two pilots on the high perch to watch for enemy fighters, while the others formed themselves into three flights of four. Two flights were to dive on the Japanese formation from out of the sun while the third flight stayed back in reserve. That was the theory, anyhow; as with Jack Newkirk's over-hasty attack, Sandell's assault pilots ignored his plan in the general excitement. To judge by their recollections, the eight pilots made it a free-for-all, every man for himself. (Sadly, this is one of the few AVG battles for which no actual combat reports are available, though some were excerpted in the War Diary maintained by Olga Greenlaw, the wife of Chennault's executive officer and one of three American women on the group's payroll.)

The Lilys were still in the porcupine cluster they'd assumed upon seeing the Panda Bears, north of the city. Now, as a dozen Tomahawks swept down on them, each bomber lowered its "dustbin," a hinged platform that supported the belly gunner, who could defend a rather narrow arc to the rear of the plane and below it. Each Kawasaki also had a nose gun, manned by the bombardier, and a top gunner at the rear of the greenhouse canopy, who had the widest field of fire, to the rear, right and left, and above. It's important not to underestimate the killing power of a 7.7 mm bullet, even when you're protected by armor plate behind and a bloody big engine in front. Most infantry rifles of the day were just that size – and these were machineguns, not a single shot at a time.

"I ROLLED AND started down," wrote Charlie Bond in his diary, as later edited for publication – one of the best of the firsthand accounts of the AVG. "As the nearest bomber eased within the gunsight ring, I squeezed the trigger on the [control] stick. Damn it, nothing happened!" Nervously checking and rechecking the toggle switch that controlled the firing circuit, he'd gone into combat with it in the off position. He broke off and climbed back to altitude.

Fritz Wolf – he who had earlier watched the Chinese stacking the bodies of their dead – meanwhile selected the outside bomber in the righthand "vee." He dived below the Kawasaki so as to attack where its defenses were weakest, as he recalled in 1942 for a wartime magazine; his recollection was thus fresh, though no doubt spiced by the editors. "At 500 yards I let go with a quick burst of all guns. It was curtains for the rear [dustbin] gunner.... I could see my bullets rip into him and cut him to pieces.... At one hundred yards I let go with a long burst, and the bullets tore into the Jap's motor and gas tanks. A wing folded and the motor tore loose, then the bomber exploded in midair."

Jim Cross was flying as Wolf's wingman, and he too wrote a magazine article about the battle, and he too claimed the same bomber: "There was the Jap plane, dead in front of me. I could see the sun glinting on the gunner's goggles.... I saw my own tracer fire almost before I realized I'd pressed the button."

Both pilots then climbed back to altitude and attacked again. So did Charlie Bond, having resolved his confusion about the toggle switch: "Two bombers began to lag behind, trailing smoke," he wrote in his diary. This was probably closer to the truth than the exploding Kawasakis reported by Fritz Wolf.

The reserve flight was chafing in its assigned location above the fray. For Camille (Joe) Rosbert, a stocky Italian-American from Philadelphia, the battle seemed "like a bunch of swarming bees. I wondered why our planes did not collide with one another, they looked so close." It was all so inviting that Ed Leibolt, the flight leader, could contain himself no longer, and gave the signal to attack. Rosbert followed him down. "As the rear bomber loomed in front of us," he recalled long after, "I pressed the gun button almost at the same time as Ed. Debris flew by as we dove down and away."

Eddie Rector of the 2nd Squadron soon joined this free-for-all. Off-duty that day because his Tomahawk's engine was undergoing a 25-hour check, he sprinted out to the flight line. "Get that goddamned cowling back on!" he shouted at Harry Fox, the head mechanic. When he told me this story, 45 years later, Colonel Rector had an especially vivid recollection of that day in December 1941. Picture him telling the story, still handsome as a movie star, banking his hands to represent the diving Tomahawks: "I fired up that P-40 and got out there. I saw eight damned airplanes out there engaging them." Rector came down in a long, sweeping turn behind one of the Japanese bombers. "I came on in, right behind the guy ... and I drove up his ass. I got target fixation. I just saw my shots going into him, and I said, *Why doesn't he blow up?* At the last moment, I realized what I was doing.... I looked at [the dustbin gunner] – right in the eye – and I'd shot away his whole jaw. And I can see him, and I can see the rivets and the camouflage pattern of that damned bomber."

Just before they collided, Rector pulled down and away. "I know that I missed him by inches," he said, in awe of his own young foolishness.

Most or all of the Americans seem to have attacked the starboard "vee" of bombers, led by a pilot named Funamoto Shigaru, and all three Lilys in that flight went down. For each engine that burst into flame, two or three pilots had been pouring machinegun fire into it – adrenalin pumping, sphincters twitching, vision tunneled down to that eruption of black smoke and scarlet flame. Diving clear, each man was understandably convinced that he alone had killed the bomber.

Fortunately for Suzuki, he wasn't in Funamoto's flight – indeed, he may have been the odd man out, piloting the tenth Kawasaki, which would have been tucked inside the Japanese formation. "I saw one of our airplanes in the right-side unit being shot and quickly going down," as he recalled the combat more than fifty years later. "Next was a closer airplane. I think the pilot was [killed or wounded because] the airplane went down in a very unbalanced way. I recognized these two, but didn't see the leading airplane, Captain Funamoto's airplane, being shot down. But when we went into formation again [after the battle], I noticed there was one more airplane missing. It had been shot down while I was not watching."

In half an hour, from that first brush with Jack Newkirk's flight to the moment when Sandy Sandell waggled his wings and led the Adam & Eves back to Wu Chia Ba, the bomber squadron had lost three planes, each with four men aboard. The survivors were also badly shot up, with two dead gunners on board. Nor was their ordeal finished yet, as Suzuki recalled: "[L]ots of us couldn't lower landing gear due to the damage from the shooting. So, some landed with only one gear, and others on their bodies. Everyone landed somehow, but all airplanes had bullets in their bodies. Even mine had about thirty shots."

As the tally went into the AVG records, Fritz Wolf accounted for two bombers, Eddie Rector a third, and Einar Mickelson a fourth. The informal claims of course were much larger, which in later years would lead to the belief that that the AVG had accounted for nine of the ten Kawasakis. (Chennault supposedly snapped at his pilots: "Next time, get them all!")

Yet each pilot, after telling how he had knocked down a bomber or two, went on to say that the formation was mostly intact when he broke off. Sandy Sandell recalled that seven Lilys were still aloft when the Adam & Eves turned back to the airport. Robert Neale, who by the following July would rank as the AVG's (and America's) top fighter ace, thought there were eight survivors, each with a dustbin gunner lying dead on his platform. Joe Rosbert said that six Lilys escaped the battle.

In any event, more claims were lodged than there were enemy bombers on the ground. And we know how exactly many of those there were: unlike in the later furballs near Rangoon, Claire Chennault's warning net was in full operation between Kunming and the Vietnam border, with both Chinese and American radiomen on duty. A Chinese listening post counted seven Japanese bombers aloft at 11:25 a.m., after Sandy Sandell had waggled his wings to lead the Adam & Eves back to Wu Chia Ba. So three Lilys had been shot down during the combat, just as Sandell had reported – and sure enough, three wrecks were later located on the ground by Chinese scavenger crews. A few days later, the Chinese Aeronautical Commission reported that a fourth bomber had exploded in midair before reaching safety at Gia Lam airport in Hanoi. No evidence was advanced for this conclusion, and it's not borne out by Suzuki-san's account, but I'm inclined to trust it. The Chinese seem to have had spies on the ground at Gia Lam airport, counting the planes that took off and those that returned; likely one of those belly landings was spectacular enough that observers reported it as destroyed.

In any event, the official tally for December 20 was four Kawasaki Lilys shot down. For its part, the AVG had lost one Tomahawk –

Eddie Rector's plane couldn't be retrieved, though he managed to scavenge the machineguns and his remaining ammunition. There were no American injuries.

Faced with more claims than known enemy losses, Chennault divided the credit among all the pilots who had joined the attack, south of Kunming: fourteen Adam & Eves plus Eddie Rector from the Panda Bears. So each man was officially credited with four-fifteenths of a Japanese bomber, and in time with $133 in his combat bonus account – the equivalent of $2,360 in 2022 greenbacks.

Compared to the great air battles that had roiled the skies over Britain the previous year, the AVG's combat of December 20 was fairly small potatoes. But its impact was huge. For nearly two weeks, Japanese army and navy squadrons had swept the skies clear of American, British, and Dutch interceptors. It wasn't just Pearl Harbor: the debacle in the Philippines on December 8 was just as bad. The Royal Air Force in Malaya and on Singapore Island had no such day of infamy, but was steadily being consumed by superior Japanese forces, and much the same was happening in the Dutch East Indies. Only the American Volunteer Group had given better than it got, a fact that was noted by *Time* in its next issue, bearing the date of December 29. "Last week," reported the magazine in its breezy style, "ten Japanese bombers came winging their carefree way up into Yunnan, heading directly for Kunming, the terminus of the Burma Road. Thirty miles south of Kunming, the Flying Tigers swooped, let the Japanese have it. Of the ten bombers ... four plummeted to earth in flames. The rest turned tail and fled. Tiger casualties: none."

The headline: *Blood for the Tigers*. So the December 20 combat not only gave the American Volunteer Group its first victory, but a fighting name as well. Forever after, they were the Flying Tigers.

For the Chinese, the fracas over the railway tracks was a game changer. The 21st Hikotai never again flew to Kunming, nor did any other Japanese formation while the AVG guarded it. In thirty minutes, the Adam & Eves (plus one) had won the battle of Kunming.

December 20 also proved a fairly accurate forecast of how the AVG would fare over the nearly seven months of its existence as a combat force. Alone of Allied air units in that first year of the Pacific War, it regularly beat the Japanese Army squadrons sent against it. Its aircraft losses were high, but most were the result of accident or abandonment, when the Japanese overran the Allied airfields. Only four AVG pilots died in aerial combat – a small fraction of Japanese aircrew fatalities in those combats. Ground fire proved the more deadly foe: five pilots died when their P-40s were hit by anti-aircraft shells, and four were shot down and taken prisoner, of whom three survived captivity.

Like all air forces of the time, the AVG's accomplishments were magnified for home consumption, and magnified again in retrospect. A more sober reading of Japanese accounts shows that the Tigers destroyed about 115 aircraft in the air and on the ground. A majority were bombers, carrying as many as six airmen; thus the Japanese toll in these engagements must have been about 400 men, of whom only a handful allowed themselves to be taken prisoner.

The Flying Tigers achieved a combat record seldom equaled, and certainly not by any Allied air force in the first year of the Pacific War. And it all began at 9:30 in the morning of December 20, 1941, less than two weeks after the Pearl Harbor attack.

Rising Sun Over Burma: How the Japanese Remember the Battle

Flying Tigers and Wild Eagles

WHAT FOLLOWS IS A CAMPAIGN HISTORY of the first Battle of Burma, from December 1941 to its conclusion in May 1942, as told in Japanese history books. For Americans who remember the Flying Tigers and Merrill's Marauders (and for Brits who remember the Chindits), the story may come as something of a surprise. But the Japanese won, after all! Not only did they conquer Burma, but they won most of the battles, even while the Anglo-Americans claimed victory after victory in a losing campaign. History is written by the winners, and what follows is the invasion of Burma as it would have been told if the Japanese army and air force had emerged as the winners of the Pacific War.

The Japanese Imperial Army invaded Malaya on December 8, 1941, the first day of the Pacific War as reckoned in Tokyo and Southeast Asia, west of the International Date Line. Air support was provided by the 3rd *Hikoshidan* (equivalent to an American geographical air force) under Lieutenant General Sugawara Michio. As part of the run-up to the invasion, army intelligence reported that there were 48 British fighters and 12 bombers in Burma, along with a squadron of the American Volunteer Group. General Sugawara was very concerned about this enemy air force, which could support a flank attack on the newly occupied territory in Thailand and the long supply line leading down to Malaya and the British fortress of Singapore. From the very first day of the war, therefore, the Japanese knew they would have to neutralize the threat from Burma.

On December 9, the JAAF 10th *Hikodan* (more or less equivalent to a British wing and consisting of several combat groups) was ordered to Thailand to keep an eye on the Anglo-American air units in Burma. To begin, the air force construction battalion "borrowed" 700 barrels of fuel from the Thai army. Next it took over the telephone line from Tha Hin to Bangkok, along with the local radio station, the airport radio, and the telegraph line from Bangkok to Phnom Penh and Saigon. Even with these improvements, the 62nd *Sentai* (a heavy bomber group, equipped with the Mitsubishi Ki-21 that Allied pilots would know by the code name of Sally) had not recovered from the losses it had suffered during the Malaya campaign. For its part, the supporting 77th Sentai (a fighter group, equipped with the obsolescent Nakajima Ki-27, known as Nate to the Allies) was still unable to reach Rangoon because it had no drop tanks.

On December 10, Japanese reconnaissance reported seeing only four enemy planes around Rangoon, type uncertain. Ominously, it seemed that the enemy fighters had moved down to the British forward bases at Moulmein, Tavoy, and Mergui, ranged from north to south on the long southern tail of Burma. The 77th Sentai was instructed to harass them with occasional attacks by a handful of its fighters. Though based in Thailand, next door to Burma, the Japanese fighters could not reach the capital city and major seaport of Rangoon. The 10th Hikodan therefore took over a small airfield at Tha Hin, 520 kilometers (323 miles) from Rangoon and comfortably within the Nakajima Nate's combat radius.

On December 15, General Sugawara sent orders to Bangkok to prepare for an attack on Rangoon with the 7th and 10th hikodans, to clear the way for his main force to advance to Sungei Patani, Malaya, in late December. Two days later, reconnaissance planes reported 19 enemy fighters, 20 light bombers, and 5 heavy bombers at Rangoon, along with 10 heavy bombers at Toungoo to the north and 5 fighters at a forward field on the southern peninsula. Fearing that the Allied air strength had been increased, General Sugawara ordered the two hikodans to attack Rangoon while the rest of his forces pressed the attack in Malaya.

So it was that, on December 19, Sugawara sent a message to Bangkok: Rangoon was to be attacked three days in succession, on December 23, 24, and 25. The 10th Hikodan commander, Major General Hirota Utaka, therefore rushed construction of facilities at Bangkok, Tha Hin, and Raheng, a forward field on the Burma-Thai border that would help make up the range deficiencies of the Nakajima Ki-27. He also sent an urgent request for drop tanks for the short-ranged fighter. The 77th Sentai meanwhile moved part of its ground crews to Raheng, with the main force to follow as soon as construction was completed. (One *chutai* or squadron of Nates remained at Bangkok to provide local air defense.) Meanwhile, the 31st Sentai (a light bomber group, equipped with Mitsubishi Ki-30 attack planes) moved its aircraft to Tha Hin, from which they could fly to Rangoon and back.

On December 20, a new commander for the 62nd Sentai arrived, but the group's strength was still not restored from its earlier losses, so General Sugawara did not plan to send it against Rangoon. However, the group demanded that it be allowed to join the mission. Sugawara agreed, and the half-strength group therefore sent its 15 serviceable Ki-21 Sally heavy bombers to Bangkok.

Two groups would not take part in the Rangoon mission. The 12th Sentai had lost 12 heavy bombers in Malaya and was now rebuilding its forces. And the 64th Sentai with its modern Ki-43 Hayabusa fighters was diverted to attack a bridge crossing in Malaya.

Meanwhile, the 21st Hikotai in Hanoi set out to attack Kunming. (A *hikotai* was a mixed group, in this case containing one squadron of Ki-48 medium bombers and another of Ki-27 fighters.) The attack force "advanced toward Kunming but realized that P-40 fighters were prevailing and a difficult foe." Thus did Japanese historians describe the first combat of the American Volunteer Group, soon to become famous as the "Flying Tigers." Of the AVG's three squadrons, two had been sent back to Kunming from the training base at Toungoo, while the 3rd Squadron bolstered the Royal Air Force units in Rangoon.

On December 21, the 60th Sentai (heavy bomber) in Phnom Penh, Cambodia, got ready to join the Rangoon mission. The following day, the 98th Sentai (heavy bomber) moved to Bangkok and likewise prepared for the Rangoon attack. The same afternoon, the reconnaissance planes of the 70th Independent Chutai scouted southern Burma and reported that the Anglo-Americans had 11 medium bombers based at Toungoo and 2 large, 16 mid-sized, and 13 small planes at Rangoon. On Burma's long tail, reaching down along the southern Thai frontier, the scouts reported seeing 2 large and 6 small planes at Tavoy, plus 1 large plane at Mergui. (The medium bombers would have been twin-engine Bristol Blenheims. The large and mid-sized planes might also have been Blenheims, or possibly Douglas DC-2 or DC-3 transports. The small planes would have been the Brewster Buffaloes of RAF 67 Squadron and the P-40 Tomahawks of the American Volunteer Group.)

For a triumphant wartime newsreel about the conquest of Burma, a Japanese film company restaged a raid on Rangoon, using Mitsubishi Ki-21 heavy bombers of the 12th Sentai. The P-40 diving to the attack was probably captured in the Philippines and put into service for training or propaganda purposes.

Japanese order of battle, December 23:
10th Hikodan (Maj Gen Hirota)
62nd Sentai (Lt Col Onishi): 15 Ki-21 Sally heavy bombers
31st Sentai (Lt Col Hayashi): 27 Ki-30 Ann attack planes
77th Sentai (Maj Yoshioka): 30 Ki-27 Nate fighters
7th Hikodan (Maj Gen Yamamoto)
60th Sentai (Col Ogawa): 27 Ki-21 Sally heavy bombers
98th Sentai (Col Usui): 18 Ki-21 Sally heavy bombers

General Sugawara chose the 10th Hikodan to lead the first attack on Rangoon. Its 15 heavy bombers set out from Don Maung airport in

Bangkok at 07:24 Tokyo time and met the fighters and light bombers over Raheng at 11:45. (For the Allied defenders at Mingaladon airport, the time was two hours earlier.) The combined formation – 72 planes altogether – crossed the Salween River at an altitude of 4,000 meters (13,000 feet). The Mitsubishi Ki-21s were in the lead, with the light bombers trailing three kilometers behind them on the left and protected by the fighters. Like the U.S. Army Air Forces this early in the war, Japanese doctrine held that heavy bombers with their multiple defensive guns could fight their way through to the target; they didn't need fighter protection.

At 12:30, the bomber crews could see the white *A* of Mingaladon's gravel runways, and even the dust trails of the Buffaloes and Tomahawks taking off to intercept them. Near Pegu, an estimated 30 enemy fighters came up to attack the heavy bombers. The Brewster Buffaloes were the first to hit them, attacking from below just as the Sallys were moving into their bombing run. The bomber crews reported that each enemy fighter was firing two streams of incendiary bullets "like a shower." In the 3rd Chutai, the Sally flown by Captain Niioka was the first to be disabled, with its right engine "belch[ing] smoke continuously." The plane slowed, dropped behind the formation, and was attacked by the AVG Tomahawks. Eventually it went down at a steep angle.

The remaining planes dropped their bombs at 12:55, five minutes ahead of schedule. The bombs "sparkled in every direction," in the words of a Japanese historian, and Mingaladon airport disappeared in "a cloud of fire." Black smoke rose into the air and lingered there.

The Sallys continued flying straight ahead, trying to gain speed to escape from the fighters attacking from every side. The crews "wanted only to be home." They later reported that they had been attacked by Buffaloes, Hurricanes, Spitfires, and Curtiss P-40s, these last three types being identified by their distinctive glycol cooling system. In fact, no liquid-cooled British fighters were stationed at Mingaladon in December 1941: the attackers were Buffaloes and Tomahawks.

Also in the 3rd Chutai, a pilot took a bullet through his right arm and hand. In the 1st Chutai, meanwhile, the Sally piloted by 1st Lt Ikura, already damaged by the Allied fighters, received a direct hit from an anti-aircraft shell and likewise plunged from the formation. The 3rd Chutai also lost a Sally at about this time, when the heavy bomber flown by Captain Chototo began to burn fiercely from a fuel leak in its left wing.

The surviving Sallys now began a left turn, which took them over downtown Rangoon and its anti-aircraft defenses. The formation by this time was thoroughly confused. The bomber crews continued to work their guns against the Allied fighter planes. One Japanese historian singled out the Number 77 Tomahawk flown by R.T. Smith as "very eager," firing his four rifle-caliber wing guns and two .50-caliber nose guns with "a sound so loud it filled the sky." This was evidently the report from a Sally that escaped Smith's attack by diving down in a spiral and then climbed back up to rejoin the formation.

The Japanese fighter planes meanwhile were still protecting the 31st Sentai light bombers as they attacked Mingaladon airport with 50 kilogram (110 pound) bombs and machinegun fire. The fighter formation too had broken up in the air-to-air combat; one fighter pilot was compared to "a duckling that has left his mother," as he was cut off from his comrades and shot down over the water. Other fighter planes now rushed to the defense of the beleaguered heavy bombers, of which five had now been shot down — one-third of the group's strength. These were the 10th Hikodan's losses, as shown in Japanese records:

1st Lieutenant Ikura, to fighters and anti-aircraft fire
Captain Sabe, to AVG Tomahawks
Captain Niioka, to Brewster Buffaloes and AVG Tomahawks
1st Lieutenant Shingansho, to Brewster Buffaloes
1st Lieutenant Shimada, to AVG Tomahawks

Each of the heavy bombers had a crew of six, for a total of 30 Japanese airmen dead. In addition, the 10 Sallys that made it home to Bangkok were badly shot up, with one plane riddled with 47 bullet holes. The gunners on the surviving bombers reported that they "fought well and shot down 10 planes certain plus 4 probable." The 77th Sentai fighters meanwhile claimed 9 Allied aircraft shot down.

The 7th Hikodan formation consisted of two heavy bomber groups, with no escorting fighters. The 60th Sentai left Phnom Penh in Cambodia at 9:35 a.m., on schedule. But by the time it reached the rendezvous, however, the 98th Sentai had already set out for the target. So the two groups went their separate ways to Rangoon, crossing the Gulf of Martaban south of Moulmein.

The 98th Sentai commander, Colonel Usui, was on board the Sally flown by Major Atsumi. The group reached Rangoon at 12:45 — five minutes early — and circled around the city at 6,000 meters (about 20,000 feet) before beginning its bombing run against the dock area. But a formation of 18 enemy fighters with the altitude advantage attacked from behind. The Sallys fought back and flew a zigzag course which made them lose the target. The bombers circled around for another run, at which time the Sally at the left side of the 2nd hintai (flight) was shot down. This was the plane flown by Captain Iteya, which crashed in a city street near the Rangoon docks, killing the pilot and his crewmen.

The 98th Sentai took up its bombing run again, but couldn't manage to line up on its intended targets, the port buildings and the freighters at anchor in the river. Instead, it bombed the government headquarters, the post office, and the telephone company. Meanwhile a bomber in the middle of the formation was mortally hit and spun out of the formation. Unusual for a Japanese airman, 1st Lieutenant Nogami and two of his crew bailed out and parachuted to the ground, where they were taken prisoner, while three crewmen were killed in the crash. Postwar, the fate of the PWs was unknown in Japan, a consequence of the "hatred" shown toward military men who were taken prisoner. (The historian is speaking of the attitude shown by others in the military and government, not of the reception that met Nogami and his comrades when they surrendered.)

Shortly after, Major Atsumi's plane was hit from behind. One bullet struck Colonel Usui in the back, exiting on the left side of his chest, killing him — not the first Japanese group commander to be killed in action in the Pacific War. Major Atsumi was wounded by shrapnel in the arm in the same burst. As the story is told by a Japanese historian, the pilot believed he too was mortally wounded, so both he and the colonel bowed and gave the *banzai* cheer: "May the Emperor live 10,000 years!" The co-pilot flew the plane thereafter. The Sallys were pursued by the enemy fighters for half an hour, with the 98th Sentai gunners claiming 12 of them certain plus 4 probable.

Meanwhile the 60th Sentai under Colonel Ogawa approached Rangoon from the ocean and flew over the east side of the city at

7,000 meters (23,000 feet) with 27 Sallys. This formation found it very quiet over the city. (23,000 feet was well above the service ceiling of the RAF Buffaloes and near the service ceiling of the AVG Tomahawks.) The Sallys reported that they had bombed the harbor facilities and destroyed a mid-sized cargo ship; afterward, they were attacked by a few enemy aircraft, with one crewman shot through the forehead and killed. All returned to Phnom Penh, but evidently one bomber was destroyed by a crash landing, its pilot unknown, as is the fate of the crew. The 60th Sentai gunners claimed 10 Allied fighters certain, plus 2 probables.

Altogether, the heavy-bomber formations had lost seven planes over the target — a loss rate of 12 percent, plus an eighth Sally crashed on returning to base. With the 98th Sentai commander, killed in a plane that managed to return, the personnel losses came to at least 43 men, including the 3 prisoners of war. In the words of a Japanese historian, it was "an unhappy experience" for the JAAF.

For their part, the Japanese pilots and gunners seem to have been credited with shooting down no fewer than 41 Allied fighters — more than were actually stationed in Burma on December 23! In fact, no Buffaloes went down that day, while three AVG Tomahawks were shot down. Two of the Americans (Neal Martin and Hank Gilbert) were killed, while the third (Paul Greene) parachuted to safety.

On December 25, General Sugawara tried again, with the 98th Sentai allowed to stay behind at Bangkok in mourning for its dead commander. Taking its place was the reconstituted 12th Sentai with 27 heavy bombers. The 60th Sentai was back and stronger than before with 36 heavy bombers. As before, their target would be downtown Rangoon.

Only the 62nd Sentai reflected the battering it had suffered two days before: the ground crews had managed to put only 8 of its Ki-21 Sallys back into the fight. They were again assigned to Mingaladon airport, and in each bomb bay the crews had put a bouquet of flowers in honor of their comrades who had died. They also carried box lunches, but they were too nervous to eat. After Tuesday's massacre, they didn't seriously expect to return alive. As before, the Mingaladon formation was accompanied by the 31st Sentai with 27 light bombers and the 77th Sentai with 32 Nakajima Nates.

The big change on Christmas Day was the 64th Sentai with 25 retractable-gear Nakajma Ki-47 Hayabusas. The army fighters looked much like the Mitsubishi A6M Zero fighters that the Japanese navy had unleashed on Hawaii and the Philippines, but their armament was less and their wings had a tendency to break up in combat. In a major breach of Japanese doctrine, the Hayabusas were to protect the heavy-bomber sentais assigned to downtown Rangoon. But just as had happened on December 23, that formation too came apart before reaching Burma's airspace. It therefore paid the higher price, with three Sallys shot down and a fourth damaged so badly that it crashed on the way home, with the crew surviving. No heavy bombers were shot down over Mingaladon airport, but three Nakajima Ki-27 Nates were lost to enemy action, along with two of the Hayabusas of which so much had been expected.

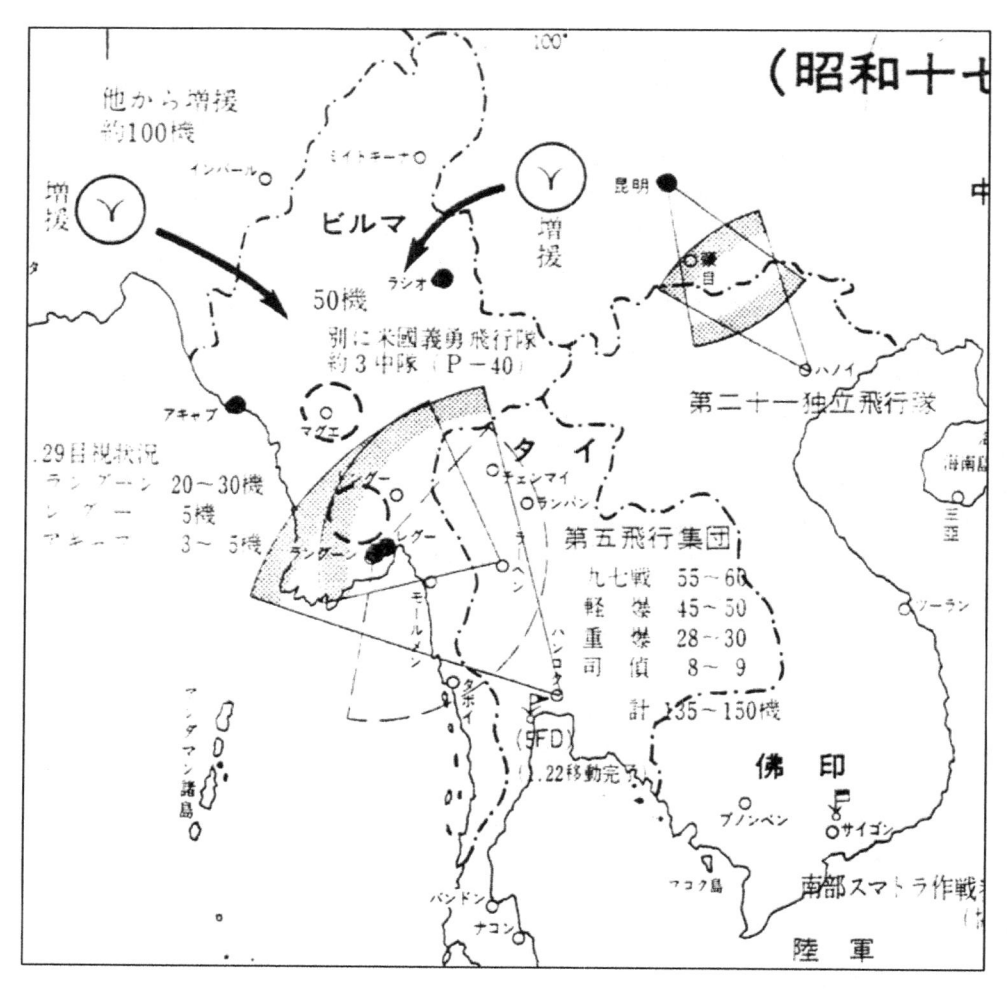

Burma, January 1942. Large arc shows the range of JAAF heavy bombers at Bangkok; smaller one shows the range of the light bombers at Phitsanulok, Thailand. (The arc of Allied response is unshaded.) Note the December 20 Hanoi-Kunming battle area at upper right. Also note how Burma and Thailand divide the thin peninsula leading down to Malaya and Singapore. Protecting their supply line was the motive for early Japanese attacks on airfields in Burma.

Air Battle for Rangoon

ON DECEMBER 28, GENERAL HIRODA of the 10th Hikodan (the equivalent of a British wing) issued orders for two combat groups to move up to central Thailand, as close to the Burma border as they could find suitable bases. The following day, two fighter squadrons of the 77th Sentai under Lieutenant Colonel Yoshioka relocated to Lampang, east and south of the Royal Air Force field at Toungoo, where the American Volunteer Group had trained. One squadron of the 77th remained in Bangkok for local air defense. To prevent a surprise attack on Lampang, Colonel Yoshioka kept a flight of two or three planes forward-based at Raheng near the Burma border. The hikodan headquarters and ground support forces also moved up to Lampang, while the 31st Sentai light bomber group went to Phitsanulok, due east of Rangoon. In their new locations, the fighters and light bombers would be well positioned to attack Tavoy and Moulmein, British airfields on the long tail of Burma that ran alongside Thailand. And once the battle for Malaya was wrapped up, they would be able to support the Japanese 15th Army when it invaded Burma itself.

Yoshioka ordered an attack on Moulmein for the morning of January 3, 1942, so the 1st Chutai (a squadron of about a dozen Ki-27 fighters) of the 77th Sentai under Captain Toyo Eto moved to the Raheng forward base, where they evidently spent the night. They took off at 8:30 a.m. Tokyo time and reached Moulmein airport at 9:05, claiming one plane destroyed and three damaged out of four seen on the ground. These were obsolete biplanes of the Indian Air Force 4 Coast Defence Fight, destroyed before they ever saw action.

The Ki-27s returned to Raheng at 9:55. The first flight landed without incident, and the second was just touching down when three "Spitfires" attacked from behind, shooting down the Ki-27 fixed-gear fighter flown by Warrant Officer Yokoyama, who survived but would require two months to heal from his injuries. The third flight then came on the scene and attacked the enemy fighters at an altitude of 400 meters, "skillfully catching them and shooting from the tail." Two of the enemy fighters were reported to be trailing white smoke. In the end, the 1st Chutai was credited with shooting down three "Spitfires" and damaging others. Besides Yokoyama's, a second Ki-27 was destroyed in this engagement and two more were rendered unflyable, but I can't tell whether these were shot down or burned on the ground.

The Allied fighters were Tomahawks of the AVG 2nd Squadron, based at Rangoon, and none was lost. The "Panda Bears," as they called themselves, were credited with three Japanese fighters shot down and four destroyed on the ground. Likely it was David "Tex" Hill who sent Warrant Officer Yokoyama to the hospital. A footnote to this engagement is Jim Howard's report that he saw "crowds of people on a grandstand," scrambling to get out of the line of fire. Since the 3rd Chutai was returning from a scheduled raid, it is indeed possible that a ceremony had been laid on to greet the victors.

General Hiroda now ordered an attack on the Rangoon airfields. Three Ki-21 Sally heavy bombers of the 62nd Sentai bombed an RAF dispersal field, north of Mingaladon airport, in the early morning hours of January 4. Then, at 1:20 p.m. Tokyo time, Major Hirose Yoshio — executive officer of the 77th Sentai — left Raheng with 31 Ki-27s. They approached Mingaladon from the north at 4,500 meters, looking for enemy fighters. The time was now 2:55 (12:55 Rangoon time). Seeing none, Hirose ordered Lieutenant Kuwabara Yoshio to take his 3rd Chutai down to strafe. The Mingaladon warning siren "rose to the sky." Major Hirose's top cover spotted six enemy planes in the air over Rangoon at 2,500 meters — "you could see the planes' shadows going down from the sky" — and promptly "veered to attack them." The Japanese pilots claimed four Tomahawks shot down. They returned to Raheng without loss, presumably satisfied that they had revenged their drubbing of the day before. The group's newspaper reported that the Allies' coordination in the air was "really awful."

For the AVG, this was the unhappy afternoon when Bert Christman, Gil Bright, and George Paxton were shot down, with all three men landing safely. For their part, the Panda Bears were credited with one kill.

Night raids of a few bombers were sent to Mingaladon and Moulmein airports over the next few days, sometimes escorted by the 77th Sentai fighters. Then, on January 8, four "Spitfires" made a return visit to Raheng. Three Ki-27s of the 1st Chutai were "on siren pose" at the airfield, ready to take off at a moment's notice, when the Allied fighters appeared at 2 p.m. In fifteen minutes they destroyed four Japanese fighters on the ground, damaging three more and a cargo plane. Anti-aircraft guns managed to shoot down two of the attackers, and three of the Ki-27s got into the air and chased the survivors out over the Bay of Martaban.

Again, the attackers were Tomahawks, and one was indeed shot down: Charlie Mott, who was badly injured, taken prisoner, and doomed to work the River Kwai "death railroad" until the war was almost over. The AVGs claimed eight planes destroyed on the ground.

The following day, January 9, the Allies fighters came back to Raheng in greater strength, to a total of seven AVG Tomahawks and six RAF Buffaloes. The strafing went on for ten minutes, destroying one Ki-27 fighter and a starter truck, and damaging two other fighters. There were no Allied losses in this attack, nor did the Japanese claim any. The Panda Bears claimed four enemy planes destroyed on the ground, and the Buffalo pilots were credited with two more.

Next day, Japanese ground support troops completed the communications system between Raheng and another advanced field at Mae Sot, enabling them to exchange information quickly. (Allied and Japanese accounts sometimes differ as to which of these fields was attacked on a given day. Adding to the confusion, the Allied pilots generally identified Raheng as Tak. I follow the Japanese usage here.)

Also on January 10, three Ki-30 light bombers of the 31st Sentai moved to Raheng for an attack on Moulmein airport. They were still at the advanced field that evening, when four Buffaloes came over and strafed them on the ground, destroying two of the bombers and badly wounding a pilot.

During this two-week period, therefore, the 77th Sentai lost a total of ten Ki-27 fighters—nearly a third of its planes—but apparently only two pilots badly injured. A starter truck had also been destroyed, and the group had expended 1,257 tracer bullets, 2,573 armor-piercing rounds, 52,740 liters of gasoline, and 1,608 liters of lubricating oil — no small matter to resource-poor Japan.

Assessing the situation in mid-January, the Japanese headquarters concluded that the enemy air force in Burma was headquartered at Mingaladon and Hlegu (Highland Queen) airports, with additional

American planes at Toungoo, to a total of about 120 aircraft — a considerable exaggeration. The 15th Army therefore established a new attack plan, and so informed the 5th Hikoshidan (area air force). This was the logic, as narrated by a Japanese historian: "Hurricanes and Tomahawks are not coming to attack our fighter planes (in the air) but instead they try to attack the bombers every time, so we need more study and a new plan for employing our bombers. Attacking Burma is difficult from bases in Thailand, so we need a Burma base." On January 15, General Obata arrived at Bangkok airport and set up a 5th Hikoshidan headquarters there. At the same time, the 50th Sentai reached Thailand and was stationed at Nakhon Sawan with its complement of 31 Ki-27 fixed-gear fighters.

The 5th Hikoshidan headquarters drew up its plan to support the 15th Army's drive into Burma. On January 20, 12 light bombers of the 31st Sentai supported the infantry as they crossed the frontier, with two squadrons of the 77th Sentai providing top cover. Heavy smoke from forest fires and burning buildings made flying difficult. Other fighters from the 77th Sentai reconnoitered Moulmein airport, shooting down two Brewster Buffaloes as they tried to take off, and killing both pilots. They were "showered with bullets," according to a Japanese news report.

The British sent their Blenheim bombers against the encroaching Japanese army, escorted by P-40s from the AVG 2nd Squadron. The six Panda Bears engaged the main force of the 77th Sentai, claiming three shot down at the cost of the Tomahawk flown by Robert "Moose" Moss, who eventually made his way back to Moulmein and Mingaladon. On the Japanese side, the accounts vary, but apparently one Ki-27 was lost along with its pilot, Lieutenant Suzuki Shigeru, while the Japanese pilots claimed three or four Tomahawks shot down.

Later the same day, the 62nd Sentai heavy bombers escorted by 50th Sentai fighters attacked Moulmein airport and its satellite at Mudon with a total of 65 planes, a major air operation as such things were measured in Southeast Asia.

Kawasaki Ki-48 medium bombers from the 8th Sentai reconnoitered Mingaladon airport, reporting four bombers and twelve fighters seen on the ground. General Obata therefore ordered an attack for the next day, January 23. The first attack was led by Major Makino of the 50th

150

Sentai, taking off from Nakhon Sawan with 24 Ki-27 fighters. After refueling at Raheng, they flew over the Gulf of Martaban in a rain squall with decreasing visibility. Circling over southern Burma at 3,800 meters, they found themselves in heavy clouds and unable to break out. At one point they spotted two "P-40s," below and to the west. These must have been two Buffaloes of RAF 67 Squadron: one British pilot was shot down and killed near Pegu, while the other claimed one fixed-gear Japanese fighter destroyed.

Finally, at 11:45 Tokyo time, the Nakajimas entered Mingaladon airspace at 3,500 meters. The 2nd Chutai found itself at a disadvantage, pressed by the newly-arrived Hurricanes of 17 Squadron RAF. (Curiously, the Hurricane pilots said much the same thing, that they were hard-pressed by the attacking Japanese.) One Ki-27 was shot down in this engagement, while RAF squadron leader Cedric "Bunny" Stone had his Hurricane shot up and rendered unserviceable.

Next the Ki-27s were attacked by three AVG Tomahawks. "Fighting now entered the stage that is very messy." At 12:10 p.m., a 3rd Chutai pilot found himself with fuel "bursting out"; he fled the scene, was chased by a Tomahawk (the Japanese identify this pilot as Bill Bartling), and finally joined up with another Ki-27 at 2,000 meters. I get the impression, reading the Japanese accounts, that the 50th Sentai ran for its life on this occasion, despite its numerical superiority. One Ki-27 disappeared on the way home: it "missed its direction and got lost" over the rain forest

Nevertheless, the Japanese claimed a rousing victory in the morning furball: three Tomahawks, a Buffalo, two "Spitfires," and an unidentified "larger aircraft" destroyed, at the cost of two of their own. (Actual Allied losses: one Buffalo and its pilot, one Tomahawk forced down; and a Hurricane that never flew again. For their part, the Americans were credited with destroying seven Ki-27s and a Buffalo pilot with one.)

That afternoon, it was the turn of the 77th Sentai fighters, 25 of them, escorting 12 light bombers of the 31st Sentai. This formation was the brain-child of General Hiroda of the 10th Hikodan (wing): he figured that with only a dozen bombers, the Ki-27s would be better able to protect them from the Allied fighters. The two groups were to have assembled near Raheng, but they missed each other in a rain squall, with the result that the bombers flew alone to Mingaladon.

(Missed rendezvous were a frequent thing in JAAF operations in Southeast Asia.) They were bounced by a reported 30 P-40s and a "Spitfire." All the Ki-30s were hit; one was shot down, three badly damaged, and seven others suffered some damage before the Japanese fighters came to their rescue 15 minutes later.

Attacking the P-40s from behind, the 77th Sentai pilots were credited with shooting down no fewer than eight of them, including the Tomahawk flown by Bert Christman, who was killed in his parachute harness. (Umemoto Hiroshi assures the reader that this was common practice in air combat since World War I, and that Japanese parachutists were similarly killed by members of the AVG.) All the Ki-27s returned safely.

January 23 saw some fairly wild discrepancies between claims and actual losses. The AVG was claiming 11 planes, with another for 67 Squadron. Actual Japanese losses were one light bomber and two fighters (three pilots and a gunner dead), though the surviving 31st Sentai bombers had been so badly shot up that the group would not play an important role for the next week or so. For their part, the Japanese claimed 14 Allied aircraft, as against one Buffalo and two Tomahawks actually shot down or crash-landed (two pilots dead).

Back at Lampang, the 77th Sentai pilots reported that "the enemy has a great will to fight but their technique in the air is not superior" to that of the Japanese — a back-handed compliment, but quite a remarkable admission that the despised westerners were fighting them on equal terms.

On January 24, it was the turn of the Mitsubishi Ki-21 heavy bombers. Six planes from the 2nd Chutai, 14th Sentai, set out from Bangkok under Captain Motomura for a rendezvous with the 50th Sentai. The fighter group's commander, Major Makino, suffered an engine failure as he was taking off from Raheng; the plane crashed, badly injuring Makino and leaving his fighters under the command of Captain Sakaguchi, the 1st Chutai squadron leader. Leading 20 Ki-27s, Sakaguchi caught up with the heavy bombers near Mingaladon, only to have them speed up and dive to a lower altitude, once again leaving the fighters behind. (It was not unusual, in the early days of the Second World War, for powerful bombers to be as fast or faster than the fighters that were supposed to protect or intercept them.)

Mingaladon airport was "full of explosions and smoking" as the heavies turned back from their bombing run, under attack from the Allied fighters — a mixed formation of Tomahawks, Hurricanes, and Buffaloes. One of the first to go down was the Ki-21 piloted by Captain Motomura; he was soon followed by the rest of his squadron mates, while the 50th Sentai did its best to protect them from the slaughter. Three Ki-27s were also shot down in the melee, including Captain Sakaguchi's aircraft. According to Umemoto Hiroshi, one of the Japanese fighter pilots parachuted to the ground, 30 kilometers east of Mingaladon. He died of his injuries, and his body was buried by Burmese villagers, who reported that he wore a white band on his forehead with his name on it. In March, a body was disinterred in this area by the Japanese; this may have been Sakaguchi. Umemoto is my source that all six bombers were lost, along with their 42 crewmen. The semi-official history gives the 14th Sentai losses at five Ki-21s.

In this one-sided battle, the Allies lost one Tomahawk force-landed, while seeming to claim 11 heavy bombers and 7 fighters shot down (the numbers conflict). The 50th Sentai apparently made no claims for January 24.

Toward the end of the day, the 77th Sentai returned with three light bombers of the 31st Sentai — evidently all that were serviceable after its travails the day before. They "wanted to revenge" their comrades lost earlier. The bombers reported several planes destroyed on the ground, while the fighters claimed one Allied aircraft shot down and others damaged. Curiously, the Allies make almost no mention of this attack, except that one Hurricane pilot was attacked as he was landing his plane. The only actual damage was six bullet-holes in an already-disabled Blenheim.

There now began a four-day air superiority battle in which the Japanese fighter units returned again and again to Mingaladon airport, hoping to wipe out the Allied air defenses and smooth the way for the Japanese 33rd Division that was now fighting its way into Burma.

On January 26, the 50th Sentai set out for Rangoon with 23 fixed-gear Nakajima Ki-27 Nate fighters, approaching Mingaladon airport at 6,000 meters (roughly 20,000 feet) at 11:40 a.m. Tokyo time. Over Moulmein, they were spotted by British observers, so the enemy was alerted. (The Royal Air Force had a primitive radar set at Moulmein.)

As a result, a dozen Allied fighters were already in the air when the Nakajimas arrived, bouncing them in pairs. "The fight was difficult," the Japanese pilots reported, but they attacked quickly and managed to shoot down four of the Allied fighters certain and six more possible, while losing one of their own. This was the Number Three aircraft in the 2nd Chutai, caught over the north shore of Bay of Martaban at 12:10 p.m. as the 50th Sentai was heading for home. He went down in a plume of black smoke. Possibly he was shot down by Bob Neale of the AVG 1st Squadron, who claimed the rearmost of the Nates as they were heading out over the bay. (The 1st Squadron "Adam & Eves" were gradually replacing the 2nd Squadron at Rangoon.) Another Japanese fighter was damaged by a P-40 and had to make a high-speed landing back at the home field, further damaging the aircraft but without injury to the pilot.

As for the Allied pilots, this was the combat in which the newly arrived Louis "Cokey" Hoffman of the AVG was shot down and killed. Moose Moss was also shot down but managed to make his way home again. Bunny Stone of RAF 17 Squadron was forced down with some damage to his Hurricane.

The following day, Japanese aerial reconnaissance showed "34 small planes and 11 large planes" still at Mingaladon, so that night four heavy bombers of the 62nd Sentai bombed the field. One was lost to the guns of Bunny Stone, with all six crewmen killed in the crash. (Two days earlier, the 62nd Sentai had moved to Nakhon Sawan in Thailand to begin transition training for the Ki-21-II heavy bomber — Sally-2, in Allies nomenclature. It's not clear if this was the type of aircraft flown on January 27.)

On January 28, General Obata ordered both his fighter groups to attack. The 77th Sentai left Lampang with 27 Nates, while the 50th set out from Nakhon Sawan with just 10 planes, testimony to the losses they had suffered in recent days. Tomahawks were waiting for them at 5,000 meters (another account says 7,000 meters). Squadron leader Captain Matsuda of the 2nd Chutai was shot down. Lieutenant Yamamoto from the same squadron was attacked by two Tomahawks; his plane on fire, he strafed the airfield and dove into Jack Newkirk's Tomahawk on the ground. (Newkirk been forced to land as a result of losing the coolant in his Allison engine, always a weak point in liquid-cooled designs.) Yamamoto received a citation to honor his sacrifice. His body, says the Japanese account, was found and buried by "the local people." Warrant Officer Kitsaka of the 77th Sentai was also shot down. The 50th Sentai escaped without loss.

The Japanese pilots claimed 15 Allied fighters certain and 5 possibles in this combat. Actual Allied losses: two Tomahawks forced down, with both pilots surviving. For their part, the AVGs claimed 6 Nates shot down.

Next day, Major Yoshioka led the 77th Sentai back to Mingaladon, this time at 7,500 meters (nearly 25,000 feet). There were 20 Nates in the formation, coming over the target at 5 p.m. Tokyo time. They were met by an estimated 20 enemy fighters, causing the Nates to go into a defensive circle, in and out of the clouds. (Called a Lufbery Circle in the west, this maneuver allowed each plane to defend the tail of the one in front, making it impossible for the enemy to get anything more than a glancing shot.) In the ensuing furball, both sides wildly over-claimed. The Japanese pilots reported that they were attacked by six Hurricanes, of which they claimed five shot down at the cost of four Japanese pilots lost in combat: Sergeants Nagashima, Kanda, and Kojima, and a warrant officer whose name has been lost. One of them — probably Nagashima — made a suicide dive on Mingaladon, aiming for but missing the Blenheim bombers in the dispersal area. (See the postwar Japanese artist's rendering on the next page.)

The Allied pilots were even more optimistic, claiming no less than 14 Nates destroyed in the melee. They had one or two aircraft forced down, with no pilots killed, though a Buffalo pilot was killed in a flying accident that day.

For the past four days, therefore, the Japanese fighter units were claiming a grand total of 19 Allied aircraft shot down. Actual Allied losses were 3 planes, with two of the pilots surviving. For their part, the Allied pilots were claiming a total of 22 victories. Actual Japanese losses were indeed severe: 8 planes together with their pilots. The 77th Sentai had taken the worst of it: in six weeks of combat with the AVG and RAF, Major Yoshioka had lost fully a third of his force — a dozen planes and a dozen pilots. The Japanese "concluded that the Tomahawks were much superior in speed and firepower [to the Nates], and always had the altitude advantage, leaving the Japanese fighters always at a disadvantage."

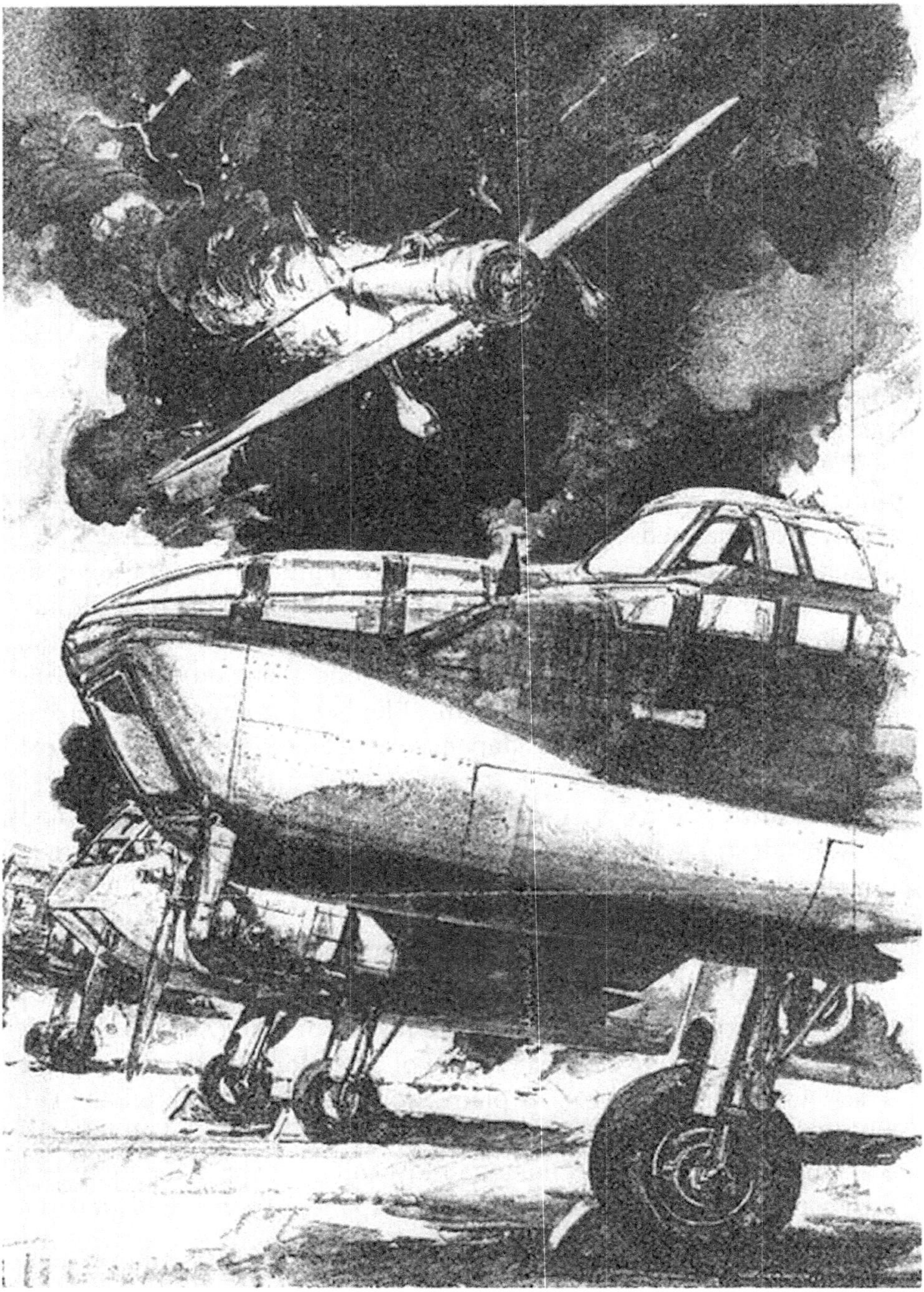

By January 30, the Japanese 33rd Division had advanced to the Salween River, where "the fight was very harsh." The infantry commanders asked General Obata for assistance, and the emphasis was accordingly shifted to army cooperation flights. Bomber squadrons (probably from the 8th Sentai, consisting of Kawasaki Ki-48 medium bombers) attacked Martaban and bombed enemy facilities there. The British evacuated the town next day, leaving its airfields (including a quantity of aviation fuel, which the Japanese called "Churchill stores") to be taken over by the Japanese air units.

Meanwhile the JAAF 7th Base Group was dispatched to Moulmein to begin the reconstruction of Mudon airport south of town, formerly an RAF dispersal field. The 4th Ground Group landed at Bangkok and was sent forward to assist in this work, but the roads were so bad that they could not begin work at Moulmein until February 16.

At left: a postwar Japanese artist reconstructs the jibaku *(self-destruction) dive at Mingaladon airport by a fixed-gear Nakajima Ki-27 on January 29, 1942. The pilot has been identified as Sergeant Nagashima of the 77th Sentai. He was apparently trying to destroy the early-model Bristol Blenheim bomber in the foreground, missing it by inches according to contemporary accounts.*

Numbers Are Not Important

ON FEBRUARY 1, GENERAL OBATA gathered his group commanders at Bangkok and ordered them to strike the Allied airfields at Rangoon and Toungoo around the clock — fighters by day, bombers by night. Meanwhile, he dispatched 450 men of the 15th Airport Group to the just-captured British airfields at Moulmein, to rebuild them for use by the JAAF. Eighty men from the 50th Sentai also joined this project, which would cut the flying distance to Rangoon by more than half. However, road conditions were so bad that actual reconstruction did not begin until the middle of the month.

The Japanese launched 17 separate attacks against Rangoon and Toungoo airfields in a three-day period, involving 120 fighter sorties, 80 light and medium bomber sorties, and 20 heavy bomber sorties. Two fighter planes were lost over Mingaladon, but there is no detail of these combats. On the evening of February 4, a reconnaissance of the Allied airfields showed disappointing results, with 50 "small planes" (probably fighters) and 10 large ones (probably bombers) still available to support the British army. For all the sacrifices of the past month, therefore, the enemy air force in Burma appeared to be larger than ever.

General Obata therefore ordered a change in plan, with the Japanese air force concentrating on ground targets at the front, to enable the army to cross the Salween and Sittang rivers into Burma proper. Allied morale was judged to be very high, causing the Japanese advance to slow down. (The Allied army on the Sittang front consisted of 17th Indian Division, made up of Indian, Gurkha, and British battalions; 7th Armoured Brigade with U.S.-made M-3 Stuart light tanks; and some Burmese frontier guards. The Chinese force around Toungoo had not yet come into contact with the invaders.)

On February 6, attacks resumed against Mingaladon, with a 77th Sentai fighter lost and another missing (but evidently landed at Moulmein and returned to base next day). The Japanese fighters claimed five planes shot down, though the Allies suffered no losses that day; for their part, the AVG was claiming six Japanese fighters and a bomber.

The 47th Independent Chutai of Type 2 fighters (Nakajima Ki-44, called *Shoki* by the Japanese and "Tojo" by Allied pilots) was now added to Obata's fighter force. When they arrived mid-month, however, there were only three fighters in the squadron, with two others left behind in Bangkok for repairs. The 62nd Sentai heavy bomber group, which had borne so much of the fighting over Rangoon, meanwhile moved to Saigon to refit with new aircraft.

Once again Obata announced a new plan: the JAAF would attack the north Burma railroad centers of Mandalay and Bassein, which he had evidently decided were the source of Allied reinforcements. Then they would again concentrate on the Rangoon area. In other developments, the Japanese construction crews at Moulmein airport were attacked by Allied aircraft, with several ground personnel killed and wounded. Further personnel arrived and began to reconstruct the airport and set up a communications system at Moulmein.

Meanwhile, reconnaissance showed 3 large, 4 medium, and 17 small planes at Mingaladon airport, plus 7 large and 6 small planes at Hlegu (known to the Allies as Highland Queen, and used for the most part as a base for the Bristol Blenheim bombers). On February 19, Ki-27 fighters of the 77th Sentai and Ki-30 light bombers of the 31st Sentai attacked Pyinmana on the railroad line to the north of Toungoo. Returning, the light bombers went off course as a result of fog (perhaps smoke from forest fires and bomb damage) and strong winds, with one Ki-30 lost and three more damaged in crash landings near Lampang. Meanwhile, the 50th Sentai escorted the 14th Sentai heavy bombers to Mandalay, where they bombed military barracks. One bomber crashed on returning. On the same day, the Japanese army crossed the Sittang River at Bilin but was stalled on the west bank. The ground commanders asked Obata for help, so the north Burma campaign was called off.

On February 21, Obata told the 31st and 77th sentais to continue supporting the army ground forces, while the 8th and 50th sentais resumed their north Burma campaign. Over the Sittang River, the 77th fighters met six Tomahawks, claiming one certain and two probable, while the AVG pilots claimed four Nates shot down. In fact, there were no losses on either side!

The Japanese accounts of this period place great emphasis on the Allied ground-cooperation units — both 1 Squadron of the Indian Air Force and 28 Squadron RAF — as "really dangerous" to the ground forces. Equipped with slow, high-wing Westland Lysanders (and often escorted by the war-weary Brewster Buffaloes of 67 Squadron), these units are usually relegated to a footnote in the Burma campaign. Ground support seldom gets the respect in military histories that bombers and especially fighters are routinely accorded.

On February 23, Captain Ohira of the 70th Independent Chutai reconnaissance unit was shot down and killed while observing a battle at the Sittang River. Evidently his antagonist was Squadron Leader Barry Sutton of RAF 135 Squadron.

Looking back on the campaign thus far, the commander of the 77th Sentai reported that although his fixed-gear Nakajima fighter had high maneuverability in combat, the enemy fighters were able to take advantage of their higher dive speed to attack from above, then leave the scene, to the disadvantage of the Japanese fighters. "One cannot count the number of (enemy) fighters," he declared. However, he added, "Numbers are not important — technique is important." The 77th Sentai by now had lost 25 fighter planes and 14 of its best pilots (including one captured and one badly wounded) in the Burma campaign. The Japanese fighter pilots were "fighting heartily" and had done very well. For its part, the 50th Sentai had lost 20 aircraft in the Burma campaign.

The Japanese commanders noted that their losses were particularly high in ground attack missions. Proportionately, their losses were much higher than those suffered by Allied pilots. They also noted that the Japanese forces tended to exhaust their fuel and ordnance supplies, and that they should emulate the Allies' "very professional" standard of training.

As of February 25, the Japanese fighter forces consisted of the 77th Sentai with 23 planes, the 50th Sentai with 21 planes, and the newly arrived 47th Independent Chutai with 3 of the new Nakajima Ki-44 Shoki fighters, essentially a retractable-gear Ki-43 with a more powerful engine, similar to that used in the Mitsubishi heavy bombers.

Toward the end of February, Colonel Tanigawa of the Japanese Southern Army toured JAAF facilities in Thailand in order to collect observations from the unit commanders. Lieutenant Colonel Hayashi of the 31st Sentai reported that he had 18 light bombers in service and that the group's policy was to work in close cooperation with its fighter escort. Major Yoshioka of the 77th Sentai reported 25 fighters in service. "The 97 Fighter [Nakajima Ki-27 Nate] is inferior to the Tomahawk," he said. "The enemy's way of attacking is to use speed from high altitude, hit-and-run, and when used this way, the 97 Fighter doesn't have any possibility to win. But right now we have a larger number of fighters, so we are confident that we will not lose."

Major Makino of the 50th Sentai likewise reported that he had 25 fighters in service. He "strongly needed" more planes, he told Colonel Tanigawa, and favored repetitive attacks, one after the other. "The technique of the enemy is very proficient," Makino concluded, "and not easy to withstand." For the 8th Sentai medium-bomber force, Colonel Honda said: "From combat experience in China we have strong confidence in attacking." He too asked for more Kawasaki bombers to replace his combat losses.

Overall, the field commanders complained that the orders from General Obata's headquarters were too precise and detailed, that the tactical units required more freedom of action.

On February 25, the JAAF mustered every fighter plane available in the area — 21 Ki-27 Nates from the 50th Sentai, 23 Ki-27s from the 77th Sentai, and 3 Ki-44 Shoki fighters of the newly arrived 47th Independent Chutai — to inflict a smashing blow on the Allied fighter forces at Mingaladon airport outside Rangoon. As they approached, the pilots could see the smoke pall rising above the city. It was, they recalled, a "unique Burma smoke." Six AVG Tomahawks and six RAF Hurricanes took off from Mingaladon. The Japanese pilots "welcomed them" and began the combat at 1:30 p.m. Tokyo time. By the time it was over, the Japanese estimated that they were opposed by 20 Allied fighters. At one point, six AVGs were concentrating on the Shoki fighters, which found themselves at a disadvantage. This was a disappointment, since great things had been expected of the speedy new fighters. Still, the Japanese pilots claimed a grand total of 16 certain kills — 11 for the 77th Sentai, 3 for the 50th Sentai, and 2 for the 47th Independent Chutai — plus a number of probables, while suffering no losses of their own.

This furball at mid-day on February 25 was probably the wildest event for over-claiming in the Burma campaign, and for both sides. Apparently only nine Allied fighters were in the air, and only four were actively engaged in the combat. Three AVG pilots were credited with four Japanese fighters shot down, and the American John "Tex" Barrick of the RAF was credited with another. (Barrick reported that at one point he was chased and nearly shot down by a "Zero," almost certainly one of the Shokis.) Adding the claims of both sides, *the fighter pilots were claiming no fewer than 21 enemy aircraft destroyed, when the actual total was zero.*

Nor was that all for the day. The Japanese fighters were back at 6:30 p.m. Tokyo time with the twin-engine Kawasaki medium bombers of the 8th Sentai added to the attacking force. (The Allies recorded the local time as 5 p.m.) They were met by AVG Tomahawks, as the Japanese pilots recalled; the P-40s were "happily shooting" at the bombers and their escort. This time the Japanese pilots were considerably less optimistic. The only claim was put in by the 50th Sentai, which reported that Lieutenant Mihara had rammed an Allied fighter while sacrificing his own life. (This could have been a close encounter with Barry Sutton's Hurricane at low level. Sutton reported that the Ki-27 spun in, whether from the Hurricane's bullets or a stall from a too-tight turn.) In addition to the lieutenant, another 50th Sentai pilot failed to return.

The AVGs were even more optimistic than they had been earlier in the day, putting in claims for no fewer than 21 Japanese fighters and a bomber. (One of the 8th Sentai medium bombers was indeed shot up, but it returned safely to base.) Thus the day's claims for both sides came to a grand total of 44, against actual losses of just two fighters, both of them Japanese. On the ground, meanwhile, five Blenheims of RAF 45 Squadron were damaged or destroyed by the bombing, and a bomber pilot was killed.

Next day, February 26, the Japanese returned with 12 Ki-30 light bombers of the 31st Sentai, which met their fighter escort — an unknown number of fighters from the 50th and 77th Sentais, plus the 47th Independent Chutai — over Moulmein. They attacked Hlegu (Highland Queen) at 9:20 a.m. Tokyo time. Afterward, the bombers went home to Phitsanulok while the fighters took up new quarters at fields recently wrested from the British, the 50th Sentai at the main RAF field at Moulmein, the 77th and the Shokis at Mudon dispersal field to the south. This was evidently the first they time refueled at their new forward bases.

Just as the 50th Sentai fighters were landing, however, they were attacked by seven "Hurricanes." The Japanese anti-aircraft crews claimed one of the enemy fighters shot down. The Allied fighters also attacked Mudon, where the 77th Sentai lost one plane destroyed on the ground, one badly damaged, and three more suffering moderate damage, and the group's commander, Major Makino, was injured badly enough to be hospitalized. In another account, a pilot of the 50th Sentai was trying to take off from Moulmein when his engine quit; the plane was badly damaged and the pilot badly injured, perhaps killed. This may also have referred to Makino's mishap.

This episode is one of the most confusing in the Burma campaign, since both the AVG and the RAF reported attacking the Moulmein airfields that day. Six Hurricanes attacked the main field as the 50th Sentai were landing, with the British pilots claiming five Nates shot down; one Hurricane was lost and its pilot captured. At about the same time, seven AVG Tomahawks strafed the 77th Sentai fighters on the ground at Moulmein, claiming two destroyed before moving on to Mudon. There the Japanese reportedly were just taking off; the AVGs claimed no fewer than 12 Japanese fighters shot down in the melee. In the Japanese account, the RAF is credited with the attack on Moulmein, while the AVG is credited with attacking Mudon.

Nor was the day finished! The 8th Sentai medium bombers raided Mingaladon, escorted by Nates from both fighter groups. They were intercepted by the Allied fighters, with the AVG claiming 7 Ki-27s and a Kawasaki bomber shot down. Two of the bombers were indeed lost, with one seen to have been shot down; the other may have crash-landed on the way home. The 77th Sentai also lost one of its planes, while the Japanese fighter pilots claimed seven Allied planes shot down. (One Hurricane was forced down with its pilot wounded and sufficient airframe damage that it had to be written off. No Tomahawks were lost.)

About this time, Japanese reconnaissance planes discovered a "new" British airfield at Magwe, 400 kilometers (240 miles) up the Irrawaddy River from Rangoon. They counted 27 aircraft on the ground. On February 28, General Obata visited Moulmein and found the airfield still under construction and still plagued with supply problems. The ingenious ground crews had been able to find gasoline locally, but no ammunition. It was decided therefore to use the heavy bombers as cargo planes, while the army pushed the completion of a road. The air force headquarters and the 4th Hikodan headquarters moved to Moulmein, while the 10th Hikodan took up residence at Mudon.

Sizing up their position at the end of the month, the 50th Sentai had only 12 planes in service while the 77th Sentai had 14; there's no mention of the 47th Independent Chutai. "The Japanese side was disadvantaged and heavily damaged," notes the historian. What was needed was a "recovering period" to bring up fuel and food, while unserviceable fighters were put back into fighting condition

On the facing page: During and after the Second World War, there was no Japanese air unit more famous than the 64th Sentai, nor a more famous pilot than its commander, Kato Tateo. Here he is shown on the cover of a postwar book about him and his unit.

檜 與平

South Burma Falls

GENERAL ALINUMA OF THE 15th ARMY visited General Obata on the last day of February and told him the British had 30,000 troops in South Burma, plus two understrength Chinese divisions between Pegu and Rangoon and a "very proficient" tank brigade. Pointing out that the British air force was very cooperative with the army, he asked for similar support from the 5th Hikoshidan in the planned offensive against the British at Rangoon and the Chinese at Pegu. General Obata agreed, assigning the 8th Sentai Kawasaki medium bombers and 50th Sentai Nakajima fighters to work with the 55th Division, while the 31st Sentai light bombers and 77th Sentai fighters worked with the 33rd Division. However, the army tended to move at night and along mountain paths, making air support very difficult, so the Japanese aircraft concentrated instead on suppressing enemy air attacks.

Heavy weather early in March also hindered the ability of the fighters to provide close air support. However, on March 3, the 33rd Division crossed the Sittang River under fighter cover from the 77th Sentai. The Shokis of the 47th Independent Chutai were also active, attacking Blenheim bombers at the Sittang and shooting one of them down.

By March 7, the 33rd Division was at the outskirts of Rangoon. The air force was planning to cooperate "with all their power," but Lampang was socked in by weather, obliging the fighters to stay put. In the afternoon, however, the 50th Sentai and one squadron of 8th Sentai medium bombers from Moulmein managed to go to the Mingaladon area and attack the British armored brigade with its Lend-Lease M-3 Stuart light tanks. According to Japanese reconnaissance reports, the British had six fighters still based at Mingaladon. (The AVG 1st Squadron under Bob Neale had already moved back to Magwe.)

March 8 was a repeat, with rain holding the fighters at Lampang. However, the 31st Sentai light bombers advanced to Mudon airport and from there attacked enemy tanks and a motorized convoy. Troops of the 33rd Division entered the Burmese capital at 10 a.m. that day.

With Rangoon in Japanese hands, additional forces joined the Burma attack. Army headquarters had already ordered the 18th and 56th divisions to get ready to join the Burma campaign, coming in by sea as soon as the port of Rangoon was secure. Three more fighter groups were also assigned to Burma: the 1st Sentai with two squadrons and a total of 15 Ki-27 Nate fighters; the 11th Sentai with two squadrons and a total of 14 Ki-27s; and the 64th Sentai, newly arrived from the Dutch Indies with 15 Ki-43 Hayabusa retractable gear fighters, 2 Ki-27s, and 2 Royal Air Force Hurricanes captured in the Indies and intended for use in "werwolf" attacks on British airfields. The two fixed-gear groups would be assigned to the Rangoon airfields, which were made ready with unprecedented speed.

On March 9, Colonel Takeuchi was sent to Mingaladon airport outside Rangoon with instructions to rebuild it and to look for additional airfields in the area. He found that Mingaladon, though pitted with bomb craters, could be fixed immediately for planes to land. Of three hangars, only one had been destroyed; the barracks were damaged but fixable. Mingaladon's three runways, he reported, were each 1,200 meters (4,000 feet) in length. He next went to Hlegu (Highland Queen to the British) and found a runway 1,800 meters by 50 meters, surrounded by woods that would make a good dispersal; the British had thoughtfully left 800 barrels of gasoline behind to fuel the Japanese fighters. He also inspected a former RAF dispersal field, but deemed it unusable in the rainy season without a month's work, and the same was true of the other dispersals. However, they could be used as emergency landing fields.

The reconstruction of Mingaladon and Hlegu began on March 13, and the craters at Mingaladon were filled in within two days.

Meanwhile, the long-range Ki-43 Hayabusas would be stationed across the border in Chiang Mai, Thailand, due east of the former AVG training field at Toungoo. Also scheduled to move to Thai bases were the Ki-21-II heavy bombers of the 12th and 98th Sentais and the single-engine reconnaissance planes of the 51st Independent Chutai, all of which had taken part in the Christmas raids on Rangoon. When this reinforcement was complete, Japanese aircraft committed to the Burma campaign would total 251 planes, including 115 fighters, 66 heavy bombers, and 70 reconnaissance aircraft and light and medium bombers.

The Allies strike from Magwe

For their part, the Allied air forces had re-established themselves at Magwe, only recently discovered by Japanese reconnaissance patrols. There was a second Allied base at Akyab on the coast, evidently not yet known to the Japanese. The combined Allied force came to 53 aircraft, including 27 Hurricanes and 6 AVG P-40s.

From Magwe, in the early morning of March 18, two AVG P-40s made a strafing attack on the Moulmein airfields. (One Japanese account says there were three P-40s, while naming only Ken Jernstedt and Bill Reed of the AVG 3rd Squadron Hell's Angels, who were the only pilots in the impromptu raid.) There were "many shots and broken pieces [of aircraft] flying in the sky." The pickings were rich, because the 31st Sentai light bombers and apparently some Mitsubishi "Sonia" reconnaissance / light attack planes had moved to Mudon from Lampang, Thailand, just the day before. At Moulmein, two Ki-21 heavy bombers and a Ki-51 Sonia were destroyed, plus a Ki-48 medium bomber either destroyed or put out of commission.

The raiders then moved on to Mudon, where even worse damage was done. The 31st Sentai had three of its Ki-30 Ann light bombers destroyed and two more badly damaged, leaving it with only one serviceable aircraft. In addition, another Ki-51 Sonia was burned, for a grand total of 10 aircraft put out of commission by the two roving pilots. (Jernstedt and Reed were credited with destroying 15 aircraft at Moulmein and Mudon.)

There was more to come: even as the JAAF was preparing to destroy the Allied air forces at Magwe, nine Blenheim bombers of RAF 45 Squadron took off from the mid-Burma base on the morning of March 21 for an attack on the Rangoon airfields. The defenders managed to put up only six Nakajima Ki-27 fighters, three from the 50th Sentai and three from the 77th. Lieutenant Nagoshi of the 77th Sentai was mortally wounded in this engagement, though he managed to put the plane down at Hmawbi; in turn, he was credited with destroying one Blenheim. Meanwhile the British bombers fought their way through to Mingaladon, where no fewer than 60 enemy planes were massed together on the runways. There was "much shooting and bombing," and one Ki-21 heavy bomber was destroyed on the ground. The five remaining interceptors continually attacked the Blenheims at "super-low speed" in a very difficult situation.

Nonetheless, the Japanese pilots claimed multiple Blenheims shot down. (Seven of the raiders were damaged, but all returned safely to Magwe. For their part, the Blenheim gunners were credited with shooting down two Nates.)

Meanwhile, 10 Hurricane fighters also made a sweep of Rangoon. An unknown number of Nates from the 50th Sentai came up to repel them. The Japanese pilots claimed five Hurricanes shot down; the British in turn claimed three Nates destroyed. Apparently none was lost on either side, though one of the Hurricanes made a forced landing as it attempted to return to Magwe, its pilot forced to hitch a ride home with 7th Armoured Brigade.

It's not possible to sort out the Japanese losses at Mingaladon. In addition to the Ki-21 destroyed by the bombers, at least one other plane (type unknown) was also destroyed and 11 more were badly damaged, whether by bombs or by the strafing Hurricanes. (It is also possible that the planes supposedly destroyed at Mingaladon actually included those burned up by Jernstedt and Reed at the Moulmein airfields.)

Payback in spades

The daring Allied raids of March 18 and 21 — Tomahawks attacking Moulmein and Mudon, Blenheims and Hurricanes raiding Mingaladon — failed to halt the huge strike the Japanese had laid on for Magwe for the 21st. The first formation to arrive had taken off from the Rangoon-area airports, and consisted of 31 Ki-27 Nate fighters of the 1st and 11th Sentais, led by Colonel Okabe, the new commander of the 11th. They entered the Magwe airspace at 3:10 p.m. Tokyo time, tasked with patrolling over the target at 4,500 meters (about 15,000 feet). At 3:20 p.m. they were joined by the heavy bombers: 51 Ki-21 Sally heavy bombers of the 12th and 98th sentais, from their bases in Thailand. (Another Sally had crashed on takeoff.) The heavies were escorted by 14 Ki-43 Hayabusa fighters of the 64th Sentai, also based in Thailand. This was, by far, the largest formation ever seen in Burma skies — nearly 100 aircraft — and more were to come.

The heavy bombers droned through Magwe airspace at an altitude of 6,000 meters (about 20,000 feet), escorted by some fighters from the 11th and 64th sentais. The bulk of the fighter pilots, however, went down to low level in order to strafe the enemy airfield.

Alas, the 12th Sentai bombardiers found Magwe airport obscured by clouds, and they had to bomb "by estimate." (A brown dirt runway in the dry season, in a nation whose sky was murky with smoke from forest fires and the burning city of Rangoon, Magwe airport wasn't easy to find even on a clear day.) Meanwhile, they found themselves under attack by two Tomahawks flown by Parker Dupouy and Tom Jones, who were soon engaged by the escorting fighters.

When the 98th Sentai came over the target, it was attacked by three other P-40s, and one of the bombers was shot down. (Ken Jernstedt of the AVG claimed a Sally in this engagement, out of a 10-plane formation that was probably one squadron of the 98th.) The formation then milled about, reorganized, and returned to its bombing run. By this time, the clouds had moved out and the Japanese were able to "bomb correctly."

Some Hurricanes of RAF 17 Squadron now joined the battle. Seeing the bombers under attack, Colonel Okabe ordered his 11th Sentai pilots to "challenge them from the back." Two of them jumped a Hurricane, "continuously shooting like a shower," and forced him down — probably the plane flown by Kenneth Hemingway, who crash-landed in a dry river bed. Alas for Colonel Okabe, while the 11th Sentai commander was firing at Hemingway, another Hurricane (perhaps flown by Pilot Officer Brooks) was shooting at him. "How sad to see his head unrecognizable and full of blood," writes the Japanese historian. Okabe's Ki-27 crashed in a dense forest.

One of the 64th Sentai Hayabusas — flown by the 1st Chutai commander, Captain Maruo — also failed to return from this engagement. A few days later, however, he turned up at Chiang Mai, having landed his plane inside Japanese lines and eventually obtaining fuel for the return flight.

The punishment continues

And the Japanese were not finished with Magwe. At 4 p.m. Tokyo time, a second formation arrived, consisting of 10 Ki-30 Ann light bombers of the 31st Sentai — their scant numbers reflecting the damage wrought by the AVG and the RAF at Moulmein and Mingaladon — along with 17 Kawasaki Ki-48 Lily medium bombers of the 8th Sentai. They were escorted by 14 Ki-27 fighters of the 77th Sentai. There were also a few high-flying Ki-46 "Dinah" observation planes assigned to the March 21 raids on Magwe, to record the devastation for General Obata. Interestingly, the Japanese historian notes that the 14 fighter pilots in this second wave each had "above 2,000 hours" of flying time — an impressive figure, which if true no doubt reflects the group's long combat experience against the Chinese and Russian air forces from 1937 to 1941.

The 77th Sentai lost one Nate shot down in this battle, likely falling to the guns of Clif Groh of the AVG.

Altogether on March 21, the Japanese claimed 8 Allied fighters shot down plus 8 destroyed and 27 badly damaged on the ground, at a cost of 4 of their own planes. In addition, 17 crewmen were injured, presumably all of them on the bombers.

The dead pilots included one mystery: Lieutenant Sugiyama of the 47th Independent Chutai had taken off that afternoon with instructions to suss out the situation at Toungoo airport, but he never returned. Later, his wrecked Ki-44 Shoki fighter was found near Bassein, riddled with bullet holes and with Sugiyama dead at the controls. Running out of fuel and attempting to land in a dry rice field, his wheels hit an obstruction and the plane flipped. It was "not clear what happened," writes the Japanese historian, but almost certainly Sugiyama had blundered into the Magwe fighting, there being no other occasion that day on which he could have picked up the bullet holes in his airplane.

Next morning at 10:18 Tokyo time, the raiders were back again. This third wave consisted of 61 Ki-27 Nate fighters of the 1st, 11th, 50th, and 77th sentais, plus 12 Ki-30 Ann light bombers of the 31st Sentai, 12 Ki-48 Lily medium bombers of the 8th Sentai, and 11 Ki-21 Sally heavy bombers of the 12th Sentai. All these groups except the 50th were making their second appearance at Magwe in 24 hours.

And there was more to come: shortly after noon Tokyo time, the *fourth* wave arrived over Magwe. This formation consisted of 27 Sallys from the 12th Sentai, 26 Lilys of the 8th Sentai, 18 Ki-43 Hayabusa fighters of the 64th Sentai, and 23 Nates from the 1st and 11th sentais at Rangoon — these last making their second assault of the day. They claimed 22 planes destroyed on the ground, while suffering no losses of their own. Two Hurricanes managed to get off the ground, but there were no claims on the Allied side. The British and American squadrons abandoned the airport to the Japanese, leaving 20 burned-out hulks behind them. The Allied air defense of Burma was now all but destroyed.

The Werwolf Hurricanes

One of the most bizarre incidents in the first Burma campaign was the fate of two Royal Air Force Hurricane fighters, captured on Sumatra in the Dutch Indies, and intended to be used against RAF bases in Burma.

Following its brief encounter with RAF Buffaloes and AVG Tomahawks on Christmas Day, 1941, the 64th Sentai and its retractable-gear Nakajima Hayabusas returned to the campaign in Malaya. The group was under the command of then-Major Kato Tateo, probably the most famous of the Japanese army's fighter pilots. On January 16, Kato and his men were diverted to support the pending attack on Sumatra in the Dutch Indies (now Indonesia). The long-range Hayabusas were based at the former British airfield at Ipoh in southern Malaya. On February 14, the group supported an airborne landing on Palembang, which succeeded in capturing the airfield and the nearby Dutch oil refineries.

At Palembang airfield, the 64th Sentai found two comparatively undamaged Hurricane fighters and put them in shape for flying. Kato himself piloted one of the British planes, and the other was assigned to squadron leader Captain Anma Katsumi of the group's 3rd Chutai. (About this time, Kato was promoted to lieutenant colonel, the grade he would hold until his death.) Predictably, the two Japanese officers found themselves under attack by friendly aircraft, as a 64th Sentai veteran recalled. Neither was damaged, evidently, and to prevent another occurrence the tails of both Hurricanes were painted white.

Soon after Rangoon fell to the Japanese on March 8, the 64th Sentai returned to the mainland. Its new base was at Chiang Mai in northern Thailand, due east of the AVG's former airbase at Toungoo. The Hurricanes came along, evidently still flown by Colonel Kato and Captain Anma. The reinforcements would have been welcome: although it had received new aircraft at intervals during January and February, the group had only 15 Hayabusas in service when it made the move tomo Malaya.

The intention was to use the Hurricanes in "werwolf" attacks on British airfields where similar aircraft were based, notably Magwe and Akyab. However, that would have to wait until the group was based nearer to the action. When the 64th Sentai took part in the big raid on Magwe on March 21-22, the Hurricanes didn't take part, since they would have been unable to make the 550-mile round-trip flight.

So it was that the "werwolf" Hurricanes were sitting on the ground at Chiang Mai on the morning of March 24, when the AVG Tomahawks swept across in their vengeance raid, ordered by Chennault to retaliate for the Allied air disaster at Magwe. When the AVG pilots claimed fifteen Japanese aircraft destroyed at Magwe — more about that later — two of them were the former RAF Hurricanes. No more was heard of the werwolves, so evidently they never flew again.

Last battles in Burma

Following the pummeling of Magwe, the Japanese concentrated on wiping out the British remnants on the west coast of Burma. Raiding Akyab on March 23, the 64th Sentai lost one Hayabusa, cause unspecified. (The British claimed two bombers and one fighter.) A return trip was almost spoiled by the AVG's March 24 raid on Chiang Mai, which destroyed three planes and sidelined 10 more to strafing damage, including the "werwolf" Hurricanes the 64th Sentai had brought from the Indies. When the raiders struck, four Hayabusas of the 3rd Chutai were apparently preparing to take off for a raid on Akyab.

The Japanese historian notes that "the immortal Jack Newkirk was shot down" by ground fire, along with William McGarry, who was captured by Thai police, brought back to Chiang Mai by boat, and there interrogated. The Japanese "strictly pushed him to answer the questions" — an ordeal that must have been very unpleasant for McGarry. It was less than satisfactory for Colonel Kato as well: there was no one at Chiang Mai who spoke both English and Japanese, so one Thai asked the questions and translated McGarry's answers into French for the second interpreter, who then rendered them — apparently ineptly — into Japanese. "Commander Kato was greatly annoyed because he could not understand the French language," the Japanese historian relates. In consequence, it was "hard for him to understand what was happening in this combat" between the AVG and the 64th Sentai. Later, the Japanese concluded that McGarry had given "a lot of incorrect information" to his questioners.

Despite the AVG raid on Chiang Mai — the worst pummeling the 64th Sentai had received during the war — "the whole troop reorganized and joined the combat again." Indeed, it was back in action the same afternoon. Eleven Hayabusas were still in service after the AVG strike, and these finally managed to get off for Akyab, escorting 26 Sally heavy bombers of the 98th Sentai.

Over the British base, Kato's pilots claimed three Hurricanes shot down at no cost to themselves. (The British did lose three fighters at Akyab, with two pilots surviving. In turn, they claimed a Hayabusa shot down, plus other probables.) Of this engagement, the Japanese historian relates that five Hayabusas had occasion to go into "a defensive circle" — what western pilots knew as a Lufbery Circle — in which each pilot protected the tail of the plane in front, the formation apparently stacked up vertically.

Afterward, the historian relates how "the Kato troop was happily talking and remembering" the battle. The "2nd Chutai tried to make themselves look like the enemy troop and shot down heavily-gunned fighter planes." I assume this mock combat was just talk, on the ground, but it's not clear. "Thus they proudly encouraged" themselves.

On March 27, after spy planes had discovered a "British secret field" near Akyab, the 64th Sentai sent 18 planes over the Arakan mountains at 2:20 p.m. Tokyo time. (Note that Kato's group had now almost made good the damage suffered at Chiang Mai, with 7 more planes back in service. Though the Allied pilots did not over-claim as heartily as the Japanese, later historians more than made up for the gap. It's frequently written that the entire fighter group at Chiang Mai had to be returned to Japan and rebuilt after its drubbing.) One squadron swept down "super low" to strafe the airfield, while the others stayed higher to engage the Hurricanes that took off. "Brave soldiers fighting even though [it was] very dangerous"; afterward, as the historian notes, they "had a great appetite." Of this battle, one pilot recalled seeing Sergeant Antai "happily pounding himself on the shoulder and chest and sighing to the sky." Afterward, they drank a victory toast of the emperor's wine.

The Japanese claimed several Hurricanes shot down in this raid, with other planes destroyed on the ground. (The British lost one Hurricane, with the pilot surviving; a transport and seven Hurricanes were wrecked on the ground.) The RAF did evacuate the Akyab airfields, though continuing to use them as advance fields for operations in Burma.

Moving north

The Chinese troops holding the line at Toungoo under General Joseph Stilwell now pulled back, meaning that the old AVG training base was in Japanese hands. On the west, the British Commonwealth forces were likewise driven back. The only RAF air defense still in Burma was based at Lashio, the last city before the Burma Road turned east over the mountains into China. For its part, the AVG was based just across the border at Loiwing, China.

As the army moved north, the air force moved with it. On March 29, near Loiwing, the Japanese historian notes that Chuck Older of the AVG's "Hell's Angels" squadron shot down a twin-engine Ki-46 Dinah reconnaissance plane of the 51st Independent Chutai. Elsewhere, the light bombers of the 31st Sentai and a squadron of 77th Sentai fighters attacked British tanks in front of the Japanese army. Medium bombers from the 8th Sentai also joined this attack, "strongly strafing till sunset." One of the Ki-27 Nate pilots "sacrificed himself and was lost," being shot down in flames. However, he was found and saved, though badly wounded.

On March 30, the Japanese occupied Kyedaw airfield at Toungoo and began putting it into service for offensive operations. During the first week of April, JAAF squadrons in Burma were devoted to supporting the army's advance and defending Rangoon from American B-17s attacking from India, while navy aircraft battled the RAF off the island of Ceylon (Sri Lanka).

Meanwhile, the JAAF sent out observation planes to locate the American airfields that had been used to launch the raid on Chiang Mai. The possibilities seemed to be the airstrips at Heho, Loilem, Lashio, Loiwing, Maymyo, and Mandalay. The 62nd Sentai heavy bombers attacked the first two of these, March 28-29, and when the runways were not repaired — indicating that they weren't being used — the Sallys bombed Lashio on March 30 with the same negative result

On April 2, General Obata went to Lampang and drew up a new plan for attacking Loiwing on the Burma-China border. This was indeed the base from which the AVG had launched its raid on Chiang

Mai. For its part, the 64th Sentai sent fighter patrols to Lashio on March 31, to Lashio and Loiwing on April 1, and to Mandalay on April 3. Finding no planes at any of these places, they decided that Mac McGarry had told them the truth and the Americans had all retreated into China.

Lieutenant Hinoki with his Nakajima Hayabusa

Duel Over Loiwing

SHORTLY AFTER NOON on April 8, Colonel Kato and seven other pilots of the 64th Sentai took off from Chiang Mai to raid the Allied airfield at Loiwing, which they had reconnoitered the week before. (This was roughly half the group's fighting strength. The other Hayabusas were escorting bombers to Maymyo, in the continuing effort to destroy any possible airfields being used by the Allied squadrons in Burma.) Unusual for the 64th Sentai, three of the pilots in Kato's formation had never before seen combat. They were replacing experienced pilots who had been called away to provide seasoning to newly formed fighter groups.

As the fighters crossed the China border, Kato heard by radio that a reconnaissance plane had seen 15 "small planes" on the ground at Loiwing. As a result, at 3:15 p.m. Tokyo time, after two hours in the air, the Hayabusas entered the Loiwing airspace at an altitude of 6,000 meters. (About 20,000 feet, though another account puts their altitude a bit higher) The winds were calm; the sky was clear. The Japanese pilots were on high alert, but sure in their minds that they would be facing an unprepared and rich target.

Kato waggled his wings and led most of the Hayabusas down to strafe the enemy airfield, destroying "one large and two small planes" on the ground. (The victims were a British Blenheim bomber and two P-40E Kittyhawks that had spent the night at Loiwing en route to China; they'd been left on the ground because they weren't armed for combat.) Meanwhile, Captain Maruo of the 2nd Chutai was supposed to be flying top cover for Kato's strike force, but for some reason he too came down to strafe. As a result, the entire group found itself at low altitude, "a very disadvantageous position."

As it happened, the American pilots were circling above the raiders, unseen by them. Kato now zoomed up to higher altitude, taking a hit from an assailant he apparently didn't see. (This may have been the 3rd Squadron leader, Arvid Olson, who was the first on the scene and claimed a "Zero" shot down.) Kato's engine began leaking oil, so he left the formation and headed home. The remaining pilots found themselves outnumbered by the enemy, which they reported as 20 Tomahawks. "The proficient pilots tried to help green ones and themselves got killed," as one pilot told the story. Lieutenant Takahasi, whose first battle this was, could think of no other expedient but to loop-the-loop, and after 30 repetitions he found that he had somehow left the battle; he too headed for home.

Among the seasoned pilots who stayed to fight and who died as a result was the 3rd Squadron leader, Captain Anma, who had been credited with 12 kills in China, Malaya, and the Dutch Indies. Also shot down that morning were Sergeant Wada, Lieutenant Kuoki (probably one of the newcomers), and Lieutenant Okumura. That amounted to half the raiding force. One of the returning Hayabusas was riddled with 40 bullet holes, and its pilot may have been wounded. The Japanese pilots apparently made no claims of enemy aircraft shot down in the air.

There was little appetite at dinner that night, as Lieutenant Hinoki Yohei would write in his memoir. Another account has pilots complaining: "The fighting leadership is wrong." As for the commander himself, Kato was "holding his right arm and striking himself, crying that Captain Anma in the China War had made a great contribution.... He expressed great sympathy for the fallen pilots."

This prompted Lieutenant Hinoki to blurt: "There was nothing you could have done."

To which Kato replied: "I'm going back there and attack again. Whatever the hardship, we must not yield. There is always a way!"

For their part, the AVG pilots claimed 12 Hayabusas shot down. Of the Allied aircraft supposedly destroyed on the ground, the actual tally was one Kittyhawk destroyed and another P-40E and the RAF Blenheim lightly damaged.

April 10: the revenge mission

Determined "to do the revenge" for their drubbing at the hands of the American Volunteer Group, Colonel Kato spent the next two days studying weather and geography and drawing up a "secret plan" for a return to Loiwing. One difficulty was posed by the fact that the JAAF calculator wasn't able to compute fuel burn beyond 600 kilometers. The one-way trip was a bit more than that, and of course the Hayabusas also had to fight on their internal fuel supply (on the way *to* the target, they would depend on their drop-tanks). Nevertheless Kato decided to make a return attack, and all his pilots agreed. In the darkness before dawn on April 10, they ate an early breakfast and afterward sat very still, with no one speaking. Their ground crews had been working all night to get 12 Hayabusas ready for the flight.

At 0540 Tokyo time (3:40 a.m. local time), the twelve fighters started down the gravel runway at Chiang Mai. The mission began badly: Captain Maruo crashed into a Ki-21 Sally heavy bomber at the side of the runway, and his two wingmen also cracked up, evidently because of their leader's accident. Then Lieutenant Endo returned to the airport when his engine began to run rough. Endo's wingmen — sergeants Yasuda and Yokoi — tried to pick up the navigation lights of their commander's plane but were misled by stars in the night. When dawn came over the mountains, they realized that they were lost, and so returned to Chiang Mai. That left only six Hayabusas on the mission, led by Colonel Kato.

At 8:05 a.m. Tokyo time, the Hayabusas entered the Loiwing airspace. Kato waggled his wings for the attack, then reached over to shut off his navigation lights — inadvertently turning off his main power switch instead. He counted 23 Tomahawks on the ground. The Hayabusas dove down to 300 meters altitude (about 1,000 feet) and strafed the enemy repeatedly, but the commander's guns of course didn't fire. The pilots saw people on the ground looking up at them: this time, the enemy had indeed been caught flat-footed.

It was "a battle of blood," as the Japanese pilots reported, and they believed that only one or two of the enemy aircraft survived destruction. To their surprise, however, the P-40s didn't explode, presumably because the fuel had been drained from their tanks. Kato waggled his wings for the return to Chiang Mai, and after they joined up, he fired a burst from his guns. Afterward, Lieutenant Hinoki asked him why, and Kato explained that that his guns had been dead throughout the strafing runs. Forming up, he discovered the error when he went to switch on his lights again; he fired the burst to determine whether he had actually done such a stupid thing.

There had been 13 Tomahawks, 7 of the newer and more powerful P-40E Kittyhawks, and 3 RAF Hurricanes on the field that morning. Half were damaged, but most only superficially; only one plane had to be written off. With just one hour's delay, three 1st Squadron pilots took off for the scheduled morning mission.

The Japanese pilots were confident they had destroyed the enemy air force in their surprise raid, and they were exhausted mentally and physically from their four-hour flight. Nevertheless, Colonel Kato decided to make a return attack that same afternoon. This time, just nine Hayabusas took off from Chiang Mai, arriving at Loiwing at 1705 (Tokyo time; 3:05 p.m. local) at an altitude of 5,000 meters in fairly heavy clouds. They were arranged in three flights:

- Colonel Kato, with sergeants Kondo and Goto as his wingmen.
- Lieutenant Hinoki, with sergeants Misago and Saeki as his wingmen.
- Lieutenant Endo, with sergeants Yasuda and Yokoi as his wingmen.

Years later, the battle was recalled in a memoir by Lieutenant Hinoki. To his surprise, as he approached the target, he looked up and saw four enemy aircraft coming out of the clouds above him with the altitude advantage. (The Tomahawks were flown by Frank Lawlor, Bill Reed, Bob Brouk, and R.T. Smith of the AVG 3rd Squadron.) Two P-40s were attacking Endo's flight, whose pilots did not seem to realize their danger. Hinoki therefore jinked in their direction and fired his guns. The Tomahawks dove down and away, with Hinoki after them. They dodged into the clouds, in and out, ten times or more at low altitude.

Hinoki caught a glimpse of a wing nearby in the clouds and fired at it. The enemy pilot fired at him at the same moment. (Hinoki's antagonist was almost certainly R. T. Smith, whose recollection of this combat matches Hinoki's like one map transparency laid over another.) Hinoki heard bullets tearing through his plane, and he found that his face was covered with blood. Believing that it was the end, he "decided to die in the mountains," and flew off toward the nearest peak. His Hayabusa had been hit in the right wing, and fuel was spilling out but did not burn.

The Tomahawks still pursued him, but two Hayabusas came after them and engaged them. One was evidently flown by his wingman, Sergeant Misago. Hinoki signaled farewell to his friends and continued toward his chosen resting place in the hills. Again a Tomahawk fired at him, and again he heard the bullets ripping through. Both wingtips disintegrated. The Tomahawk then broke off.

Hinoki looked down and saw the Salween River, the agreed-upon rendezvous for their return to Chiang Mai. Realizing that both the

Hayabusa and he still seemed to be functioning, he decided to forego suicide for the moment and instead attempt to fly back to Chiang Mai. Throughout the two-hour flight, he worried about his fuel supply, meanwhile suffering extreme pain from his wounds. Finally he saw the airport ahead. In his final glide onto the runway, his engine cut out and he made a dead-stick landing with dry fuel tanks. The ground crew counted 21 bullet holes in the Hayabusa's fuselage, and Hinoki himself was wounded in the back.

As Colonel Kato recalled the battle, he zoomed back to altitude when the Tomahawks first appeared. After 15 minutes of combat, the enemy aircraft disappeared and he signaled for a return to base. They headed south. After flying for five minutes, Kato noticed an enemy aircraft following them. Sergeant Goto, in the rearmost plane of the commander's flight, evidently did not see the danger, so Kato turned and took up an attack position — too late. Goto was shot down, crashing 10 kilometers southeast of Loiwing. Again, there is virtually no question but that R. T. Smith shot down Goto.

Sergeant Misago also did not return from this battle. In the first engagement, when Hinoki had dashed to the rescue of Sergeant Endo's flight, Misago had stayed as top cover and lost sight of his leader because of scattered clouds. Misago found Hinoki again when he was already hit by R.T. Smith's P-40 and trailing fuel. Then Misago saw that two more P-40s were about to attack Hinoki. He drove them off, but a P-40 (probably flown by Bob Brouk) attacked him from out of the sun. When last seen by his comrades, the left wing fuel tank of his Hayabusa was burning and he was going down to a corner of the enemy airfield.

Sergeant Yasuda and Lieutenant Endo each claimed a P-40 in the battle. (The AVG lost no aircraft on April 10, but two RAF Hurricanes went down, so this may have been a rare case of accurate reporting of aerial combat.) Having exhausted his ammunition and lost his flight leader, Yasuda turned south toward Thailand. Suddenly he "found some orange balls" in front of him and felt some hits on his airplane. He saw a P-40 about 600 meters behind him, and maneuvered to evade it. The enemy aircraft was then joined by another, and the limping Hayabusa struggled to survive against the two P-40s (flown by Chuck Older and Duke Hedman of the AVG 3rd Squadron) for 30 minutes. Yasuda's mouth was dry, his throat sore, and he found it difficult to breathe. Finally he escaped, his plane trailing oil. But he managed to fly one and half hours more. One thousand meters short of Chiang Mai airfield, his engine quit, and he landed dead stick on the runway with 17 hits on his plane. (Older and Hedman were credited with one "Zero" shot down.)

The 64th Sentai lost two planes in the afternoon raid, with two more damaged during the battle, in exchange for two confirmed kills which were credited to Lieutenant Endo and Sergeant Yasuda.

Too badly wounded to be treated in the Chiang Mai infirmary, Lieutenant Hinoki was evacuated to a hospital in Bangkok. After a month of treatment and convalescence, he was discharged on May 18, went to Don Muang airport, and caught a flight to Toungoo, where the 64th Sentai was now located.

The great Lashio Turkey Shoot

Following Jimmy Doolittle's B-25 raid on the Japanese homeland on April 9, 1942, the Japanese Army Air Force was told to beef up its home defense formations, with the result that the 47th Independent Chutai flew back to Japan. Similarly, JAAF squadrons in China were moved about as part of an effort to roll back the line of airfields that Chennault and the Chinese had established within striking distance of Japan. The squadrons in Burma were also repositioned as a result of the new realities there.

By the beginning of April, the motorized 56th Division on the Japanese right flank was in position to threaten Lashio, the last Allied stronghold before the Chinese frontier. The plan was to prepare for the army's main force by dropping parachute troops, who were training at Phnom Penh in Cambodia. On April 12, they flew to Rangoon and were attached to the 5th Hikodan at Mingaladon airport. Their orders were to land and capture Lashio on April 29 — the Emperor Hirohito's birthday. The drop would consist of 440 jumpers in 40 license-built Lockheed transports, built by Kawasaki and designated "Type LO." The unit's heavy gear would be dropped by Sally bombers adapted as cargo planes.

In the center, meanwhile, the Japanese 55th Division advanced north along the Sittang River into Pyinmana with the help of the 50th Sentai fighters and 8th Sentai medium bombers in close cooperation. By April 20 the front had moved far enough that the 64th Sentai

Hayabusas and the 98th Sentai heavy bombers were able to take up residence at Toungoo airfield, the former AVG training base on the Sittang River, moving there from their previous bases in Thailand.

And on the left flank the Japanese 33rd Division captured Magwe airfield on April 17 and the Yennanyuang oilfields on April 20. That enabled the 77th Sentai fighters and the 31st Sentai light bombers to take up new quarters at Magwe, recently evacuated by the Allied air squadrons. Also at Magwe was the 70th Independent Chutai, probably a ground-cooperation squadron. The plan for cleaning the Allies out of Burma was "all on schedule," wrote a Japanese historian.

Except for occasional skirmishes with the enemy air force, most JAAF activity during these two weeks concentrated on supporting the ground forces as they finished the conquest of central Burma. While of great interest to the men involved, I skip these battles since they didn't involve air-to-air combat with the AVG — which, for its part, was also concentrating on carrying out ground-support missions for the Chinese army. The Japanese records do confirm that the AVG shot down a handful of reconnaissance and ground cooperation aircraft during this period, but there are no details in the Japanese record because there were no witnesses.

In preparation for the airborne assault on Lashio, Colonel Kato's 64th Sentai probed that city on the three preceding days. On April 28, 20 of his Hayabusa fighters also escorted 24 Sally bombers from the 12th Sentai with the intention of bombing Loiwing. Meanwhile, the paratroops moved up to Toungoo by rail, ready for their big day on the 29th.

This activity set the stage for what the AVG believed was one of its greatest victories over the Japanese in Burma. Later, Chennault would write that the battle represented a JAAF effort to achieve a big Emperor's Birthday victory for Hirohito. That it took place a day before the actual date, he explained as a Japanese effort to achieve surprise — a bit of a stretch. Foreseeing exactly this, he wrote, he positioned his squadrons to meet them at Lashio. According to the AVG tally, 13 "Zeroes" were shot down in a wide-ranging combat, with no losses to the Tomahawks and Kittyhawks engaged.

Seen from the Japanese viewpoint, April 28 was indeed a defeat, but it was far from the rout shown in the AVG records. The escorting Hayabusas were at 3,000 meters (about 10,000 feet) when they sighted 12 P-40s catching up to them from approximately 1,000 meters behind and an estimated 2,400 meters above. In fact, there were 10 Tomahawks and 4 P-40E Kittyhawks at various altitudes. The first to engage was Tex Hill's flight of Kittyhawks; Hill reported that he spotted the Japanese formation below him and on the reciprocal course. As he led his element down to attack the bombers, he saw six "Zeros" drop their auxiliary fuel tanks and turn to meet him.

As the Japanese reported the engagement, the four trailing Hayabusas immediately began to spiral up to meet the attackers, while the Ki-21 Sallys began their bombing run. (Among the Allied aircraft on the ground that day was a Douglas C-47 piloted by Colonel Robert Scott, who later commanded the 23rd Fighter Group that succeeded the AVG in China.) This was the 3rd Chutai under the command of Captain Kuroe Yasuhiko, formerly of the 47th Independent Chutai. He had stayed in Burma when his squadron was ordered home, and he was replacing Captain Anma, killed at Loiwing on April 8. A veteran of air combat in China and in the Nomonhan border war with Russia, Kuroe would end the war as one of the JAAF's leading aces, credited with 30 victories; postwar, he would become a jet pilot and group commander in the Japan Self Defense Force, only to be killed in a fishing accident.

In the battle, the Hayabusa flown by Corporal Hirano was apparently hit in one wing (Tex Hill and Lew Bishop both claimed kills in this encounter) with the result that the wing came off. According to his squadron mates, Hirano's plane was shot up by one P-40 and then collided with another; but the AVG pilots reported no such collision, and more likely the Hayabusa was crippled by the same structural weakness that had caused the group's retractable-gear fighters to shed wings from the first day of the war. Hirano bailed out, landed safely, and eventually joined up with the advancing 56th Division ground troops.

Later, Captain Kuroe and his remaining two pilots encountered a pair of P-40s, which feinted toward him and then turned away toward a lone Hayabusa. This was the plane flown by 1st Lieutenant Kataoka Masashi of the 3rd Chutai, who had broken flight discipline and left his squadron in search of enemy aircraft. He was shot down and killed. (The P-40s might have been flown by Parker Dupouy and Tom Haywood, or perhaps by Paul Greene and R.T. Smith. Both flights claimed a "Zero" in circumstances like this one.) Kataoka was a graduate of the 53rd class of the Japanese Army Military Academy, where he had learned to fly.

Back at Toungoo, Captain Kuroe apologized to Colonel Kato for breaking formation to engage the fighters. "We knew you were battling the enemy," Kato replied, "but we did not come to help because the principle was to protect the bombers.... Forget those pilots. Work for the group."

Next day, the Emperor's Birthday jump into Lashio was foiled by bad weather. Of 100 aircraft that set out from Mingaladon and Toungoo, only 4 light bombers managed to reach Lashio, to support the 56th Division when it stormed into the city at noon.

A Japanese artist's conception of the duel between Major Kato and Sergeant McLuckie, as shown on the cover of Hinoki Yohei's memoir of the 64th Sentai; reprinted with permission.

Last Days in Burma

IN THE EVENING OF MAY 3, the Japanese Army 56th Division captured the American base and factory at Loiwing, with 6 Tomahawks on the "production line" and sufficient parts to build 20 more. This was a factory belonging to the Central Aircraft Manufacturing Company that served as the AVG's housekeeping unit. CAMCO had assembled the Tomahawks in Rangoon the previous year, and its Loiwing factory had since been turned into a repair facility. The P-40s were wrecks trucked up from Rangoon in March, or brought in for repair more recently. (Another account says the Japanese found 22 burned airplanes at Loiwing.) The AVG, meanwhile, had pulled back into China, where they could "get more Chinese soldiers to help them." Their new base was at Baoshan.

The JAAF pursued the AVG to China next day. Taking off from Mingaladon airport near Rangoon, Ki-21 heavy bombers of the 98th Sentai attacked Baoshan with an escort of 64th Sentai Ki-43s. They reported being met by two AVG P-40s. "Lots of bullets" sprayed the heavy bombers, with one Sally destroyed and several damaged with three crew members badly wounded. Their return fire (or, more likely, the escorting Hayabusas) damaged the armor plate on Charlie Bond's P-40 and forced him to make a parachute landing. Though grazed by bullets and burned when his plane caught fire, Bond landed safely in a Chinese graveyard. He was the only Flying Tiger pilot to get off the ground that day.

On May 5 a return visit was spoiled by an overnight raid on Mingaladon by an American B-17 Flying Fortress based in India, which destroyed two heavy bombers on the ground, damaged at least 10 more, and also destroyed a cargo plane. Thus it was only fighter planes and light bombers that attacked Baoshan, with dismal results: the 27th Sentai (newly arrived from China) lost two Ki-30 Ann light bombers, the 11th Sentai three or four of its Ki-27 Nate fighters while claiming two P-40s shot down, and the 64th Sentai one Hayabusa damaged or destroyed in a crash landing on its return from Baoshan. The Flying Tigers meanwhile claimed 7 Japanese planes destroyed — fairly close to the mark — while losing no aircraft of their own.

On May 9, Royal Air Force Blenheim bombers, based in India, launched their first raid on Japanese bases in Burma, destroying four

77th Sentai fighters and a Lockheed transport on the ground at Magwe. This was followed by a second raid on Magwe and another on Akyab, on the west coast of Burma. The 64th Sentai therefore moved cross-country from Toungoo to defend Akyab, arriving just in time to encounter an attack by a British Lockheed Hudson, for all practical purposes the same plane as the Type LO Electra the group was using to transport its ground crews and equipment. It was now the rainy season in Burma, with high temperatures and high humidity; many of the airmen came down with dengue fever, including Colonel Kato. "Many soldiers lost their physical condition and also their spirit," as the Japanese historian notes.

Again, the Akyab garrison was attacked by a Hudson on May 17. The 64th Sentai was caught by surprise — "in a mess," says the historian — and one pilot was wounded. The Hayabusas were unable to catch the British plane, which flew 50 meters above the water, too low for them to get a favorable attack position from below. (The Hudson evidently was lost, either to battle damage or mechanical breakdown, because it did not return to base.) The British attacked two more times over the next two days, but the 64th Sentai was able to strengthen its Akyab garrison with Colonel Kato and six other pilots who flew over from Toungoo.

Heavy rains gave a respite, but the weather broke on May 21, when the British returned. Kato and six others chased them across the Bay of Bengal to Chittagong, but lost them in clouds. Returning empty-handed, they lost one of their number when Lieutenant Shimizu — out of fuel or experiencing an engine breakdown — parachuted from his plane into the palm trees on the Burma shores. Kato led a search for him without success. At Akyab, the 64th Sentai was almost out of ammunition and food, with their meals now down to eggplant eaten raw or boiled in salt water for breakfast and again for dinner. Next day, May 22, Kato waited until 2 p.m. Tokyo time, hoping Shimizu would walk in or be reported by the Burmese volunteers who were searching for him. At this moment, the main RAF base at Akyab, which the 64th Sentai had recently abandoned in favor of the dispersal field, was bombed by a lone RAF Blenheim.

The 64th Sentai pilots took off in pursuit of the attacker, catching the Blenheim over the water. This was the plane flown by Warrant Officer M.H. Huggard of RAF 60 Squadron, who flew at wave-top height to prevent the enemy fighters from getting beneath him, and to give the best defensive position to his turret gunner, Flight Sergeant John McLuckie. (60 Squadron had been based at Rangoon until it moved back to Magwe and finally to India earlier in the spring.)

Sergeant Yasuda was the first to attack. His Hayabusa was badly damaged by McLuckie's twin Browning machineguns, so he peeled off and returned to Akyab. The second to attack was Captain Otami, who made some hits but in turn had his fuel tank holed; he followed Yasuda back to base. Otami's plane was a write-off.

Colonel Kato now attacked the Blenheim in his turn, to become the third Hayabusa winged by the aptly-named McLuckie. As seen by the Japanese pilots who had not yet joined the combat, his right wing burst into flame. Realizing he was doomed, as the story is told in Japanese accounts, Kato did a wing-over and dove into the sea, "thus dying a noble death" of his own choosing — a phrase that regularly appears in popular Japanese histories of the Pacific War. The score: McLuckie 3, JAAF 0. (See page 185 for a Japanese artist's conception of this encounter.)

Kato died at 2:30 p.m. Tokyo time, 10 kilometers west of Asanyo, Burma. In their grief, the remaining pilots let the Blenheim escape (though some Japanese accounts claim wrongly that Kato shot it down), and returned to Akyab with the news of "the hero's sacrifice." As the Japanese historian relates, they wept and struck their shoulders as they told the story. Kato became the first Japanese army officer to be promoted posthumously two grades instead of the customary one, from lieutenant colonel to brigadier general. One account of his death ends with these words:

"The spirit of fighting in the Japanese air force was shaken. Everyone was crying with sadness, and the fighting spirit was down."

I often think of Flight Sergeant McLuckie's clean sweep when aviation buffs scoff at the notion of rear-facing, rifle-caliber, flexible guns on a bomber or scout plane, as compared to the more and usually heavier fixed guns on the attacking fighters. Real life is very different than a scenario on a computer screen!

And of course it wasn't just luck that brought Colonel Kato down. After I published this account on the Annals of the Flying Tigers, I was pleased to get an email from Keith McLuckie, the gunner's son.

He pointed out that his father was meticulous about maintaining his Browning machineguns, and that he daily practiced with a shotgun on moving targets, honing the distance required to bring down a bird — or an enemy fighter plane. The same was true after he returned to civilian life: "He rarely missed and was annoyed with himself if given the opportunity he missed a 'left and right,' meaning one bird with the left barrel and one with the right using a double barrel shotgun."

Keith's email continued:

"In his description of the action my dad said he shot at and hit two of the flight of five Hayabusas and they turned back and the other three hung back.... It was then Kato came in slightly from the side and rear almost level and turning. Dad said he just started firing at the point in space where Kato was committed to fly through and he saw the wing, engine canopy and cockpit hit by his fire. It seemed likely from this account that Kato was dead before he hit the water. I believe it was this sight of death that made my dad reluctant to speak about the action for the rest of his life.... My dad wasn't clear what had happened ... because he was worried about the other two Hayabusas. However, shortly after that the other two turned and left for their base."

Final tally of the Burma campaign

With the Allies having retreated into China and India, and the rainy season in full force, the air war in Burma was effectively over. The JAAF fighter squadrons now regrouped, several of them returning to Japan to re-equip. This was the final tally of their losses, from December 11 to June 10:

- The **77th Sentai** had lost 16 pilots, including one who survived as a prisoner of war, another who died from wounds, and two who were shot down by ground fire. Altogether, 18 of its Ki-27 fighters were lost in combat.
- The **50th Sentai**, with two squadrons in Burma, had lost 9 pilots and 8 Ki-27s in combat.
- The **11th Sentai** had lost 5 pilots and 5 Ki-27s.
- The **64th Sentai** had lost 11 pilots, including one taken prisoner, along with 13 Ki-43 Hayabusa fighters. Two other fighters crashed after experiencing engine problems, for a total of 15 aircraft, several of them to British bomber gunners.

- And the **47th Independent Chutai** had lost 1 plane and its pilot.

Making a total of 42 fighter pilots who were killed, captured, or died of wounds, and 47 fighter planes destroyed by enemy aircraft, ground fire, or crash landings after combat.

These numbers pale beside the victories claimed by the AVG Flying Tigers, and to a lesser extent the claims of British Commonwealth pilots who fought in Burma. But remember that, if the Anglo-American pilots over-claimed, their exaggerations were dwarfed by those of the Japanese airmen who met them in combat.

AVG Confidential: A Flying Tiger Reports to the U.S. Navy, April 1942

Becoming a Flying Tiger

LIKE MANY OF THE "Flying Tigers" of the Second World War, Noel Bacon was an engaging young man from the heartland of America. Born in June 1917, he grew up in Randalia (population 125 at the time, but only half as many today) in the flatlands of northeastern Iowa. Corn and soybeans were the crops that kept Randalia in business. Officially, it was a city, and Noel's mother was the mayor. There were two boys in the family; their father died when they were small, and Mrs. Bacon later married a pharmacist from a neighboring town.

Noel joined the Boy Scouts, played the clarinet, and joined the Randalia High School basketball team, such as it was. Less predictably, he had his first taste of flight. In 1930, when he was thirteen, he met Slim Freitag, who played the trombone for a mid-western dance band, and who also piloted a small plane owned by Charles Correll, then famous for playing Andy Brown in the nationally syndicated "Amos 'n' Andy" sitcom. One of the first radio comedy series, the show was hugely popular in the 1930s and 1940s, but would be condemned as racist today, with white actors portraying sterotypical black residents of Harlem.

"Slim and I struck up a friendship," Noel recalled years later, "and I would hitchhike into Chicago and spend a weekend with him. We would fly around Chicago in Charles Correll's airplane, and I got enthused about flying. That's how it all got started."

Noel went off to Iowa State Teachers College in Cedar Falls, now the University of Northern Iowa. Here he seems to have joined every organization in sight, including the marching band and the mostly male "Pep" squad. He also worked on the *College Eye* student newspaper, which a few years later would remember him this way:

The young man is none other than smiling, taciturn Noel Bacon, the boy who in 1938, as head cheerleader for Teachers College, broke the ladies' hearts, and set the stands yelling themselves hoarse for their alma mater.

After receiving his Bachelor of Science degree in commercial studies in June 1938, Noel taught high-school business classes for a year in Soldier, Iowa. This was a somewhat more substantial "city" than his hometown, north of Omaha, Nebraska.

In 1939, with war clouds over Europe and Asia, Noel followed the example of thousands of young Americans, leaving home to become a military pilot – in his case, a naval aviator. (The U.S. Navy reserved the title of "pilot" for the specialist who guides ships into harbor.) His brother Royden also went into Navy officer training about this time.

Noel learned to fly at Pensacola, Florida, winning his "wings of gold" and an ensign's commission in April 1940. His assignment was a good one, to America's first purpose-built aircraft carrier, USS *Ranger*, which was then assigned to what was euphemistically called the "neutrality patrol," combing the Atlantic Ocean from Bermuda to Newfoundland.

In the summer of 1940, the view from the White House was a bleak one. In Asia, Japan had set up a puppet government in Manchuria, fought a bloody border war with the Soviet Union, seized much of seacoast China and its fertile Yangtze River valley, and invaded what we now know as Vietnam, then the French colony of Indochina. In Europe, Germany had conquered most of the continent, leaving a few scraps to be taken by Italy and a larger portion by the Soviet Union. The only significant capitals still standing were Chongqing, ruled by the Chinese dictator Chiang Kai-shek; and London, where the redoubtable Winston Churchill had pitted his country's arms and his own splendid oratory against the German onslaught.

President Franklin Roosevelt was determined to aid these very different allies any way he could. With astonishing chutzpah, he drew a line at mid-Atlantic, from Iceland to the Azores, and declared that anything west of that line belonged to the United States. It was *Ranger's* task, along with U.S. Navy destroyers, to patrol this vast expanse of ocean so as to safeguard freighters heading for England from submarine attack. The Americans weren't to attack the subs: if found, they were to be shadowed and their position reported to Washington "in the clear." Royal Navy destroyers could then listen to the transmissions, intercept the German subs, and sink them.

Roosevelt also turned a blind eye to the hundreds of American military pilots who resigned their commissions, joined the British and Canadian air forces, and fought the German *Luftwaffe*. Soon enough, he would sign on to an even more audacious plan to bolster the Chinese Air Force.

Ranger bore the hull designation of CV-4, and her air squadrons were therefore VF-4 for fighters, VB-4 for bombers. Noel was assigned to "Fighting Four," piloting the stubby, radial-engine Grumman F4F-2 Wildcat, arguably the best American fighter plane of 1940. It was armed with four fifty-caliber (half-inch) machineguns, at a time when U.S. Army fighters relied on just one or two "fifties" and a few thirty-caliber guns.

"Bombing Four" flew the Vought SB2U Vindicator, soon to be replaced by the much more formidable Douglas SBD Dauntless dive bomber. Among the VB-4 aviators were David "Tex" Hill and Eddie Rector. Early in 1941, when *Ranger* was docked at Norfolk Naval Base for resupply, they were approached by a retired Navy commander, Rutledge Irvine. Would they be interested in going to Asia? He explained that the government of China would pay them $600 a month – a fabulous salary in 1940, with the Great Depression barely over, and double what they were earning from the U.S. Navy – and a combat bonus of $500 for each Japanese plane they shot down. To put these sums in perspective, a Manhattan hotel room could be rented for two dollars a night in the spring of 1941.

"Well, hell, we're interested," Tex replied.

Not only Hill and Rector, but John Petach and Bert Christman from Bombing Four signed on to join the American Volunteer Group, as it was called, and so in time did Noel Bacon from Fighting Four. Though they believed they were working for China, the AVG was in fact a covert operation, run by the White House through a front organization called China Defense Supplies, whose lawyer was the President's uncle. Years later, Noel would explain what inspired him to join the AVG:

> The Japanese pilots were meeting no resistance at all and were having a heyday. Japan was just sweeping through China. At the same time, there was tremendous American sympathy for China. Eventually the idea was sold to Franklin D. Roosevelt, who

authorized the release of 100 military pilots and 100 P-40s to help the Chinese.

It was pretty damn exciting to think about going to the other side of the world. I don't think any one of us who signed up gave much serious consideration that we'd be shot at.

On July 8, 1941, a cold and foggy morning, Noel Bacon passed beneath San Francisco's Golden Gate Bridge aboard the Dutch liner *Jaegersfontein*. He had mixed feelings about leaving the country, because at some point in the past few months he had met and fallen in love with Elizabeth Jane Kennedy, the daughter of a Navy medical officer. "I only hope the little Honey waits for me," he wrote in his diary as he left.

The *Jaegersfontein* contingent – thirty-seven pilots, eighty-four clerks and ground crew, and two women nurses – had a riotous layover in Singapore, then continued to Burma on a coastwise steamer, *Penang Trader*, which landed them at Rangoon on July 28. Their final destination was a Royal Air Force base at Toungoo, one hundred and seventy-five miles upcountry. There they trained through the summer and fall, their numbers growing as additional contingents arrived from the United States.

In September, Noel flew the Curtiss P-40 for the first time. A very different beast than the stubby Grumman Wildcat, the long-nosed U.S. Army fighter had been dubbed "Tomahawk" by the British, who purchased it in quantity for their fighter squadrons in North Africa, meanwhile reserving their own Hawker Hurricane and especially the Supermarine Spitfire to defend the home island. Of the British production run, at the request of the White House, one hundred Tomahawks were diverted to Rangoon to equip the American Volunteer Group. These were basically the "B" model of the P-40, a pretty plane with two fifty-caliber machineguns synchronized to fire through the propeller arc, plus four thirty-caliber guns in the wings. However, the planes had been altered to suit British requirements, and some standard equipment was missing, a combination that would lead to endless technical difficulties in readying them for combat.

Noel and most of the other Navy aviators were chosen for the AVG Second Squadron under the command of Jack Newkirk, "a persuasive guy," as Noel described him; "gets along with people better than anybody in the outfit. He is at home anywhere."

The war broke upon the Flying Tigers (the name was bestowed on them by the lads at China Defense Supplies in Washington) on December 8, local time, while they were still training at Toungoo. One squadron moved down to Rangoon's Mingaladon Airport to support 67 Squadron RAF, defending Burma with a handful of pilots and planes. The other AVG squadrons moved up to Kunming, at the far end of the fabled "Burma Road" that supplied war material to China. The Americans' mission was to protect this supply route from Japanese bombing attack. For the time being, however, most of the fighting was at Rangoon, so Claire Chennault, the AVG commander, rotated his squadrons through that hotspot.

At the end of December 1941, it was the turn of Jack Newkirk and his Navy aviators. Two vicious air battles over the Burmese capital at Christmas had persuaded the Japanese Army Air Force to back off, turning instead to night bombing. Newkirk therefore took take the battle to the enemy, strafing Japanese airfields across the border in Thailand, often in cooperation with 67 Squadron, whose pilots were mostly from New Zealand, and whose planes were American-built Brewster Buffaloes, intended for the Navy but no longer in front-line service on American carriers. The Buffalo was a much inferior plane to the Grumman Wildcat Noel had flown from USS *Ranger*.

He made his first combat foray on January 9, 1942, attacking a dirt airfield at Tak, recently constructed near the Thai-Burma border. (The Japanese knew this field as Raheng.) As Noel described the mission in his diary:

> I was sick last night (dysentery). Today I feel like hell. Jack Newkirk was called to Operations at noon – some deal on. We took off at 4:30 p.m. (seven P-40s and six Buffaloes) to strafe Tak.
>
> We dove out of the sun and strafed the whole field. I got one fighter (an I-96) and a truck. We returned to satellite [dispersal field] at 6:40 p.m. and I found two holes in my plane (7.7 calibre).

The Americans claimed three fighters destroyed on the ground at Tak, with two attributed to the squadron leader and the third divided between Noel Bacon and Bob Layher. As was typical of aerial combat during the Second World War, this was something of an exaggeration. Japanese records show just one fighter plane destroyed at Tak that afternoon, plus a second fighter "disabled" – along with the starter truck, no small loss to a force that relied on an external source for firing up its engines. They belonged to the 77th Sentai, a combat force somewhat smaller than an American group or British wing.

Japanese equipment was often identified by its year of adoption, using a calendar dating from the mythical founding of the Imperial line in 660 BC. By "I-96," Noel meant the open-cockpit Mitsubishi A5M, which the Japanese Navy had adopted in the year 2596 (1936 by western reckoning) and accordingly known as Type 96 Carrier Fighter. This was a common error among western pilots, who did not understand that the Japanese army and navy each had its own distinct air force, and that they usually did not operate in the same geographical area. The 77th Sentai was an army unit, and Noel's target was the slightly more modern Nakajima Ki-27, with a protective canopy for the pilot but still with fixed landing gear. It was also called the Type 97 Army Fighter – "I-97" to the Americans.

Not for another two weeks did Noel earn his first air-to-air victory, the traditional test of a fighter pilot. In the morning of January 23, 1942, he set off as part of an escort for RAF bombers raiding Tak, but the mission was scrubbed when the weather turned bad. Noel brought his flight back to the dispersal field, north of Mingaladon airport:

> I landed the group at satellite and we gassed up five P-40s, just in time to engage twenty-five Jap fighters. We got four of them. We went back to Rangoon, serviced [the Tomahawks] and answered an alarm at 12:30 p.m.

The morning fracas involved the 50th Sentai, another Japanese Army fighter group. Altogether, the Americans claimed six Ki-27s shot down, and the RAF pilots another, though only two of the Japanese fighters were actually lost.

George Rodger of *Life* magazine was visiting the Rangoon airfield that morning, and he photographed six AVG pilots examining the rudder from a Ki-27. "This is an extremely handy group of men," Rodger wrote in the caption. Noel was among them, wearing sunglasses, overseas cap, and a radio headset, because he was serving as Operations officer while his Tomahawk – fuselage number 59 – was being repaired. For that reason, he was late taking off for the 12:30 scramble:

I was held up because a new starter was being installed in old 59. I got out ten minutes after the others. Had a radio report informing me: "The bandits are northeast of the base." I headed that way, hoping to join the other P-40s. Soon I saw twelve Jap bombers. Our boys were attacking them.

I came in on the bombers' beam and fell in behind them, just as they dropped their explosives.... I dodged the bombs as they dropped and, still climbing, found four Jap fighters (I-96s) over me. Down they came and I got one head-on. He spun in aflame. It was most encouraging to me. I dove out ... and came back up, firing on the bomber formation, bow to stern.

The other three I-96s jumped me again, and the sky looked like it was full of them. Got another one head-on and dove out with one on my tail. He put twelve slugs in [my plane]: one across the top of the engine, one through the cockpit at my right heel and the rest in my gas tanks and wings.

The raiders were twelve single-engine Mitsubishi Ki-30 light bombers, escorted by fighters from the 77th Sentai – the same group Noel had strafed on the ground on January 9. The Americans claimed no fewer than thirteen enemy aircraft shot down, including two by Noel Bacon – his first air-to-air victories, duly confirmed by the British commander at Mingaladon. The cost however was high. Bert Christman, Noel's shipmate from USS *Ranger*, was killed while parachuting from his crippled Tomahawk, and the RAF also lost a pilot, Colin Pinckney of 67 Squadron, flying one of the Buffaloes. Three Tomahawks were forced down with battle damage though without injury to the pilots, Squadron Leader Jack Newkirk among them.

As often happened in the Rangoon combats, both sides celebrated January 23 as a victory. In the morning, the 50th Sentai pilots reported shooting down two Tomahawks, one Buffalo, and a "Spitfire." (This last was probably one of the first Hawker Hurricane fighters to reach Rangoon. They sortied that morning, and the RAF squadron leader suffered some battle damage, but the British pilots did their best to avoid combat because they were still burdened with the bolt-on ferry tanks that had enabled them to fly from India to Burma.) In the afternoon combat, the 77th Sentai pilots claimed eight Tomahawks shot down.

Alarms and scrambles became a regular feature of life at Mingaladon airport and the dispersal fields, as Japanese bomber and fighter units tried to wear the Allied defenders down in advance of a ground invasion from Thailand and Malaya. Thus it came to January 29, when Noel chalked up his final air-to-air victory:

> Another alarm at 3:15 p.m. We went up to 19,000 feet northwest of the base and ran into twenty-four Jap Navy fighters. When the Japs dived on our planes Jack Newkirk and a wingman climbed and dove on them.
>
> The dives brought the Japs and Newkirk and his wingman under me, so my wingman and I jumped the Japs. I made a pass, went into a cloud, turned while in it and climbed again and attacked.
>
> One Jap turned up at me and I got a 45-degree shot in his bow. His prop immediately began to windmill and he started to spiral down. I dove through the clouds and met him beneath them. He was still in a slow spiral. I dove on his tail and opened all guns, setting fire to his left [fuel] tank. I went on past and saw the pilot was dead.
>
> I watched him crash and burn ten miles northeast of the base, then I followed another little old devil out over the bay. He was running for home, and I got too eager and lost him.

Again the enemy was the 77th Sentai, this time with twenty Ki-27s. They were intercepted by eight Tomahawks and two RAF Hurricanes. Jack Newkirk's pilots were credited with five Nakajimas shot down, including one for Noel Bacon. The AVG First Squadron was also being phased into combat at Rangoon at the end of January, and its pilots were credited with no fewer than *nine* enemy aircraft. Alas for the American claims, the 77th Sentai lost just four planes that afternoon. That was bad enough, bringing its total losses to twelve planes shot down and six more burned on the ground in strafing raids – one-third of its strength, in six weeks of combat with the defenders of Rangoon.

For the fortunate among war veterans, the fear and exhaustion of combat fade from memory as the years go by, until only the exhilaration remains. Forty-four years later, Noel would tell the story of his month in Rangoon as entirely upbeat:

> We'd scramble and get our planes up and wait for the Japanese bombers and go down and just pick 'em off. Boy, the Japanese pilots were gung-ho. Our attacks didn't scatter their bombers,

didn't bother them. But more often than not, we got every damn one of them before they got to the port of Rangoon.

This was exciting, exciting, exciting! All of us were 23 to 25 years old at the most and we were on the other side of the world fighting the Japanese. Our flying skills were honed by a lot of close calls.

Jack Newkirk's squadron was pulled back to Kunming on February 4. (The replacements included Greg Boyington, future Medal of Honor winner and commander of the Marine Corps' "Black Sheep" squadron. He was credited with his first air-to-air victory on February 2.) About this time, as the head of AVG veterans' group told me when I was researching the history of the Flying Tigers, Noel was granted home leave to see his father, who was ailing. He evidently parted on good terms with Claire Chennault, for the Old Man entrusted him with a packet of mail to take back to the United States.

Noel flew out of Kunming on February 19. "My ticket to the United States," he wrote in his diary, "cost $2,785 (Chinese). My excess baggage cost $1,980 (Chinese)." In greenback dollars, that came to $95.30, not an insubstantial sum in 1942 — the equivalent today would be $1,600. On the other hand, Noel had $1,750 in his combat bonus account in New York City, or nearly $30,000 in our debauched dollars.

He may have been the first American pilot to return from Asia with aerial victories to his credit, and he was certainly one of the earliest, and journalists and military officers alike were anxious to hear what he had to say about the seemingly invincible Japanese air forces. On April 22, at the U.S. Navy's Bureau of Aeronautics in Washington, D.C., he was interviewed for the record. Fifteen years ago, that interview was discovered in the National Archives by the historian John Lundstrom, who passed it on to me. I have corrected typographical errors in the transcript, and added some context in the form of bracketed words and the occasional paragraph in italic font. Otherwise the words are is just as Noel Bacon and his questioners spoke them, that hot spring day in Washington, less than five months after the United States was plunged into the Second World War. – *Daniel Ford, March 2022*

The 'Confidential' Interview

IN THE INTERVIEW that follows, at least three officers are questioning Noel Bacon: a Navy commander, a Marine Corps colonel, and a Marine major, all apparently aviators. The speaker is never identified, and because different individuals are asking questions, the conversation sometimes darts off in a different direction or reverts to something that was said before. Any words in square brackets, and any paragraphs in italics, have been added by me. - *Daniel Ford*

Interview of Flight Leader Bacon
AVG Pilot
In the Bureau of Aeronautics
22 April 1942

Interviewer: How does the speed of the P-40 compare with the Japanese fighters that you saw over Burma?

Bacon: Well, I think we've got easily forty miles on them.

Interviewer: What kind were they?

Bacon: I-96s and I-97s.

Interviewer: No Zeros?

Bacon: No Zeros. Well, one of the boys in the group reported that he contested one Zero and that he stayed in a dogfight with it. The results of which were nothing to boast about on either pilot's part. Evidently it was broken up. I know nothing about it. That's the only Navy "Naught" we saw.

[As noted in the introduction, most Japanese Army Air Force squadrons were equipped with the Nakajima Ki-27, also known as the Type 97 Army Fighter. It was not as fast, sturdy, or heavily armed as the Curtiss P-40. Less often, the AVG encountered the more modern Nakajima Ki-43, which was invariably mistaken for the Mitsubishi A6M – Type Zero Carrier Fighter – which Noel calls a "Naught." - DF]

Interviewer: Did you have any difficulty in keeping your P-40s in commission out there?

Bacon: Definitely.

Interviewer: What were your principal difficulties?

Bacon: Tires, thrust bearings, generator drive gears.

Interviewer: How did the planes themselves, as well as the tires, the brakes – did they stand up all right?

Bacon: Yes.

Interviewer: Did you have air cleaners?

Bacon: Negative. We flew in very little dust, naturally. *[Something about this question, or the questioner, seems to have made Noel uneasy.]* The information that is being recorded is – going to be used against me. Anything I say will be as close to the truth, within reasonable limits, as I can get it.

Interviewer: Is it true that you make only one pass in your P-40s? You do not pull out and go into a dogfight?

Bacon: No. I should say we are forced to employ hit-and-run tactics ... due to the fact that the I-96 and I-97 can outmaneuver us quite easily. We had two [Japanese] planes crash right on the field, one on the runway after it collided with one of our P-40s, and one in a bomb crypt [berms that protected the British bomber aircraft]. We got some good information from that. I'd be only too glad to give you any information regarding the plane's equipment.

Interviewer: No armament, no self-sealing tanks?

Bacon: No. Two small caliber Vickers.

Interviewer: Is that no armor?

Bacon: No armor plate. They had the two Vickers guns synchronized [to fire through the propeller arc].

Interviewer: Radio?

Bacon: It has radio equipment.

[This must be an error, either in Noel's memory or in the transcription, because the Nakajima Ki-27 had no radio. Instead, the pilots relied on visual signals from the flight leader, a major reason for the swarm tactics he later describes. The Japanese fighters had to stay close to one another because otherwise they could not cooperate or follow orders. - DF]

Interviewer: What outfit were you in before you left [the Navy]?

Bacon: Fighting Four.

Interviewer: What were the characteristics of the I-96 or I-97 you shot down?

Bacon: The enemy plane had mechanical brakes, an all metal plane [that is, no fabric surfaces], a camouflage color well known to everybody. The tires on the plane were very small. It had fixed landing gear with pants over the wheel, no tail wheel, the tail [skid is] nothing more than a straight beam with a big ball of metal on the end of it. The plane had trim-tabs all over it. It had flaps, cowl flaps; a fixed pitch screw [propeller]; and an engine like I have never seen before – it wasn't similar to anything I had recognized. The stern end of the crankshaft was covered with a fuel injection unit that was very small in itself, and from that nine individual lines ran to the cylinders, probably about an eighteen-inch line.

The screw on every Japanese plane that I saw come down – all the air screws have an attachment on the leading edge or I should say forward on the hub, like the old automobiles used to have down on their crankshaft to stick a crank in, with two prongs, one on either side, to stick a crank in and twist the thing. Evidently these used some kind of an accessory engine or starting gear, and just stand right out in front of the thing and turn it over, which would scare me to death if I thought that [the pilot] didn't have the brakes locked.

[To save weight, the Nakajima Ki-27 had no battery or starter motor. Instead, the squadron had one or two starter trucks, each with an auxiliary engine in the back and a rod projecting over its cab. The truck driver nosed up to the Nakajima so that a claw on that overhead rod engaged those "prongs" on the propeller hub. The driver then engaged a clutch, so the truck's auxiliary engine would spin the propeller and cause the engine to fire. It was one of these trucks that Noel destroyed at Tak on January 9, 1942. The Ki-27's air-cooled, nine-cylinder Nakajima Ha-1b engine could also be started by hand-propping, and this was often done in field conditions.

[The conversation now changes to the gun sight on the Curtiss P-40. The AVG received a shipment of U.S. Army reflector sights, a kind of "heads-up" display that imposed bright, concentric circles and a "pipper" onto the pilot's view of the enemy aircraft, rather than have him use two-point mechanical sights or peer through a telescope tube. The U.S. Army reflector sight was meant to sit on the instrument panel, but that proved impossible because Curtiss had installed thick "armourglass" behind the windshield, in accordance with Royal Air Force specifications. Then, too, the charging handles of the Tomahawk's nose guns projected back from the instrument panel. AVG mechanics therefore had to jury-rig a floor mount, as

Noel explains. - DF]

Interviewer: Gun sights?

Bacon: Well, as far as the long nose of the plane hindering our sight, if that's what you mean to bring in, that didn't affect us in any way. I might say that we manufactured our own electric sights, a good lot of them. We had the sights shipped out to us, but we couldn't install any gear in the plane or any electric device to give us only single image, with any gear that they sent us. And we didn't want the [reflector sight] mounted up there where our teeth would take a bite out of it if we went into the ground.

[Furthermore, with the reflector sight on the instrument panel], we had to lean to the side to charge our guns. We didn't want to be bothered with that. So we installed the thing down on the deck, just forward of the stick control, and then dropped a mirror, not a mirror, a glass plate about three by four [inches], from the ... top of the windshield, that runs along the top of the flaps. We fixed it on about an eight- or ten-inch arm on either side holding it in that position. So you can see it was rather a crude affair, and any vibration in the plane would cause the image to fluctuate. But we got away from the double image, and we took all the mirrors out of our gun sights, and with the aid of our small lamp for blacking them – just holding them over this oil lamp to get a good black [carbon] surface – we would re-cut the image (?) smaller than they were originally because of the focal lamp.

[The question mark is in the original. I confess that neither am I able to follow Noel's explanation. The field-installed AVG gun sight was indeed a Rube Goldberg contraption, and in the heat of combat a pilot would sometimes knock it out of alignment.

[The U.S. Navy trained its aviators in deflection shooting, in which a pilot learns to "lead" a target much as a hunter fires in front of the duck he hopes to hit. They learned the technique by attacking a canvas sleeve being towed by another aircraft. The AVG's ex-Army pilots did not have this training, and therefore tended to rely on attacks from directly ahead or astern, rather than from the side. It turns out that Noel preferred this approach as well. - DF]

Interviewer: How much deflection did you figure?

Bacon: Personally, very little. Most of my shots were head-on, right into the engine.

Interviewer: Was that against bomber aircraft?

Bacon: No, that was against fighter aircraft. I had very little contact with bombers while I was out there. Once with a twin-engine, and once with a single-engine light bomber, which looks an awful lot like our SB2U-2 with its landing gear extended.

[Noel knew the SB2U from his months aboard USS Ranger, *whose Bombing Four squadron had been equipped with the scarcely adequate Vought Vindicator dive bomber. Tex Hill was among the Flying Tigers who had flown the Vindicator from the carrier's flight deck in search of German submarines.*

[The Japanese light bomber was the Mitsubishi Ki-30, called "Ann" by Allied pilots; it had fixed landing gear, a long plexiglass greenhouse, two machineguns in the wings and another on a swivel at the rear of the greenhouse, and carried 400 kilograms (880 pounds) of bombs. The twin-engine bomber mentioned by Noel was probably the much more formidable Mitsubishi Ki-21 "Sally." The interview then turned to the P-40's armament, with the Marine Corps major apparently asking the questions. - DF]

Interviewer: You had four fifties?

Bacon: No, sir. We had two fifty calibers synchronized [to fire through the propeller arc, plus four thirty-caliber guns in the wings].

Interviewer: Do you like the thirty caliber?

Bacon: Well, it hasn't got the range of the fifty, and I think the fifty is the one that does the damage with a head-on shot, putting the engine out of commission. The thirty caliber was responsible for small disintegration of the airplane.

Interviewer: Do you use tracers?

Bacon: Yes.

Interviewer: How did you have them belted [with respect to tracer, armor-piercing, and incendiary bullets]?

Bacon: No uniform belting, Major, it depended entirely upon our mission. Some days we would load a full load of incendiaries to strafe enemy airdromes, and oftentimes the availability of our ammunition regulated our belting.

Our crew chiefs would spend [the night maintaining our planes], for I have found them, after our planes had been dispersed off the ground, off the airdrome, that is – out in the trees, out in the rice paddies – wherever we might locate them in order to steer clear of damage [from Japanese bombs] during night raids. We'd find them out there during a bombing raid pulling chocks with pinpoint flashlights. They didn't seem to mind, they didn't do any growling about it. We had wonderful personnel out there in the ground crews.

Interviewer: Were there any losses among the ground personnel?

Bacon: None that I know of.

Interviewer: Where did they come from?

Bacon: They're all service personnel, Commander. Army, Navy, and Marine Corps. We have a few natives working around, rolling gas drums, pushing the planes, but those who are working on the airplanes are all [former] service personnel.

Interviewer: What are your gassing facilities?

Bacon: We had gasoline on the airdromes in drums. We exhausted it as they would fill it. It came from Rangoon, that's about all I can offer on that score.

Interviewer: Could you explain something of the system of training you had?

Bacon: The Colonel [Claire Chennault] gave — he guided us, of course, but he left an awful lot up to the units themselves. Shortly after we got there we were divided into three squadrons, most of which we did again by ourselves [with] the Colonel's permission, and we made up our own training program of indoctrination, which would hinge on an awful lot of combat [training].

Interviewer: Dog fights?

Bacon: Yes, actual dog fights.

Interviewer: Camera guns?

Bacon: No, sir. We had no camera gun equipment.

Interviewer: Would you have used it?

Bacon: I don't know if we'd have taken the time to install it if we had had it. Would not even have taken the time to develop the films. All those facilities were not as good as they could have been. The Colonel was far-sighted in having a camera shop in the group [for reconnaissance photographs among other purposes] but the heat and a few other things spoiled a lot of our personal camera gear, so I don't know.

Interviewer: What did you use for targets?

Bacon: We used a P-40 for the target plane and made runs on him. That was for, well, we probably had fifteen hours of that work, making our Navy runs right on the P-40, flying about five thousand feet, north and south. We had five or six runs that we developed from the Navy that we used, similar to the overhead, high side, low side [attacks], all the same. We used about a four-thousand-foot step-up on the overhead, rather than what we used on the F4F at fifteen hundred [feet].

But it worked quite well, and then when we began to put the guns in commission and start firing them, we had the butts [set up for test firing on the ground, with the P-40's tail jacked up]. We built our own butts and [sighted] the guns in – bore sighted them – and then took them out on the gunnery range that we had policed [cleaned up] by natives. We set up a gunnery range command, we had a radio set over at the range, had a series of flags, and we'd fire on the targets [from the air] as we'd get a white flag. When a red flag would run up, we'd close the area. But that's actually the only firing we did. We got very little of it before we ran into the Rangoon battle.

Interviewer: How did you have your guns bore sighted?

Bacon: The Colonel advised us to bore sight our guns at a certain distance, but if a pilot had a definite idea that he could just fire the guns and get results with them at [a different] distance then he could have them bore sighted differently. I had mine bore sighted at five hundred yards to begin with, and then when I found out I had to fire at closer range, I had it cut down to three hundred yards.

[The more aggressive and more experienced the pilot, the closer he would press against the target, and he would "harmonize" the bullets from his wing guns so that they would converge at his preferred firing distance. Three hundred yards was typical for the American Volunteer Group pilots after they got into combat. - DF]

Interviewer: Against a maneuvering opponent what was your best run or approach?

Bacon: All depending on where we found him. If he was above me, my first movement would be away from him and down. There's nothing you can do in combat [with] those fellows when they have the advantage [of altitude]. So I think you'll find most of the boys will agree with me. Unless you find yourself on an equal basis with them, you've got to get out and get yourself on an equal basis with them. We were outnumbered as many as six and eight of their planes to one of ours. Fighting a maneuverable craft and having five others beside the one you're concentrating on, it makes a pretty tough schedule. We would, at least, try to be at the same altitude so we could have a head-on shot at him, and [then] we'd just keep going. Of course, if we could find ourselves losing him sufficiently to expedite a chandelle [180-degree climbing turn] and pick up some altitude before we came at him again, we would do so. If not, we would turn right where we were and head back at him rather than sacrifice our speed. But very, very few times did you ever fire on a I-96 or I-97 without having to look right at his engine, because he could work himself right into that [head-on] position while you were getting your gun switches on.

Interviewer: Do you think your fifty-caliber would have been effecttive in the wings?

Bacon: I don't know. I don't know why they shouldn't have been.

Interviewer: Well, do you think that parallel [as when mounted on the cowling of the P-40B] they would be more effective ... at low range than they would be converging from the wings?

Bacon: No. I would have them converging from the wings, yes. Fighting with the bombers especially, you can park yourself right at a given range practically, and set there where your guns are most effecttive. Then it's to your advantage to have them bore sighted [at that distance]. But with the little fighter it is a different proposition. I myself would rather have [the convergence] at a given point, provided I know where that is, the concentration of fire rather than the dispersed. Is that what you meant?

Interviewer: No. What I really meant was, would you prefer to have synchronized guns parallel [firing straight ahead through the propeller arc] rather than converging [from out on the wings]?

Bacon: Well, I don't know. To me it wouldn't make any difference.

[The newer Curtiss fighters, P-40D and P-40E, were equipped with four or six fifty-caliber guns in the wings. Indeed, this armament had become standard for American fighter planes. Some P-40E's reached the American Volunteer Group after Noel went home on leave. These were known as Kittyhawks in RAF service, and the Flying Tigers used the same terminology. - DF]

Interviewer: Could you tell what the range was, the true range?

Bacon: Well, within reasonable limits, yes, after one or two fights. Just like firing on a [towed target] sleeve continually for three or four weeks. You begin to picture without having to judge it on a gauge [range finder?] that you might have within the sight just how it should look.

Interviewer: Did you have any fires at all?

Bacon: Yes, we had one boy come in from a hop, started to ground loop, and crash into a plane that was parked on the side of the runway. At least he thought that it [a crash] was inevitable so he gave it the throttle too quickly, and the engine I'm sure tried to pull about sixty inches of manifold pressure, with a forty-one inch allowance. He took off again with a terrific roar – you could almost hear the engine cry – and he came around and landed, signed his yellow sheet and went inside. Then the next boy who was scheduled for that plane the next hour, took it off and got about one hundred and fifty feet in the air, and fire burst out in the nose section. Evidently there had been a strain there somewhere.

Interviewer: Did you get any facts [about that fire]?

Bacon: Well, [the pilot was] one hundred and fifty feet in the air, and at about one hundred and ten knots [airspeed]; he had his wheels up.... He put it down, wheels up, in a rice paddy, bounced a little bit when he hit one of those bridges [dikes] where the natives walk across during the wet weather, but stayed right side up and [he got out] and started to put [the fire] out with his fire extinguisher until his fifty-caliber ammunition started going off in the ammunition boxes, and then he had to leave the plane and it burned up.

Then one boy, Gil Bright, from Fighting Four as well, was shot up pretty badly and had to bail out because his plane was on fire and the flames were coming in the cockpit. We had fire fighting equipment.

Interviewer: Were you trained at all in your ground strafing?

Bacon: Yes. The only targets we had for firing our guns was either at the butts in the park position or targets on the ground were used for strafing attacks.

Interviewer: Do you think our pilots should be trained in delayed drops [a free fall before opening the parachute] to avoid being shot up when coming down?

Bacon: Well, I don't know. You don't mean to take it up as a training program but at least advise them or caution them to withhold pulling the ripcord until they have gotten to a decent altitude. Is that what you mean?

Interviewer: Something along that line. I merely wanted your opinion.

Bacon: Yes. As a matter of fact, the boys were using that. Because shortly after the fight started one of our boys, Paul Greene, an Army pilot, had to bail out from his plane, and he floated down from about, well, he floated for about eight thousand feet, and he had three I-96s making runs on him all the way. Well, a crew chief who had a camera with him, and I'm sure you have all seen the film, some of you at least, had pictures of that Christmas Day raid on Rangoon, and it showed Paul coming down in his chute with the Japs making runs on him, and the tracers were evident, and they were all above him. He didn't get touched. They shot at his chute, but they were firing too high. After that, most of the times when the boys would bail out, providing they thought about it, they would delay pulling the ripcord until they got down to three thousand feet or so.

Interviewer: That's a good point to tell our people....

Interviewer: What is going to happen to the AVG?

Bacon: I wish I knew, Commander. I don't know.

Interviewer: Did you speak to the men, the personnel [about] coming back to the Army, Navy? How do they feel about it?

Bacon: Well, I think they'd just as soon remain in their present status. I think they'd rather be untouched. Actually, I'm not criticizing [the U.S. military], but the Group does run pretty freely, and when we get information that there is an enemy force at a given area, we run right to the planes and take off. We don't wire headquarters and ask for permission to go, etc., and – do you get what I mean?

Interviewer: When you said before that you thought the Group might pass out of existence due to the war, did you mean the personnel would come back into the Navy, Army, or what?

[This question seems to refer to a conversation before the formal interview began. Noel then recounts a rumor that was new to me: that the Flying Tigers might rejoin their original branches of the military while remaining part of the American Volunteer Group. - DF]

Bacon: I meant that I think that there is a plan underway to recall the personnel to their original service, whether they were Army, Navy, or Marine Corps, and reinstate them where they are. But to make it officially an American military force. As I understood it before I left – most of it was scuttlebutt, understand – but they would make it into a pursuit group so that the Navy boys could have their naval commissions back with detached service, and the Marine Corps would have their commissions back with detached service as well.

Interviewer: Did you have any contact with Chinese planes out there?

Bacon: Well, with the Chinese – not operating [with] them, but they took care of us wonderfully well when we were moving in and around South China, yes. But we didn't operate with them at all.

Interviewer: What is the fight psychology of the Japanese pilot? Is he aggressive, will he give up?

Bacon: Well, I think I can give you a few examples that might answer that question more easily. The Jap bomber pilot has never broken formation from my observations. The leaders have been shot so that their engines were blown right off the wing, and consequently he's out, and another one will move right up in his position, without flinching the formation will maintain their course and speed – never afraid. Five, six, seven of them came over Rangoon one day with the Brewster Buffaloes and our P-40s sitting on their tail. Evidently we had drawn most of their stern fire and were getting in pretty close, and every once in a while one [of the Japanese bombers] would start a white stream of smoke and spin down, down he'd go, and they'd get another one, until before they turned over the Gulf of Martaban on the way home all seven of them had been done away with.

[Noel is describing a fight that took place on January 24, 1942, involving what Japanese accounts say were six Mitsubishi Ki-21 heavy bombers under the command of Captain Motomura Rhosuki of the 14th Sentai. They were intercepted by four Tomahawks, four Buffaloes, and two newly arrived Hurricanes. Whatever the number of Japanese bombers, they were all shot down. "They all fell in a straight line," marveled one AVG pilot who watched the carnage from the ground, "as though someone were dropping smoke pots." - DF]

Bacon: The Japanese fighters – I wouldn't say they were aggressive. Because once you make contact with them, the sky looks like you had hit a beehive. They're all over the place, and you never will find one of them alone – I mean, very seldom. He's always got two or three [of his squadron mates] within easy reach. At least they are very sportsmanlike, and they look after a buddy who is in trouble, which is quite natural. I rather think, rather than saying they tend to stick together in their combat, which [as] I have experienced is an impossibility, but it is just that they've outnumbered us a great deal. We always found two or three of them in a spot, and each one [of us] would try to catch one.

The oddest thing I have seen happen as far as their ability to go to great ends to accomplish anything, was one day during my day off I was riding around with the chief [of his P-40's ground crew] enjoying the sunlight and fresh air, and the air raid warning sounded, so I tore to our Operations shack, which is well dispersed, and watched for the [radio] reports to come in, and followed them in over the area.

High altitude formation was reported, so our boys took off and climbed to the ordered altitude and stood by up there for probably thirty-five minutes, and all of a sudden six of us that were standing out at the shack – all the fellows that had the day off – happened to be just looking down at the airfield. We were at this vantage point where we could see what was going on. Right at the tree tops at the west end of the field was a formation of no less than twenty-seven Jap fighters already opening their guns to strafe the airdrome. And all our people were at twenty thousand feet!

We immediately told Operations to send out our key [alert the patrolling Tomahawks], and a hell of a noise took place right then with all the [Japanese] planes diving down, flames and screams galore. In the meantime a Hawker Hurricane, with engine trouble it seemed, he was in the landing circle trying to land, when he came around and met this Japanese formation and flew right through the boys – flew right through them – well, he had his wheels coming up just like *this*, and away he went, right over the Shwe Dagon Pagoda and a few other places out there, and a couple of the Japs tried to tail him but they didn't catch him.

But I think he saved the airdrome. They scattered in every direction. Evidently they figured they hadn't pulled quite the surprise that they might, but it was only one boy that broke them up. But at least it shows that they were aggressive to put a decoy up [at twenty thousand feet] and then come in unnoticed, absolutely unnoticed, from the opposite direction that we expected.

Interviewer: But will they give up, will they run away?

Bacon: No, they can't. Not their fighter [pilot]. He's helpless. It's kind of hard to distinguish the value of a Japanese pilot [compared to] our pilot because of the difference of the equipment we were using and of the equipment they were using, if you could appreciate that. We had advantages in the P-40 that they didn't have in the I-96 and I-97, and they had advantages in the I-96 and I-97 that we couldn't combat with. When we combatted them, we used the advantages we had, and consequently they did [the same] with theirs.

Interviewer: Plane for plane, which would you rather have, the speed or the maneuverability?

Bacon: If you don't want to fight, you can always get away in a P-40. Speed is quite to the advantage, I am sure. Because with the speed you can get yourself out of range of that fellow and orient yourself and put yourself in a position to make an attack on him while he is wondering what you are doing, or trying to catch up with you.

Interviewer: Even though he has a climb [advantage]?

Bacon: Yes, even though he has a climb. We would make, well now, that might not stand up if there was just this little Jap and this little P-40 out in a given area, but when there's a group of them so that everyone is busy, you [can] make a hit-and-run attack on one of these fellows and you just keep going. Well, he's gotta get back into the fracas or he'll be shot down by another P-40 that's in reasonable proximity. See, you just take a couple of minutes' time and keep on going for a while. After you get out of the proximity battle, [you can] climb up to altitude and [dive down] and come back into the fracas again.

It makes it a little slower process but it's a little safer as well. A fellow doesn't have to show that he's afraid of fighting to pull a maneuver like that. I mean, that's no indication that he's afraid to battle. That's only good common sense.

Interviewer: How many planes did you have? How many were delivered to the Group out there?

Bacon: Well, I'd like to withhold some of this information. I'm sure that within reasonable limits we got around one hundred.

[*Noel's reticence is odd, since BuAer could easily obtain this infomation elsewhere. – DF*]

Interviewer: If you were going out there, going to start all over again, and you were running the Squadron and could run your own training, what changes in the Navy training you had, would you recommend? That is, for work with the AVG. What would you knock off? What would you add to?

Bacon: I can't say that I'd delete it one particle. I'm pretty proud of the training I have gotten [in the Navy], and I think that it is only that that brought me back here.

Interviewer: How about dive bombing?

Bacon: Well now, that might be one thing, yes.

Interviewer: You might get more strafing [practice]?

Bacon: Yes, I would add to that. I had had no strafing experience at all until I got over to an enemy airdrome and found that I'd better [start learning]. The strafing, if you're going to use bombs for a pursuit group. I don't think it's necessary. However, we did begin to experiment with that in our leisure hours.

[The conversation here is confusing, probably because it involves two questioners. Noel is saying that a fighter pilot would benefit from additional training in using his machineguns to strafe ground targets. However, using a fighter as a bomber was more difficult because it had no dive brakes. This would change as the war went on, and even the AVG would employ its new Kittyhawks to bomb Japanese targets. - DF]

Interviewer: That would be strafing, not dive bombing.

Bacon: Yes. Dive bombing in one of those planes makes it a pretty helter-skelter business, because of not being able to set on your target long enough with the sights. Same thing with the Grumman, the F4F. We tried that a little bit with the Grumman [in Fighting Four], but it didn't seem to prove too successful.

Interviewer: If you had to fight against the P-40s, and wanted to improve your P-40, what would you do, sacrifice maneuverability in favor of speed, or would you stick to the speed?

Bacon: I'm all in favor of the speed, yes, sir.

Interviewer: How does that rate against the climb?

Bacon: Well, maybe this will appear to you to be a bit on the "fraidy cat" side, shall I say. But if I can break off a fight when I desire to, I think that I'll last to get in another fight, where possibly I can have the advantage.

Interviewer: In other words, if you're able to break off a fight, then that automatically means that you're able to make [a] fight any time you want to?

Bacon: Yes, it does. If you can break off a fight, you have an opportunity to start another one. That's one advantage you have with speed over climb.

Interviewer: Would you sacrifice any of your leak-proofing [fuel tanks]?

Bacon: No, sir. Because I got two slugs in a tank of mine, and I never would have gotten out of enemy territory if I hadn't had leak-proof tanks. They held a very, very slow leak, caused by armor-piercing shells, which doesn't put quite the hole that the ball cartridge might.

Interviewer: How about your armor plate? Would you add any more or take out some?

Bacon: No. The armor plate seems to be quite satisfactory. However, I tried to get away from the break in the [joining of the] back-piece and the head-piece, you know, that comes right at the fittings at the top of the seat. There's a small three-quarter-inch break in there where the two pieces of armor plate are pulled. Because of that, one of our boys got a couple of slugs in the shoulder. The armor plate stopped [the bullets] down here in the back, but they came through that break in the top.

[The Curtiss P-40B had half-inch armor plate to protect the pilot's back. Noel is describing the injuries suffered by George Paxton on January 4. In addition to this gap between the two pieces of armor plate, the Tomahawk had another vulnerability, one shared by all liquid-cooled fighters. Like an automobile engine, it was equipped with a radiator to cool the Prestone fluid, and a single bullet could cause a leak that would destroy the engine. This was of particular interest to the Navy and Marine aviators, who had been trained in air-cooled fighters like the Grumman Wildcat. - DF]

Interviewer: How about trying to protect your cooling?

Bacon: Well, there is actually no protection for that whatever.

Interviewer: Don't you think it would be advisable to consider that?

Bacon: Well, I don't see how you can. Do you mean the [Prestone] tank or the radiators? The radiators are huge, and actually you can't, well, the only way you can protect those would be to put a band of armor plate around the sides. I don't think the advantage you would gain would be sufficient to merit putting it on there. Because you still have those vulnerable openings. They'll come through you from a below belly shot, right out through your radiators.

Interviewer: Do you recall an incident where one of your pilots got a casualty in his radiator, or something like that?

Bacon: No. I recall that he got a slug in the Prestone line running out of the cylinder.

Interviewer: How long could he fly?

Bacon: He went right back to the field and overshot [the runway] and cracked up. He ran over a machinegun nest we had set up. He lost his cooling. I don't know that his engine froze before he hit the ground; I don't think so. I don't know how long he flew before he was caught. That was the only incident of all the scrapping we did out there – that was the only incident I remember where they got hit in the cooler.

[Noel is probably remembering a crash on January 28, when Robert Sandell was forced down after a hit to his coolant system. He landed hard, but his Tomahawk was actually damaged by a Nakajima Ki-27 whose pilot made a suicide dive on the runway. This was one of two such incidents mentioned earlier by Noel.

[The conversation now turns to the question of high-altitude combat. The Curtiss P-40 had only a single-stage supercharger, which made it ineffective in combat above eighteen thousand feet. That was why the Royal Air Force deployed the Tomahawk to North Africa, where most combat was at lower altitudes, like the Pacific theater but unlike the aerial warfare in Europe. - DF]

Interviewer: Did you find it any handicap not to have a higher altitude rating in your engine?

Bacon: We seemed to contact the Japanese right where the P-40 would operate seemingly best, and so I would say no.

Interviewer: Would you cut down the strength [of the aircraft] in order to reduce the weight?

Bacon: No. You're speaking of stress put on the plane by a dive or that you might have to forfeit the pullout speed or something? Because in breaking off a fight, the P-40 picks up its speed so quickly [in a dive] that before you know it you've got 475 indicated [airspeed], and a pullout at low altitude has to be made rather quickly. Is that excessive speed, do you think, Colonel? I wouldn't know.

[The RAF manual for the Tomahawk states that "The maximum permissible diving speed is 470 m.p.h. indicated." The questioner, a

Marine Corps officer, next wants to know about G forces. One G is a normal gravity. At five G's, a 160-pound pilot finds himself weighing 800 pounds, so that the blood rushes from his head and perhaps causes him to lose consciousness. This was an era before "G-suits" were in common use to buffer the effects of gravity. Noel describes one technique to avoid blacking out, by leaning down and tightening his torso muscles to keep the blood from leaving his head. Greg Boyington similarly tightened his neck muscles, a trick he had learned as a college wrestler. - DF]

Interviewer: What G's do you pull on these things, six or seven?

Bacon: Well, I keep from going black if I can. Probably, with leaning over in the plane, [I could handle] six, five. I always stoop over and strain like everything.

Interviewer: What is the P-40 stressed to?

Bacon: I would say anywhere about seven and one-half. I know it will take a terrific beating. We dove straight for the ground from 16,000 feet and pulled out about 4,500 with cruising throttle on, and my wingman told me we were nearing 475 [mph], and that's why I quoted that figure a minute ago. I didn't have my eyes on the airspeed meter because the section of planes I was following with my section made a turn, and I said, "No soap – I'm gonna keep my ailerons" [rather than risk tearing them off], so I still went on straight. He made a pullout in a turn, which I considered very foolish at the time. I thought he was going to lose his ailerons sure at that speed.

Interviewer: There are several devices which tend to reduce the tendency to black out in a pullout. Do you think something like that would help in the fighters?

Bacon: Well, I don't know; I haven't had any experience [with them]. Every time I would pull out of a dive I would lean over in the seat, so that my head is, oh, down by the instrument panel, and that seems to prove very beneficial.

Interviewer: Suppose you didn't have to [lean over]. Suppose you had a [G-]suit on or a belt that would keep you from blacking out up to about nine [G's]?

Bacon: Well, I could keep anything in sight that I might be following, or someone behind me [even when leaning over].

Interviewer: What type [harness] did you have, belt or shoulder?

Bacon: We had only the seat strap, the simple old buckle strap.

Interviewer: When did you leave [China]?

Bacon: The latter part of February, the 20th or 21st.

Interviewer: What do you think of the Brewsters?

Bacon: I don't think much of the Brewsters because the record they made in the Rangoon operations, flown by the RAF, is nothing to write home to mother about.

[The BuAir interviewers had a particular interest in the Brewster F2A, called Buffalo by the Royal Air Force. It was the first monoplane carrier fighter to go into service with the U.S. Navy, which in 1936 regarded it as a more promising plane than a biplane design from the Grumman Corporation. Grumman therefore modified its entry as the single-wing F4F-2 Wildcat, which events proved to be a much superior aircraft. The Brewsters were then sold to European air forces, with the first lot going to Finland and providing good service against Soviet Russia in 1941-42. Those still in U.S. Navy service were handed off to the Marines and used as island-based fighters in the Pacific theater. - DF]

Interviewer: How about the Grumman [Wildcat]?

Bacon: Well, I'd like to fight some of the Japs in a Grumman. I had 250 hours in the F4F before I left here [to join the AVG].

Interviewer: How would you compare the P-40 with the Grumman?

Bacon: Well, the Grumman had a nice climb.

Interviewer: Well, look, we'd like to ask you some more questions because what you have to say affects the future airplanes of the Navy, and we don't care what you say about them, you can say as much as you want, but we want you to do it now, so we can improve the airplanes.

Bacon: Yes, I understand. Well, why I hesitate to talk is because as I stand here among you people I am wholly an inexperienced pilot so I hold my tongue thinking I may be trying to tell you people, who have been flying a lot longer than I, how it should be done, and I don't feel comfortable doing it.

Interviewer: Have you any idea why the Brewster didn't show up so well?

Bacon: No. I flew a P-40 in Rangoon, flying near a Brewster Buffalo, and he was supposed to be a pretty good pilot, so he came over looking for a fight one day, and I told him I'd take him up, and we went up and had three [mock] fights. The first one we drew on was a regular combat using the Army starting procedure – using the same altitude – and the minute the wings passed [abreast] we started wrapping it up. He finally drew on it, just making a mad circle, one after another. The fight took place at 10,000 feet. The second fight, rather than make a sharp turn on the same level that we passed at, I pulled into just as steep and sharp a chandelle as I could, and cut across my path as well. Coming in this way, I pulled up and nearly did an Immelmann actually, and got him in the sights right off the bat.

Why he didn't do [the same], I think, is because he couldn't with a Brewster. And then I got on his tail and rode him around in a circle, and as we were going around he was slipping off, beginning to fall off on the wing. Well, my plane was just about doing it [falling off] but as yet there wasn't any movement in the wingtips themselves.

[The Immelmann turn, invented by a German ace of the First World War, was a favorite of Japanese pilots with their lightweight, highly maneuverable fighters. When chased by an enemy fighter, the pilot yanked his aircraft into the first half of a vertical loop, meanwhile rolling upright, so that he ended by facing in the other direction and at a higher altitude. He was now in a position for a head-on attack with the altitude advantage.

[The final page is missing, either mislaid or taken by someone who found it interesting. - DF]

The Tigers Come Home

NOEL BACON WAS THE FIRST of many Flying Tigers to return to the United States, though the U.S. Army did its best to recruit them in China. In the end, only five AVG pilots stayed on with the 23rd Fighter Group that replaced the American Volunteer Group when it was disbanded in July 1942. A larger number went to work for CNAC, the Chinese national airline, flying cargo over the "Hump" of the Himalayas, from India to China. The rest headed home by whatever means they could find, typically a slow boat from Bombay to New York City around the Cape of Good Hope.

And all along that route, U.S. military officers snagged the returning heroes for a debriefing. They were the first to have flown in combat against the Japanese air forces with any considerable success, and the military was desperate to learn about their tactics and equipment, and about those of their Japanese opponents. Thus, toward the end of April 1942, officers of the U.S. 10th Air Force in India managed to sit down with three AVG pilots – Charlie Sawyer, Bob Layher, and Robert (Snuffy) Smith – who passed through Delhi on a ferry flight. The result was a four-page Confidential report, dated May 2, which was later picked up and reissued by no less a personage than Henry (Hap) Arnold, the Army Air Forces commanding general. He divided the information into "universal rules" and "basic tactics." There were two universals:

1. Take advantage of the sun and clouds whenever possible.

2. Keep looking around. Never remain intent on a target, a flight of the enemy, or even one part of the sky for very long. Danger might be coming from any direction. Take one last good look around before making an attack, and take another good look as you break away. If possible, also take a good look around just before you come within firing range of your target.

As for the tactics used by AVG pilots, flying their Curtiss P-40s against the nimble Japanese, General Arnold wrote:

1. Never use climbing maneuvers unless you have excess speed from a dive, because the Jap plane can outclimb you.

2. Use P-40's best characteristics, namely speed, diving, and fire

power (head-on runs). Never use maneuverability. Avoid aerobatics because the Jap planes can do them faster and in much less space. Never dogfight them.

3. Altitude is good life insurance. If the enemy has two or three thousand feet altitude advantage on you, turn at right angles to his course, or even directly away from him, and avoid him until you have enough distance to climb safely.... Climbing straight up into an enemy formation at 150 m.p.h. is almost a sure way to lose pilots and equipment.

4. If you have to bail out while the enemy is in the vicinity, wait as long as possible before opening your chute, because if a Jap sees you, he will machine-gun you.

5. Be patient, use the clouds and sun [to hide in], and wait until you have an altitude advantage before attacking. If you have to dive away from an attack, it will take you twenty minutes to get back into it again. If you have an initial altitude advantage, you can dive, fire, and climb again to repeat at very close intervals, thus doing more damage.

There were other interviews with George Paxton (the pilot wounded in combat because of the gaps in the P-40 seat armor), apparently also in India; with John Farrell, Chuck Older, Ken Jernstedt, and Bob Brouk in Africa on their way home; with Frank Metasavage, an AVG mechanic; and with Walter Pentecost, who had helped assemble the P-40s at Rangoon in the summer of 1941. Reading them now, these reports seem mostly unremarkable. That they were treasured by the U.S. military in 1942 is evidence of how unprepared the United States was to go to war with the Empire of Japan, and to how little the U.S. military knew about the men and equipment it would encounter in the field.

In U.S. service

Of the two dozen Flying Tiger pilots who returned to the United States in the spring and summer of 1942, about half took civilian jobs as test pilots for aircraft companies or ferry pilots for the airlines. The others returned to the branch of the U.S. military from which they had been recruited the previous year, often serving heroically in their nation's service, with two of them (Greg Boyington and Jim Howard) earning the Medal of Honor, America's highest award for valor. As for

Noel Bacon, already in the U.S., he elected not to return to China and finish his year with the American Volunteer Group:

> I turned down some lucrative offers with private aviation companies. What talents I may have possessed at that point the Navy had given me. Besides the country was at war.

His decision not to return to China was probably a tribute to the "little Honey" whom he had missed so much when he sailed from San Francisco in July 1941. He rejoined the U.S. Navy with a modest promotion to lieutenant (junior grade), and in his new uniform he married Elizabeth Kennedy on May 10, 1942. Their daughter, Jane, was born the following year in Jacksonville, Florida. By this time Noel was on sea duty, serving aboard the flagship of a division of six aircraft carriers and thirteen escort destroyers. He finished the war as a lieutenant commander.

Postwar, Noel remained in the Navy as a career officer, assigned to the U.S. embassy in Cairo as naval attaché. In 1961 he retired from active duty as a captain to work for a Metro Goldwyn Mayer subsidiary in Connecticut, later moving to Florida to become the director of Port Everglades, a cruise-ship terminal in Fort Lauderdale. By 1990, he was retired and living in Boca Raton, where I managed to interview him by telephone for my history of the Flying Tigers, published by Smithsonian Institution Press the following year. I enjoyed the chat, and I especially appreciated the photo he mailed me, showing him in British Army khakis on the occasion of his first flight in the Curtiss P-40, in September 1941. It appears as the frontispiece of this book – and note that the Tomahawk's nose is barren of the shark-face paint job that would help make the Flying Tigers immortal. That would be added later, as Noel and the other early arrivals developed the spirit that goes with a fighting unit with its own private traditions and heraldry.

I was very excited to have found a "lost" Flying Tiger (Noel was identified that way on the AVG roster), so I forwarded his mailing address to Richard Rossi, head of the AVG veterans' group, in the belief that he would be equally pleased. He wasn't, alas, and to the best of my knowledge Noel was never able to get together with his onetime comrades of the American Volunteer Group. It seems that, once the war began in December 1941, Claire Chennault decided to give a "dishonorable discharge" to any member of the AVG who went home before the group was officially disbanded in July 1942. Whatever this term might have meant in what was, after all, a civilian organization, it was applied not only to those who dodged combat but also to such veteran pilots as Noel Bacon and Greg Boyington. Both had served honorably and well in combat, with three air-to-air victory credits for Noel and two for Boyington, plus additional credit for planes destroyed on the ground in strafing attacks.

Noel died in Boca Raton on April 12, 1996, at the age of seventy-eight. He was survived by "the little Honey," by his daughter, three grandchildren, and two great-grandchildren. After all these years, his name still doesn't appear on the website of the Flying Tiger veterans website, on what the organization claims is the "Complete Roster of the American Volunteer Group, 1941-42." Those interested can see a much more complete roster on the Annals of the Flying Tigers at my website WarbirdForum.Com. – *Daniel Ford, March 2022*

Notes and Sources

Throughout this book, I have followed Asian word order for personal names, except where citing the author of a book published for the American market. Thus the full name of Lieutenant Hinoki is Hinoki Yohei, with his family name appearing first. All interviews were by the author, in person or by telephone.

100 Fair Pilots

"Boy, if the Chinese": letter to Haywood Hansell 09/14/1937; see Daniel Ford, *Flying Tigers: Claire Chennault and His American Volunteers, 1941-1942* (Warbird Books 2016), a revised and updated edition of the history first published by Smithsonian Institution Press. Unattributed biographical information comes from this book and from the websites danfordbooks.com/tigers and flyingtigersavg.com.

Adkins: "Two More Flying Tigers Now Testing P-47's Here," *Republic Aviation News* 01/22/1943.

Armstrong: In 2015 we learned that the bodies of the pilots killed in training accidents were exhumed postwar and reburied, first in India and later at the Punchbowl Cemetery in Hawaii. After much badgering by relatives, they were identified through DNA testing and brought back to the continental United States for burial. See warbirdforum.com/topeka.htm for more about Armstrong.

Bacon: Noel Bacon, "Diary of a Flying Tiger," *NY Sunday News* 08/02/1942 and "AVG Confidential" in this omnibus.

Bartelt: Osbourne Groethe, "Deceased DL 'Ace' served as Flying Tiger," *Detroit Lakes Tribune* 07/07/2015.

Baumler: Kirk Setzer, "Flying Tiger? The AVG's Missing 100th Pilot" online at warbirdforum.com/baumler.htm

Bishop: Lewis Bishop & Sheila Irwin, *Escape From Hell: An AVG Flying Tiger's Journey* (privately printed 2005).

Bond: Charles Bond & Terry Anderson: *A Flying Tiger's Diary* (Texas A&M University Press 1984).

Boyington: Gregory Boyington, *Baa Baa Black Sheep*, Putnam 1958; Bruce Gamble, *Black Sheep One: The Life of Gregory "Pappy" Boyington*, Presidio 2000.

Bright: J. Gilpin Bright, "From a Flying Tiger," *Atlantic* October 1942.

Brouk: Jennifer Holik-Urban & Scott Sloan, *To Soar with the Tigers: The Life and War Diary of Robert Brouk*, Createspace 2011.

Burgard: His son's website "George Burgard's Flying Tiger Days" (seen 07/07/2015).

Cavanah: "Three Flying Tigers Home for a Rest," press photo 08/03/1942, and other wartime memorabilia, online at "Flying Tigers Antiques" (seen 07/07/2015).

Christman: Andrew Glaess, "Remembering Bert Christman," warbirdforum.com/scorch.htm (seen 07/07/2015).

Conant: Joseph Brown, "Will the Real Flying Faker Please Stand Up," *Argosy* September 1963.

Cook: USAAF accident report.

Criz: "General Airborne Transport XCG-16," Wikipedia (seen 12/28/2021).

Cross: James Cross, "We Kept the Tigers Flying," *Mechanix Illustrated* December 1942.

Dupouy: Okuyuma's death: Hinoki Yohei, *Hayabusa sentotai cho Kato*, Kojinsha 1987.

Farrell: "No more flying" in Bond above p75.

Fuller: "Henry Fuller Was Lawyer, Wartime Pilot," *Miami News* 04/08/1958.

Gilbert: "Huge conglomeration": Charles Older interview 1986.

Groh: Major Tadashi from Hiroshi Umemoto, *Burma Kokusen Jyo*, Dai Nippon Kaiga 2003; Captain Anma from Hinoki above.

Gunvordahl: "Secret mission" in *Chicago Tribune* 04/05/1942.

Hall: "Route Over China," *Salina Journal* 08/18/1943.

Hedman: Yasuda Yoshito, "Muteki Hayabusa sentai," from *Eiko Hayabusa sentai*, Konnichi no Wadaisha 1978.

Hennessy: "One damn good" etc. in Bond above p50.

Hill: David Lee Hill & Reagan Schaupp, *Tex Hill: Flying Tiger* (privately printed 2003). "Y'all follow me": Donald Lopez interview 1989.

Howard: James Howard, *Roar Of The Tiger: From Flying Tigers to Mustangs, A Fighter Ace's Memoir*, Crown 1991.

Jones: "When he suddenly failed" from Chuck Baisden on AVG veterans' forum (seen 07/09/2015).

McGarry: Myrna Oliver, ""William McGarry, 74, of World War II Flying Tigers Fame," *Los Angeles Times* 04/13/1990. Photos of the wrecked Tomahawk online at Thai Tango Squadron website.

McMillan: togetherweserved.com (seen 07/10/2015).

Martin: "Turned away" from Umemoto above.

Merritt: See Peter Wright below.

Mickelson: "Flying Tiger Hero Missing on China Flight," *Rattle of Theta Chi* March 1944; "Mickelson Featured in 'Flying Tigers',"

Fergus Falls Journal 04/26/2008.

Moss: Drew Jubera, "A Diving Powerhouse Springs From Georgia's Sandy Soil," *NY Times* 08/10/2009. Michael Helms, "The legacy of Robert C. 'Moose' Moss," *Moultrie Observer* 12/06/2005.

Mott: "There was a big": Charles Mott interview 1988.

Neale: His AVG diary in the Pistole Collection, see below.

Newkirk: "Scarsdale" etc.: John Newkirk, *The Old Man and the Harley*, Thomas Nelson 2008. For the dispute about his death, see www.warbirdforum.com/avg.htm.

Olson: I can find no obituary for him, nor does the Flying Tigers Association website have his biography. His collection of AVG documents ("A Story of the American Volunteer Group," "Activities of the Third Pursuit Squadron," combat reports, and his letters as squadron leader) was acquired by Larry Pistole, son of an AVG ground crewman. In 1989-1990, machine copies of the "Pistole Collection" were housed at the National Air & Space Museum archives. The originals were eventually purchased by the Flying Tigers Association, and some were lost or pilfered.

Paxton: Robert Hotz, *With General Chennault*, Coward McCann 1943.

Probst: "En route to Washington," *Chicago Tribune* 09/17/1942.

Reed: Meehan Family dot com (seen 07/11/2015).

Ricketts: "Ricketts, one of the new," R.T. Smith below. "Chewed it up," Bond above p58.

Rosbert: C. Joseph Rosbert, *Flying Tiger Joe's Adventure Story Cookbook*, privately printed 1985.

Sandell: "A small fellow," Bond above p63. "The boys had to dig," Fritz Wolf & Douglas Ingells, "It's Hell Over China!," *Air Trails Pictorial* Oct 1942.

Sawyer: "Emmett WWII veteran's memorabilia brings in thousands at auction" on KTVB website (seen 07/11/2015).

Schiel: Find A Grave (seen 07/11/2015).

Shamblin: Letter home: www.warbirdforum.com/shamblin.htm (seen 07/11/2015). Capture: *Japan Times & Advertiser* 07/15/1942.

Shapard: biographies on Wikipedia and confederatevets.com (seen 07/12/2015). "Hey you guys": Melvin Woodward diary on warbirdforum.com/avg.htm (seen 07/11/2015).

Shilling: "Had a dog fight": Wilfred Schaper diary, Larry Pistole Collection above. Also Erik Shilling, *Destiny: A Flying Tiger's Rendezvous With Fate*, privately printed 1993.

R.T. Smith: His *Tale of a Tiger*, privately printed 1986, contains a reproduction of his handwritten diary, so we can rely on it absolutely, unlike postwar memoirs or a diary like Charlie Bond's that was edited for publication. The dust cover shows a retractable-gear Nakajima Hayabusa, making it the first book about the AVG to concede that the Tigers did not battle the infamous "Zero" but the similar but somewhat less formidable Japanese army fighter. This information (and the identity of some of the Japanese army air force units that encountered the AVG) was long known to historians but not the public. Almost to the turn of the 21st century, most AVG veterans believed they'd fought the Mitsubishi A6M Zero over Burma and China.

Stubbs: "Col. Gail L. Stubbs," *St. Louis Post-Dispatch* 02/06/-2002.

Swartz: "One big bomb": Wolf & Ingells above. "Swartz had part of his hand": "Dick Rossi's Story," Flying Tigers Association website (seen 07/13/2015).

Swindle: USAAF accident report.

Wallace: "Veteran Of AVG Back At Lashio" and "Apology," *India-Burma Theater Roundup* 04/19/1945 and 05/24/1945.

Watson: USAAF accident reports.

Wolf: "About this time": Wolf's biography on the Flying Tigers Association website (seen 07/13/2015).

Allen Wright: "CNAC Captain Allen M. Wright," CNAC dot org (seen 07/13/2015).

Peter Wright: Peter Wright, "I Learned About Flying From That," *Flying* May 1944. Gayle Sims, "Peter Wright Sr., 90, a pioneer in helicopters," *Philadelphia Inquirer* 06/05/2007.

"Well, that's a good start": Jennifer MacNeil, "Fallbrook man recalls days as a Flying Tiger," *San Diego Union-Tribune* 04/01/-2001. Robert Hotz, *With General Chennault: The Story of the Flying Tigers*, Coward McCann 1943 p22. "Bullshit": R.T. Smith, "Smithsonian Slanders Flying Tigers," *Air Classics* February 1992.

"Indeed, over claiming": Christopher Shores via Ruy Horta, "Re: Flying Tigers VS Christopher Shores?" on Twelve O'Clock High! forum (seen 07/05/2015). Of particular interest to students of the AVG are the first two volumes of Christopher Shores, Brian Cull, and Yasuho Izawa, *Bloody Shambles*, Grub Street 1992, 1993. For the combat claims of USN and IJN fighter pilots, see John Lundstrom, *The First Team* and *The First Team and the Guadalcanal Campaign*, Naval Institute Press, 1984, 1994. "Upwards of a thousand": *AVG-CNAC Reunion*, Ojai CA 1989.

100 Hawks for China

Section titled "How the Hawks Reached China" first appeared in *Air & Space / Smithsonian,* April-May 1988. The undated and mimeographed *Pilot's Notes: Tomahawk I*, Publication 2013A of the Royal Air Force, apparently accompanied the airplanes to China and was part of the Pistole Papers cited above. Other sections are drawn from web pages first published on www.warbirdforum.com/avg.htm.

In addition to aircraft identified in "What We Know About the Hawks," several fuselage numbers have been tied to their pilots but not to a specific aircraft. Thus number 17 was flown by Croft, 19 by Hoffman, 30 by Moss, and 67 by Prescott. And of course pilots often flew whatever plane happened to be available.

The list of AVG aircraft was compiled from books and articles by Walter Pentecost, Peter Bowers, Joe Christy, Terrill Clements, John Rawlings, Thomas Tullis, Charles Baisden, and Frank Losonsky; from documents in the Chennault Papers at Stanford University and the AVG Archives; and from emails from Jim Settle, Craig Busby, Paul McMillan, and James Atkinson.

First Blood for the Flying Tigers

This is an expanded version of an article published in *America in WWII* in its edition of December 2010, copyright 2010 by 310 Publishing LLC. The *Time* story was published in the issue of December 29, 1941, and is the first time the term "Flying Tigers" appeared in print. The author was probably Theodore White, a friend of Chennault from the early days of the Sino-Japanese War.

Rising Sun Over Burma

Based on material in the following Japanese-language texts: Japan Defense Agency, *Nanpo shinko rikugun koku sakusen* (Army Air Operations in Southeast Asia), Asagumo Shimbunsha 1970; Hinoki Yohei, *Tsubasa no kessen* (Desperate Winged Combat), Kojinsha 1984, and *Hayabusa sentotai cho Kato* (Commander Kato's Falcon Corps), Kojinsha 1987; Tagata Takeo, *Hien tai Guramen* (Swallow vs. Grumman), Konnichi no Wadaisha 1973; and Umemoto Hiroshi. *Burma Air War*, vol 1, Dai Nippon Kaiga 2003. Translations by Miyuki Rogers and Difei Zhang.

AVG Confidential

"Alumnus Is Up In The Air – But How He Comes Down!" *College Eye* 03/14/1941.

Arnold, H.H. "Fighter Tactics of the A.V.G.," Air Forces General Information Bulletin No. 3. Intelligence Service, Headquarters Army Air Forces 08/12/1942.

Bacon, Noel. "Diary of a Flying Tiger: AVG Officer Comes Back With China Air War Story" NY *Sunday News* 08/02/1942.

Bacon, Mrs. Royden. Interview 09/20/2014.

Boyington, Gregory. *Baa Baa Black Sheep*. Putnam 1958.

Ford, Daniel. warbirdforum.com/avg.htm; *Flying Tigers: Claire Chennault and His American Volunteers, 1941-1942* (3rd edition). Warbird Books 2016; and Noel Bacon interview 1990.

Hussey, Brian. "The U.S. Navy, the Neutrality Patrol, and Atlantic Fleet Escort Operations," Trident Scholar Project Report. U.S. Naval Academy 1991.

Jones, Steve, "Alumni Profile: Noel Bacon," *Nonpareil* Jul 1988.

"Obituary: Bacon – Noel Richard," *Fort Lauderdale Sun-Sentinel* 04/15/1996.

Olynyk, Frank. *AVG and USAAF (China-Burma-India Theater) Credits for the Destruction of Enemy Aircraft in Air-to-Air Combat, World War 2*, privately printed 1986.

Peterson, Gerald. "Noel Bacon 1938," emails 08/09/2014, 08/28/2014, and 09/18/2014.

Rodger, George. "Flying Tigers in Burma: Handful of American Pilots Shoot Down 300 Jap Warplanes in 90 Days" *Life* 04/30/1942.

Rossi, J. Richard. Undated letter 1990.

Smith, Patricia. "Re: Noel Bacon 1938," email 08/09/2014.

About the Author

DANIEL FORD has spent a lifetime reading and writing about the wars of the 20th Century. He studied at the University of New Hampshire (B.A. political science 1954), University of Manchester (Fulbright Fellow 1954-55), and King's College London (M.A. War Studies 2010) and served the then-obligatory two years as a enlisted man in the U.S. Army, at Fort Dix, Fort Bragg, and Orléans, France. He then worked as a reporter for the *Overseas Weekly* in Frankfurt, Germany, an English-language newspaper for American servicemen in Europe. Since 1959, he has been a free-lance writer based in Durham, N.H.

He received a Stern Fund Magazine Writer's award in 1964 for his dispatches from Vietnam, published in *The Nation*; a Verville Fellowship in 1989 to study the Japanese air war in Southeast Asia in the opening months of the Pacific War; and an Aviation-Space Writer's award in 1992 for his history of the Flying Tigers (see below). Most recently, he wrote *Looking Back From Ninety: The Depression, the War, and the Good Life that Followed* (Warbird Books 2021).

You may be interested in his other books about the American Volunteer Group. For more information, point your web browser at the web address following its description.

Flying Tigers: Claire Chennault and His American Volunteers, 1941-1942 - During World War II, in the skies over Burma, a handful of American pilots met and bloodied the "Imperial Wild Eagles" of Japan and were immortalized as the Flying Tigers. To bring his prize-winning history of the American Volunteer Group up to date, Daniel Ford has completely rewritten his 1991 text, drawing on the most recent U.S., British, and Japanese research. "Admirable," wrote Chennault biographer Martha Byrd of Ford's original text. "A readable book based on sound sources. Expect some surprises." Even more could that be said of this new and more complete third edition, published by Warbird Books in 2016. Paperback and digital editions.
danfordbooks.com/tigers

Remains: A Story of the Flying Tigers - When young Eddie Gillespie discovers a World War II airplane in the jungle, with a grinning skeleton at the controls, he sets a story in motion. Two American fighter pilots in the Chinese Air Force, with their English and Burmese girlfriends, and a Japanese suicide pilot whose name happens to mean "tree of the sun" – they clash at Rangoon, while the British empire falls about their ears. Here Daniel Ford deftly melds fact and fiction in an unforgettable wartime romance. "You can't beat remains, kid," Lieutenant Atherton says in a beautifully limned conclusion. "They'll tell the story every time." Paperback and digital editions.

danfordbooks.com/remains.htm

The Lady and the Tigers - Olga Greenlaw kept the War Diary of the American Volunteer Group – the Flying Tigers – while those gallant mercenaries defended Burma and China from Japanese aggression during the opening months of the Pacific War. Returning to the United States in 1942, she wrote *The Lady and the Tigers.* Out of print for more than half a century, it has been brought up to date by Daniel Ford, who explains for the first time where Olga and Harvey Greenlaw came from, how they became caught up in the saga of the Flying Tigers, and what happened to them after their year with the AVG. Paperback and digital editions.

warbirdforum.com/greenlaw.htm

Made in the USA
Las Vegas, NV
12 June 2022